Focus on Theology

An Adult Faith-Formation Discussion Program

Edited by
Kathleen Foley, C.S.J.
and
Peggy O'Leary, C.S.J.

A Liturgical Press Book

THE LITURGICAL PRESS
Collegeville, Minnesota

Nihil Obstat: Frederick F. Campbell
               Censor Librorum/Deputatus
               February 22, 1999

Imprimatur: ✠ Harry J. Flynn
             Archbishop of Saint Paul and Minneapolis
             February 26, 1999

Cover design by Ann Blattner. Illustration: *Trinity* by Andrei Rublev, 1425.

1   2   3   4   5   6   7   8   9

Library of Congress Cataloging-in-Publication Data

Focus on theology : an adult faith-formation discussion program /
   edited by Kathleen Foley and Peggy O'Leary.
        p.   cm.
     Includes bibliographical references (p.   ) and index.
     ISBN 0-8146-2530-4 (alk. paper)
     1. Christian education—Textbooks for adults—Catholic.
   2. Catholic Church—Doctrines.   I. Foley, Kathleen.   II. O'Leary,
   Peggy.
   BX930.F65   1999
   230'.2—dc21
                                                      99-22624
                                                      CIP

About the Cover

"Trinity" by Andrei Rublev, 1425

"For we shall be made equal to the angels of God, and in equal measure with them, we shall by vision, have the fruition of that Trinity in which we now walk by faith."

—St. Augustine

"Yes, suddenly our eyes are opened and we see the invisible Trinity which Rublev painted as three angels having supper. It is a strange icon. Perhaps it is the most beautiful expression of the 'Holy' ever made. Rublev was a Russian, but his Trinity has captured the hearts of millions of people—people who understood something more than art and who know that icon painters depart at times into a deep void in which their icons are painted by another hand and, in a manner of speaking, they just copy what is in front of the eyes of their heart."

—Catherine de Hueck Doherty, *Sobornost*, 36, 37

"In the Trinity icon, each figure has a slightly different posture. The Son, the redeemer and healer of humankind, gazes upon the Father. The Father, the fountain of mercy, gazes upon the Spirit, the giver of life. The Spirit, the consoler, the advocate who proceeds from the Father and the Son, gazes to the open space at the center of the icon. The open space on which the Spirit gazes is the place at table left for us. The Spirit looks to this open space in invitation. Each and every one of us is invited to join them at table. The Trinity invites us to share their equality, to share their power, to share their hospitality, to share their openness and dialogue, to share their festivity and joy as they celebrate their distinctiveness within their absolute unity. For the Trinity is the source for all of us. The Spirit's gaze invites us to share that freedom, that security, that fulfillment. Their relationship with each other is a ministry we are invited to share and to extend."

—Author unknown

Art Depicted in Videotape Headings

Sister Palladia, a joyous Hungarian Sister of Notre Dame, lives in Budapest. During her lifetime, Hungary endured World War II, the revolution of 1956, and the Soviet regime that lasted until 1991. How does the culture of war, revolution, and oppression affect one's life and art?

We offer Sister Palladia's paintings as a meditation on the meaning of the resurrection for a twentieth-century Christian artist in a particular culture. In her art we see worry, sadness, exuberance, effort, and joy on the part of the followers of Jesus. We see an image of Jesus that shows immense love and the nearness of the risen Lord even when not recognized.

Contents

Contents

PART FOUR: REFERENCE

"Should anyone ask you
the reason for this hope of yours
be ever ready to reply,
but speak gently and respectfully."

—1 Peter 3:15

Preface

Focus on Theology is a comprehensive adult approach to Catholic Christianity. The entire program allows a coherent examination of the important religious insights of our tradition.

Sometimes a cloud of controversy obscures Catholic learning because it is too theologically oriented or, on the other hand, too formation oriented. We have experienced the necessary oneness of the two aspects of our journey to God. We begin with theology, which, when interiorized, affects the formation of the learner.

PURPOSE

Focus on Theology is a course for adults who have a desire to learn or to renew and expand their understanding of the Catholic faith tradition. The goal is to give participants the opportunity to enrich their intellectual and spiritual life and to reflect on and articulate foundational issues of the Catholic faith and belief. *Focus on Theology* accepts the challenge to help participants develop sufficient knowledge in theology, a desire for personal growth in spirituality, and confidence in the ability to communicate Christian truth and life to others.

We hope that as you study the contents, you will find a comprehensive overview of the basic components of the Christian life.

Many learned about these topics long ago; others never had an opportunity to study these areas adequately. The aim of *Focus on Theology* is to challenge participants to think about the foundations of the Catholic Christian tradition on a mature level.

As adults we have the advantage of seeing interconnections and seeing the way they affect one's life. The program has two movements: God speaks to us and we respond to God. Familiar names that address the first movement are vocation, spirituality, revelation, redemption, and doctrine. In the Church we find the second movement in sacramental life, moral life, and one's own spirituality.

LIMITATIONS

The focus of the program is thinking about and discussing the basic teachings of the Catholic Church as they relate to our present experience. While this is basically a comprehensive program, not every topic concerning the Catholic Church is found here. The program aims for a better understanding of fundamentals so that more sophisticated and controversial topics can later be argued with background, vigor, and confidence. Priorities in the *Focus on Theology* program lie in input from the videos and discussion.

Because the emphasis is on discussion, the book contains only simple and brief questions to stimulate conversations. The facilitator or participants can choose which questions will be most beneficial for the group while at the same time incorporating questions and concerns that arise within a group.

PROGRAM DESCRIPTION

The book contains each presenter's paper with accompanying focal points, reflection questions, and other helps; it puts theological understandings into a format that is more easily comprehended. The book is designed to assist and support those who have participated in the program as well as those who are involved in faith formation professionally and personally. The program strives to help the participant identify issues and formulate questions concerning Catholic belief and faith with a continuing respect for historical background, development of doctrine, and experiences of the culture. The *Catechism of the Catholic Church* serves as a main resource.

As participants and facilitators prepare for each session, they will be aided by the book.

Each topic includes activities before the session and discussion questions for use after the video presentation. Following most essays are references to the *Catechism of the Catholic Church* and questions for further reflection, as well as a bibliography.

A unique and invaluable feature of the book is a section with prayers to open each session. The prayers can be used as they are or may be adapted to accommodate each group.

Participants may find it helpful to keep notebooks for thoughts that summarize a session. These notes may serve as a way to think about the content presented each day and as a cumulative summary of the program.

Other participant aids in the book are a glossary, a bibliography, and an index. The words in the glossary, for the most part, came from the first participants in the program. Participants will find it helpful to be familiar with the rich references and other aids in the book.

The book and videos are integrally related and together lead to the discussion that is at the heart of the program. The book serves as a preparation for the videos as well as a discussion guide. With its many resources it is also a valuable aid in reviewing the program.

The videotapes contain the twenty-eight presentations of the program that assume preparation using the essays in the book and allowing sufficient time for discussion. The book and videotapes are central to the program; the discussion is indispensable.

The methodological goal of *Focus on Theology* is to give participants an opportunity to reflect on and articulate foundational issues of Catholic belief in relation to their own lives. Considerable time is afforded participants to engage in conversation and clarification following each presentation. The dynamic interaction between tradition and experience is the basis for transmitting the Christian message. The participants come to know one another in a community of faith through these conversations and through prayer together.

The presenters—with their different personalities, backgrounds, and ways of teaching—reflect the Church in its rich variety.

The program offers participants the opportunity to reflect on theological understandings and internalize values while they engage in a humble and fruitful journey toward God.

CONTENT OUTLINE

Focus on Theology addresses foundational aspects of the Catholic tradition using two components: a book and video presentations. The process is to read, listen, and discuss.

The program is divided into four major parts. Part One, "Scripture," addresses basic content and its relationship to the culture of the day. The topics include Genesis, spirituality, gospels, vocation, christology, and redemption.

Part Two, "The Church," explores the Catholic belief of the Church as mystery, mission, and doctrine and speaks to the need for the believer to respond to God in gratitude for the gifts received. This part addresses the role of the Church as manifested and lived out in the sacraments, worship, liturgical life, virtue, the Christian moral life, the common good, and human dignity. Music and art, which play an important liturgical role in the life of the Christian, are addressed in this section. Other areas addressed are the role of Mary, the place of ecumenism, and the importance of understanding the relationship between intellectual learning and learning on the level of faith. As in Part One, we see that cultural ways of thinking often negate or ignore the messages and way of life in the Catholic tradition.

Part Three, "Prayers," consists of a variety of prayers to be used at the session. The facilitator may want to choose the prayer most appropriate for the season, day, or topic. The prayers may be adapted to fulfill the needs of the group.

Part Four, "References," begins with a glossary of terms. With few exceptions, former participants identified the terms. A bibliography, a list of contributors, and an index are included as references.

The twenty-eight sessions of the program are arranged in eight chapters. Chapter One addresses the creation stories and providence. After an introduction of the creation story according to science and its limitations, we hear the Genesis creation stories and the story of the Fall. We discuss why they are so important in daily life. The providential aspects of God's continuing love and care for us are also addressed here.

Chapter Two speaks of spirituality as a relationship with God and the things of God. What effect does God have on daily decisions? To give an example of this, a segment from "Robert Coles: An Intimate Biographical Interview" is used. Robert Coles tells of his remarkable encounter with six-year-old Ruby Bridges. This is a poignant example of the two movements mentioned above: God seeks us, and we respond to God. In Scripture God reveals to us realities that we could not determine with our own natural ability, no matter how enlightened we are. In order to make complete our view of the one God, human beings, and all creation, we need both the natural and the supernatural. Often we encounter barriers in understanding the words of Scripture. Sometimes when we have an insight, we notice that a blanket has been covering up a truth that was there all the time. We will call these barriers cover stories.

Chapter Three invites the reader to think of approaches to the Gospels that will aid in the interpretation of Scripture as we read it or listen to it. Parables give us an example of Scripture interpretation and cover story.

Chapter Four explores our beliefs about Christ and suggests that early in our lives we intuitively understand our constant need for redemption because of our own thoughts and behavior. Redemption has significant meaning and application for daily life and also for eternal life. The final essay in this chapter recalls the meaning and importance of vocation in the life of a Christian.

Chapter Five considers the Church as mystery and gives us an opportunity to think about our community relationship to God. We find that the mission of the Church is the mission of Jesus. We continue to see the two movements of God inviting us and of us responding in the sacramental and moral life of the Church. The important understandings written over the years by Catholic Christians have been formed into statements called doctrines that have developed over the past two thousand years and continue to develop in the life of the Church today.

Chapter Six considers sacramental life in the Church by helping us relate to God using human signs of life such as bread, wine, water, oil, incense, and gestures. The role of music and art play an integral part in our sacramental life; a proper understanding of these aspects will enhance and deepen our prayer life.

Chapter Seven, on moral life in the Church, reminds us to act on our belief that God loves us with a faithful and everlasting love. The Church sheds more light on this love in teachings on the theological and cardinal virtues, and in its emphasis on human dignity and the common good.

Chapter Eight shows Mary as the person who most richly embodies the movements of God's asking and humankind's positive response of "Hail Mary, the Lord is with you." "Be it done unto me according to your Word." We look to Mary, as well as to all the saints, as role models who show us the way and help us to achieve our own responses to God. Our continuing work in the area of ecumenism is our response to Jesus' words, "That they all may be one." In the final two sessions participants look at religious information, formation, and transformation to see how essential they are to one's religious life and in our communication with others.

This is the entire program: Scripture, spirituality, redemption, doctrine, vocation, and Church. God speaks to us and we respond.

We owe a debt of gratitude to Fr. Dennis Dease, president of the University of St. Thomas, Dr. Ralph Pearson, vice president of Academic Affairs at the University of St. Thomas, and Monsignor Terrence J. Murphy, chancellor of the University of St. Thomas and chair of the Aquinas Foundation, for funding the *Focus on Theology* program since 1988 and for additional funding for the video project. We also thank Dr. Don Briel, director of the Center for Catholic Studies, in which the program now resides.

We also offer our heartfelt thanks to those who assisted with the *Focus on Theology* project: the principals, facilitators, and participants of the five schools and parishes that piloted the program, for their dedication and honesty in critiquing the original work; the managers of the television studio and the Instructional Support Services Department at the University of St. Thomas for their expertise in producing the videotapes.

We thank Fr. Gerald Keefe, author of "A Trinitarian Examen of Praise"; *First Things* for the use of "Journal of an Illness"; The State Tretyakovsky Gallery in Moscow for the use of Rublev's *Trinity* icon; The Madonna House Publication for the use of the quotation from

Sobornost by Catherine de Hueck Doherty; Crossroads Publishing for the use of quotations from *Prayers for a Lifetime* by Karl Rahner; Ignatius Press for the use of a quote from *Splendor of the Church* by Henri de Lubac; University of Missouri Press for the use of selected quotes from *Kontakia of Romanos, Byzantine Melodist I: On the Person of Christ* translated and annotated by Marjorie Carpenter; and Sister Palladia, S.N.D., of Budapest, Hungary for the use of her resurrection paintings in the videos.

We thank Fr. Arthur Kennedy and Dr. Don Briel, former chairs of the theology department, for their inspiration and sustaining support without whom the project would never have been initiated. We thank Harry J. Flynn, Archbishop of Saint Paul and Minneapolis, and John R. Roach, retired Archbishop of Saint Paul and Minneapolis, for their encouragement, support, and contribution to the *Focus on Theology* program through the years of its development and completion.

During the ten years that *Focus on Theology* was an on-site program at the University of St. Thomas, participants consistently informed us that their knowledge had increased, their confidence to speak about and model the faith had improved, and their own spirituality had deepened. We hope the same for you.

Notes for Facilitators

Focus on Theology addresses, through a resource book and video presentations, non-controversial issues with an emphasis on foundational aspects of the Catholic tradition. Because of the content and its relationship to the culture of the day, we urge you to allow sufficient time for discussion, clarification, and reflection following each presentation. The logistics of your local situation and community will determine the schedule for completion of the program. You may wish to set as your goal the completion of Part One the first year and Part Two the second year. The time element is flexible, but pace it in a way that it will allow for consistency so participants will keep focused on the purpose of the program and their own personal commitment. The goal of each session is quality discussion, rather than the quantity of material covered.

Part One addresses Scripture and the Catholic tradition (God speaks to us) and establishes the foundation for the remainder of the program. Part Two addresses the mystery and mission of the Church (our response to God) and enriches our understanding and appreciation of what it means to be Catholic.

It is important to go slowly in Part One so that the participants can reflect and discuss the issues most important to them individually and as a group. This will help to establish a comfortable rapport among all persons in the group. Both you and the participants are learning together, and sharing ideas and concerns will motivate good discussion. Remind the group that the goal of the program is not to learn and recite all the answers, but to grow in knowledge and faith. The purpose of the resource book and the tapes is to enable each facilitator and participant to discuss, clarify, and increase the understandings presented in each of the videotapes.

The Focus on Theology facilitator assumes responsibility for the smooth running of the program by organizing the logistics for the sessions, preparing for presentation, and initiating the discussion. It would be an advantage to have more than one facilitator to assist in planning and introducing the discussions.

Familiarize yourself with the procedure for each session so that you can determine what will be of help and what you may decide to omit. Briefly discuss the focal points and be familiar with the contents of the video you are introducing so the group will be comfortable, receptive, and confident as they enter into discussion. Encourage everyone to participate as fully as possible. Each person's contribution is valuable and essential to the success of the program.

Begin each session with prayer. A number of prayer services are included in the resource book for your use and convenience. They can be adapted to fit the needs and wishes of the group. Give participants the opportunity to help in the preparation of prayer and prayer environment.

Keep in mind that the book and the videotapes are integrally related and together lead to the discussion that is at the heart of the program. The book with all of its resources is a valuable aid for the participants as they continue their own further study and reflection.

INTRODUCING THE PROGRAM

Invite participants to speak briefly about their expectations as they begin the program. If each person speaks aloud in the group, it will create a more open discussion in future sessions.

An introduction to the program is most important. Take sufficient time to call attention to the contents of the book with all of its components. One way might be to guide the group through the topics to be considered and an overview of the book.

PROCESS FOR FACILITATING SESSIONS

Before the Session

Remind participants of the need to read the focal points, the essay, and other background information. Call attention to the importance of accepting personal responsibility for this preparation, which will enhance the time spent together.

At the Session

First, spend a few minutes reviewing the key concepts. Then watch the video (time allotment is stated for each video). After the video, refer to discussion activities at the end of the essay, encouraging new insights, questions, and concerns related to the topic.

After the Session

Additional questions or statements and references are listed for further personal reflection.

Abbreviations

B.C.E.	Before the Common Era (formerly B.C.)
CCC	*Catechism of the Catholic Church*
C.E.	Common Era (formerly A.D.)
CA	*Centesimus annus* (one hundred years)
DV	*Dei verbum* (Dogmatic Constitution on Divine Revelation)
GIRM	General Instruction of the Roman Missal
GNLYC	General Norms for the Liturgical Year and the Calendar
GS	*Gaudium et spes* (Pastoral Constitution on the Church in the Modern World)
ICEL	International Committee on English in the Liturgy
LE	*Laboren exescens* (In Proclaiming Justice and Peace)
MCW	Music in Catholic Worship
RCIA	Rite of Christian Initiation of Adults
SC	*Sacrosanctum Concilium* (Constitution on the Sacred Liturgy)

PART ONE

SCRIPTURE

CHAPTER ONE

GENESIS 1–11

Scientific Background and Biblical Inspiration

TERENCE NICHOLS

Before Arriving at the Session

Read Focal Points and General Introduction.

Focal Points

Because Catholic teaching on creation is complex, we will need:

(1) to understand a sophisticated reading of Genesis 1–11;
(2) to acquire knowledge of recent scientific thinking about how the world was created and how humans developed through evolution; and
(3) to understand the Catholic concept of inspiration.

GENERAL INTRODUCTION

Current scientific theory explains creation with the "Big Bang Theory," but this has been widely accepted only since about 1965. According to this theory the universe originated about fifteen billion years ago in a titanic explosion of energy from which evolved, over billions of years, all present forms of matter and life.

The scientific account of creation is partial—it only presents half the picture. Scientifically, we read nothing about God, angels, the human soul, the afterlife, or the purpose or meaning of creation. We read nothing about values, sin, or the origin of evil. Genesis complements the scientific account. Although its cosmology is outdated, Genesis gives a spiritual or theological account of creation that is still true. For Catholics and most Christians, this is not just opinion but is revelation, it is a story whose basic spiritual truths have been revealed by God to humans.

At the Session

Review Focal Points; view video "Scientific Backgroud and Biblical Inspiration" on Videocassette 1 (41 minutes).

After the Video

1. How can science and Genesis both be true?
2. Summarize the meaning of biblical inspiration and its significance.

NOTES FOR BIBLICAL INSPIRATION*

*These notes can be used before the session or for review

I. Main Points of Catholic and Mainline Protestant Views

   A. Inspiration applies to the authors of the Bible, not to the readers.

   B. The root meaning of "inspiration" is from Latin inspiro, "to breathe on." The image is of the Holy Spirit, that is, God breathing on (inspiring) the authors to write the truth about God.

   C. A definition is that the Bible is the word of God in the words of human beings. The authors of the Bible were inspired or moved by God so that what they wrote revealed the truth about God. But the authors remained fully human instruments and used the language, images, understanding, literary forms, and metaphors with which they were familiar.

   D. Therefore, in the Bible we have a divine author speaking through human authors. The Bible tells us about past time, but it also conveys the revelation that is necessary for our salvation. In short, it tells of spiritual or theological truths, not scientific truths (DV 11).

   E. Problems: God did not dictate the Bible. The human authors had a limited understanding of science, history, geography, and, in the Old Testament, even of morals. Hence parts of the Bible are inconsistent with modern knowledge in these areas.

     1. Science: The cosmology (picture of the universe or cosmos) given in Genesis is primitive and incorrect.

     2. History: Genesis greatly underestimates the age of humanity, the earth, and the universe. The story of a universal flood is not supported by scientific evidence.

     3. Geography: The geography of Eden is mythical. Where exactly was it?

   4. Morality: Does God command genocide (Josh 11:14-15)?

   5. Contradictions: Did the flood last 40 days or 150 days (see Gen 7:17-24)? Did Jesus cleanse the Temple early (John 2) or late (Matthew 21) in his public ministry?

F. Question: Given these errors, how can we hold that the Bible is inspired and that it speaks God's truth?

G. Response:

   1. Revelation concerns spiritual truths about God and humanity that are valid for all times and places (e.g., humans are created by God and do not "just happen"). Scientific knowledge, however, changes every few generations. Our present picture of the origin of the universe—the Big Bang Theory—is only some thirty years old. But errors in non-essential details do not detract from the truth of what is revealed. God meets us where we are. God did not reveal modern physics and astronomy to the authors of Genesis 1–11 because no one in their own time would have believed them. Rather, God reveals permanent spiritual truths through human authors who use the knowledge, concepts, images, and language of their day. Thus the authors of Genesis used the knowledge of their times in writing the creation story. Their cosmology is outdated, but this does not vitiate the revealed spiritual truth that they are presenting.

   2. We must consider the literary form of the passage or book. For example: Genesis 1–11 is myth; Jonah is a parable or fable; Job is a drama; Kings is history. We cannot demand scientific and historical accuracy from a myth. The parables and sayings of Christ are not meant to be taken literally because they convey a spiritual message: "The letter killeth, but the spirit giveth life."

   3. We must read the Bible as a whole (DV 11). There is moral development in the Bible: war, slavery, and afterlife. The full revelation of God is given in Christ, not in the Old Testament.

   4. Inspiration applies to the Bible in its original text, and to copies and translations only insofar as they reflect that text.

   5. We must consider the overall theme of the author. Both Matthew and Luke change Mark's chronology and details to better fit their editorial theme (e.g., Matt 8:28-34, Luke 4).

   6. For Roman Catholics, the final interpretative authority in matters of Scripture and revelation is the Magisterium, the

teaching office of the Church, or more loosely, those who occupy that office, that is, the bishops and the pope. For example, is the story of the expulsion from Eden in Genesis 3 just myth, or does it also contain a deep spiritual truth? The doctrines and teachings of the Church that were usually affirmed by councils of bishops (e.g., Council of Chalcedon) are important in safeguarding and passing on the spiritual truths which generations of Christian believers have seen revealed in the Scriptures.

II. The Catholic and mainline Protestant view is midway between rationalism and fundamentalism.

   A. Rationalism: That is, no appeal beyond reason. Denies any revelation of higher truth in the Bible. Genesis 1–11 is just myth; the Bible is just the words of human beings (not the word of God).

   B. Fundamentalism: Protestant Christians who, reacting against liberalism, insist on maintaining the fundamentals of the faith. Fundamentalists typically deny that there are any errors in the Bible. Rather, they believe it is all literally true. These people are forced to deny many of the truths of modern science, such as evolution, age of the earth, etc. This position insists that the Bible is dictated by God and is the word of God only, not really the words of humans.

Creation

TERENCE NICHOLS

Before Arriving at the Session

Read Background of Genesis 1–11, Notes, The Creation Story in Genesis 1–11 (all below), and Genesis 1–2 in your Bible.

BACKGROUND OF GENESIS 1–11

The literary genre of these chapters is myth, not literal history. It is a story that contains spiritual truth, but is inaccurate in its scientific account of creation. Genesis 1:1–2:4b is by one author, the Priestly author, and was written about 500 B.C.E. during the Babylonian Exile. Genesis 2:5–4:26 is by an earlier author, the Yahwist, and was written about 1000 B.C.E. The Priestly author is abstract, theological, loves numbers and lists (e.g., Genesis 5), and sees God as transcendent, majestic, kingly. The Yahwist author is intimate, familiar, down to earth, sees God as intimate and personal. Both perspectives are necessary.

NOTES

General

The doctrine of creation is one of the most fundamental of all Christian doctrines.

The creation of each human soul by God makes each person a special child of God. Genesis 1–3 teaches us that the world and each human life are especially created by God, and are therefore gifts with special purposes. It also teaches us that God is active in our lives to bring the purpose for which we were created to fulfillment. If we understand that a loving God who wants to bring us to fulfillment personally creates us, we will live our lives differently than if we think we came into the world without any purpose to our lives.

The study of Genesis helps us gain a theological sense of why the idea of creation is important in Christianity and what difference it makes in our lives.

The Christian belief of creation is opposed by a cover story which says that we and the world we live in are just accidents of nature—we just happen. In this view there is no god or transcendent power that wants to bring humanity to fulfillment. We are controlled by fate or powers greater than we are which are hostile or indifferent to our happiness.

The Priestly Account of Creation, Genesis 1:1–2:4

"In the beginning God created the heavens and the earth." Creation means that all is created by God *ex nihilo* (from nothing). God pre-exists all creation; all else is created. The Son pre-exists as God and became incarnate in the man Jesus. Hence God is sovereign over all creation; there is no pre-existent matter, or fate, which governs God. In *When Bad Things Happen to Good People* Harold Kushner says that God consoles us in suffering, but the evil in creation is due to fate. Creation points back to God as its creator. Creation is good. It is not a case of fatalism; it did not "just happen."

There are two stages of creation: (1) creation of all matter from nothing and the creation of each human soul from nothing, and (2) arranging creation into an ordered, harmonious whole. Creation happens by God's word (an analogy for this is that I have an idea and tell it to another).

The seven days of creation are schematic. The time and cosmology of Genesis cannot be taken literally, although the order of creation in Genesis 1 is roughly accurate. The scientific account sees the creation of elements, galaxies, earth, plants, animals, and humans as occurring over billions of years. Theistic evolution is the Catholic position, namely: (1) God directs evolution and (2) God creates each human soul. The human body is the result of eons of evolution, but each soul is uniquely created by God. Hence each human life is "sacred."

The climax of Creation is Gen 1:27-28: "So God created humankind in his image, / . . . / male and female he created them. / God blessed them, and God said to them, '. . . have dominion over the fish of the sea . . . and over every living thing that moves upon the earth.'"

Humans are created in God's image and likeness. Like angels (and unlike animals) humans are spiritual, have free will, intellect, and can know, love, and worship God. We are God's representatives and stewards on earth; we are here to care for it. (See Gen 2:15: "The LORD God took the man and put him in the garden of Eden to till it and keep it.")

We do not participate in the creation *ex nihilo*, but we do participate in God's world of ordering and caring for creation (providence): agriculture, forestry, care of other creatures (animals), and care of other people. The reverse is uncreation, anti-stewardship, ecological destruction, e.g., torching the rain forests in Brazil, acid rain, land and water pollution, loss of topsoil, extinction of species. Children can understand this point.

We are created in relationship with God and others. Indeed, all creation is. We are called to friendship with God and others (children can understand this, too). Genesis 1:20 tells us that humankind does not eat animals, or even plants, only seed-bearing fruit, vegetables, nuts. First creation was harmonious: "God saw all he had made and it was very good." God, as triune, exists in a relationship of love.

Yahwist Account of Creation (Second Creation Story): Gen 2:5-25

This is an intimate, down-to-earth account. People talk with God in the garden. The tree of life is equal to immortality. The tree of the knowledge of good and evil is equal to being like God; that is, deciding for oneself what is good and evil, rather than obeying God. Note the order of creation is different. Here animals are created after man. (Is this historical? No and yes. Recent genetic findings trace the origin of the human race to one human couple, about 200,000 years ago.) Note that there is total trust, innocence, and no defenses, dissimulation, envy, exploitation, or domination.

THE CREATION STORY IN GENESIS 1–11

Background

The stories that make up Genesis 1–11 were written between three thousand and twenty-five hundred years ago by at least three authors. Thus Gen 1:1–2:4, the first creation story, is the work of one author (the Priestly author), written about 550 B.C.E. Gen 2:4–3:24, the second creation story, is by the Yahwist author, written about 1000 B.C.E. (Any good Bible with notes, e.g., the *Jerusalem Bible* or the *Oxford Revised Standard Version,* will explain the textual differences.) The viewpoint of these two authors is very different: compare the image of God in Genesis 1 with the image of God in Genesis 2–3. Because there were originally two different stories and authors, the details of the two creation stories are at times inconsistent. For example, in Genesis 1 God creates the animals before humanity; in Genesis 2, the animals are created after humanity. What we now have in Genesis 1–11 is the result

of a final editing or harmonization done probably at the time of the
Babylonian Exile of the Jews, about 550 B.C.E.

Why Is This Story Important?

Creation stories are important because they tell us of our origins;
these stories, in turn, shape our identity as persons. If we think of our
parents as inferior, we are apt to think of ourselves as inferior. The
worldwide movement of people to rediscover their roots or origins is
at bottom a movement to discover who they are.

There are at least four reasons to study and teach the creation story.
First, it reveals spiritual (theological) truths about God, humanity, the
origin of evil, and the nature of creation. For example, it teaches that
God is the creator of the universe and each human being, that these do
not "just happen." It teaches that the primary source of evil is not bad
technology or lack of resources or poor social planning in the government; it is sin.

Second, the basic Jewish, Christian, and Islamic teaching about
God is that God is Creator and that humans are creatures. Hence all
we have and are, are gifts from God. Our response is gratitude—
thanksgiving or praise (see Psalms 145–150). Young people can understand this as well as anyone. The core of worship is thanksgiving. The
Greek verb *eucharistein,* from which we get "Eucharist," means "to
give thanks." The heart of the Mass is the long prayer of thanksgiving
to God.

Third, the creation story tells us about our origins and hence about
our identity—who we are. According to some scientific writers
(Monod), we are chemical machines that just happened—products of
blind natural forces. According to Judaism, Christianity, and Islam, we
are embodied spirits, created by God out of love and destined for
fellowship with God in love. Though Genesis says that God creates
the human species, Catholic doctrine is that God creates directly each
human soul, even though the body proceeds from the cells of one's
parents, and ultimately from ape-like ancestors. Thus each person is
truly a child of God and is loved by God; this is his or her *primary*
identity.

Finally, the Creation—the natural world—is a good place to start
talking about God; it reflects God. Romans 1:20 reads: "Ever since the
creation of the world his [God's] eternal power and divine nature,
invisible though they are, have been understood and seen through the
things he has made." Creation exhibits design, beauty, order, immen-
sity, intricacy, and harmony. But it is an imperfect reflection of God.
Nature is indifferent to the good of any individual creature, including

humans. Hence we need revelation to supplement what we can learn about God from nature. Since Darwin, nature has more and more been seen not as reflecting God, but as a theater for competition among species. "Nature-red in tooth and claw."

How Should We Read Genesis 1–11 Today?

There are problems that arise in the reading of Genesis 1–11 that do not arise so sharply with other biblical texts. Today we all learn that earth and humanity emerged through a long process of evolution requiring some billions of years. This appears to contradict the Genesis account in which God creates the earth and humanity in seven "days." Human beings, according to modern evolutionary theory, had animal ancestors; they were not created directly by God from the dust of the earth. Again, though there is archaeological evidence for a local flood which covered the Tigris-Euphrates Valley, there is no evidence in the geological record of a universal flood, covering the whole earth and even the mountains (Gen 7:20). Furthermore, there are inconsistencies in the Genesis story itself: Were the animals created before or after humanity? Did the flood last 40 days (Gen 7:17) or 150 days (Gen 7:24)? How then are we to reconcile the inconsistencies between the Genesis account and the findings of modern science? Is the Bible simply wrong?

Faith and Reason

Many groups of Christians called Fundamentalists insist that the Bible must be inerrant, even in details; they insist that Genesis must be a literally true account of physical and scientific history. Thus they reject most of the findings of modern science and drive a wedge between faith and reason: in their view, faith contradicts the findings of reason. This is not, however, the tradition or teaching of the Catholic Church. In Catholicism, faith and reason are complementary, not contradictory. Reason supports what we accept in faith, and faith adds to what we can know through reason, without contradicting it. The basic principle here is the Catholic conviction that there is a unity in our knowledge of reality. What we come to know about the world through natural science will in the end complement and not contradict what we know about God through revelation. Why? The world, according to St. Paul, reveals its Creator through the things which have been made (Rom 1:20). God also reveals himself through the prophets (e.g., Moses, Elijah, and Isaiah) and through Jesus the Christ. If these two types of revelation prove to be ultimately contradictory, we would have to conclude either (1) that God contradicts himself, (2) that God did not make the world, or (3) that God is not revealed through Jesus. But according to Catholic (and Christian) faith, none of these suppositions is true.

Catholics (along with many other Christian believers) therefore accept what appear to be well-established scientific generalizations (such as the theory of evolution) as the legitimate products of reason. This, in turn, has forced Catholics to read Genesis 1–11 somewhat differently from the past. Scripture scholars argue that Genesis 1–11 was and is not meant to be an account of physics or astronomy or even of literal history. It was meant to convey who made the earth and humans, not how they were made. The literary genre of Genesis 1–11 is now thought to be myth, not history. "Myth" in theology does not mean a fiction or untruth (as it means in common speech); it means a story that conveys by means of symbols spiritual truth about human beings. It is thus similar to a parable. And the point of a parable, such as the parable of the prodigal son, is not: "Did this actually happen?" or "How historically accurate is this story?" The point of a parable is its moral and spiritual message conveyed by symbols and allegory.

We might ask "Why didn't God reveal the truth about the physical construction of the universe, as well as spiritual truth, to the people who wrote Genesis?" The answer is that, like a good teacher, God meets us where we are. If I want to communicate with a dog, the best way might be for me to become a dog. Similarly, God became human to teach us the message of salvation. This principle, which we might call the incarnational principle, is the pattern for all of God's revelation. If God had revealed to the authors of Genesis three thousand years ago our modern conception of the universe, no one would have believed them! And we are not sure that our conceptions of the universe are right! Scientific theories change every 60 to 150 years. They are provisional hypotheses, always subject to future revision. So God met the people three thousand years ago where they were. In revealing the spiritual truths necessary for salvation, God allowed the human authors to use the images and concepts of the universe which were familiar to that culture. If God had not done so, and had tried to reveal modern scientific theories of the universe, people would not have been able to understand the message and probably would have rejected the whole thing, including the spiritual truths. God knows, after all, that we can discover the physical truth about the universe for ourselves, by using our intellect. It is the spiritual truths necessary for salvation that we cannot completely discover, and which hence need to be revealed. Furthermore, the best way to convey spiritual truth is through symbols, not concepts, because symbols, like parables, contain many levels of meaning which enrich one another, like harmonic tones in music.

There are, then, two levels of authorship in Genesis (and other biblical texts): God and the human authors. God does not dictate the language of the biblical texts. Rather, God guides the human authors, but gives them liberty to use the language, images, concepts, and literary forms of their own time.

Thus Genesis 1–11 requires careful interpretation. But even children can grasp its basic messages: the world and humanity were created by a good and loving God and did not "just happen." Creation, including us, is good, not evil or fated. Humans are made in the "image" of God, unlike all other animals. Sin causes human beings to become separated from God and from one another.

What Does Genesis Tell Us about the World?

Israel's creation story differed markedly from the creation stories of her neighbors. In the Babylonian creation epic *Enuma Elish* the universe is created as a result of warfare between the gods. The hero Marduk defeats Tiamet, the evil monster-goddess, and Marduk makes the sky and earth from Tiamet's carcass. The universe is made from the dead body of an evil monster-god! Similarly, Marduk makes humanity from the blood of another evil god, Kingu, as Marduk exclaims: "Savage-man I will create. He will be charged with the service of the gods that they may be at ease!" (Pritchard, 36). Thus, in the Babylonian vision, both the universe and humanity originate from evil gods, and humans are created to be the slaves of the gods.

The Greeks also had myths telling of the origin of the gods, the universe, and humanity, but the gods, the universe, and humanity all were subject to fate, a power greater than even the gods. This belief gave Greek thought its characteristic tragic character; even heroes, such as Achilles, Hector, and Oedipus, are fated to suffer tragic destinies.

For many other ancient peoples, such as the Canaanites, who occupied the land of Palestine before Israel entered it, the gods were essentially divinized natural forces, to which humans had to make sacrifices in order to gain their favor or appease their wrath. Thus the Canaanites occasionally burned their first-born child as an appeasement offering to the gods, a practice condemned in Israel.

Some of the stories that might be called "cover stories" of the ancient world are (1) that the world and people are evil, (2) that human life is controlled by fate so that tragedy is inescapable, (3) that humans were created to be the slaves of higher powers, and (4) that the gods were nature-gods demanding appeasement. These stories were believed by vast numbers of people because they were the commonly-accepted "official" explanations of origins in their cultures. They functioned as self-fulfilling prophecies: those who believed these stories were doomed to repeat them.

By contrast, in the Genesis account there is no fate or other gods or previously existing evil force to limit God's creative freedom. God freely creates the world, and all that is created is good. The world itself is not to be worshiped, nor do evil forces control it. God is sovereign over all nature and all evil, and the heavens themselves declare the glory of their creator. Furthermore, the universe in Genesis has a beginning in time. It is not eternal, nor is time a series of eternally repetitive cycles, which bind human life to a never-ending tragic circle, a belief common in the ancient world.

In summary, the world is good but not divine. It points beyond itself to the God who is its Creator, and who alone is to be worshiped. It has a history and develops through time.

What Does Genesis Tell Us about Human Beings?

According to Genesis 1, the "cosmic" creation story, God made humans as the completion and fulfillment of creation; they did not just happen by accident. And Gen 1:26-27 says that humans, and only humans, were created "in the image of God." This is a wonderful example of a symbol carrying a wealth of meaning which the Church is still reflecting upon. What do you think that might mean? Scripture scholars now think that the literal meaning of this symbol may be as follows: Since ancient kings could not be present in all corners of their kingdoms simultaneously, they used to set up statues, or images, of themselves to remind the people who was king. Alternatively, they might appoint deputies or stewards to act as their representatives (or images). Following this theory, the literal or surface meaning of Gen 1:27 would be that human beings have been set up as God's stewards or custodians of the world God created. This is implied also in Gen 2:15 which states that God set Adam in the Garden of Eden "to till it and keep it." (What kind of job are humans doing in caring for God's earth?)

Over the centuries, however, Christian (and Jewish) thinkers have discerned deeper levels of meaning—allegorical, moral, and anagogical—in this symbolic text. A common interpretation has been that the "image" is spiritual. Like God, we have intellect, free choice, and knowledge of spiritual things, so that unlike any other animal we can know and thank God. We are created with an intrinsic relationship and orientation to God! Morally, the lesson might be that if all people are images of God, we have no right to use them as objects for our own ends (Gen 1:26-27 is frequently referred to by Catholic bishops to support this moral teaching). And anagogically, this text would seem to say that, as images of God, we have a multiple responsibility: to steward God's creation wisely, to honor and respect others as living images of God, and to know, love, and thank God as our Creator. The greatest of all gifts that we have from God is not mere biological life (which plants and animals have also). It is the privilege to have been made in God's image and to be gifted with a spiritual as well as a physical vocation.

Genesis 2–3, the second creation story, which we might call the "garden" story, tells us more about human beings from a perspective different than that of Genesis 1. Here the first human is made from the dust of the ground (the Hebrew word for man is "adam," a cognate for the word for "ground" [*adamah*]) and is put in the Garden of Eden "to till and to keep it." The animals are made as man's helpmates, and, finally, woman is made by God as man's companion. The mythical story of God making Eve from Adam's rib does not symbolize that woman is inferior to man, but that the two share a deep, intimate relationship. This point is made in the verse immediately following Gen 2:22, the woman is "bone of my bones, flesh of my flesh." In a striking symbol, the two humans are naked and unashamed before each other and before God. They have a perfect relationship with each other, with the animals (there is no warfare between humans and animals in Genesis; humans eat only plants, not animals), and with God, who converses directly with the human creatures and who walks in the garden with them in the evening (Gen 3:8). This, indeed, is probably the allegorical meaning of the garden: it symbolizes a state of unbroken relationship with God, others, and nature. To such a state we give the name "paradise." We find this in Ps 16:11: "You show me the path of life. / In your presence there is fullness of joy."

In summary, Genesis 1–2 tells us that human beings have been created by God as the completion of creation, are made in God's image, in a perfect relationship with God, other humans, and nature. (The Catholic Church teaches that although the first humans may have had animal ancestors, and it is our parents who give birth to our bodies, the soul of every person is created by God, so that each person is truly a child of God and is precious to God.) Note that this opposes the ancient "cover stories" that saw humans as created out of evil material, to be slaves of the gods, and to be governed by fate rather than by a loving Creator. But this story also opposes certain modern cover stories. We are told over and over again by the media that happiness is to be found in the accumulation of material possessions, rather than in fulfilled relationships with God and one another. We are told to "look out for number one" rather than to care for others and for the earth. We are told to gratify our desires for money, sex, power, and possessions because these are "natural" desires. But are they "natural"? Are they what God wants? This brings us to the question of what went wrong with God's good creation.

At the Session

Review key ideas from your reading; view video "Creation" on Videocassette 1 (40 minutes), using the following outline as a guide during the video:

I. How does a culture's belief in the stories of their beginnings impact a person's life?

A. In the Genesis accounts of creation, the writers were opposing the prevailing pre-revelation view of the beginnings of human life.

B. Listen for ways that one's view of the origin of human life impacts daily life and decisions.

II. What does the Babylonian story of our beginnings teach?

A. More melancholy forces beyond humans.

B. Humans are slaves of the gods.

III. What do the Genesis stories teach about the beginnings of human beings?

A. All is good. Stories stem from God and God's word.

B. Humans are made in the image of God.

C. All is gift for which we will be accountable and responsible.

D. Spirit is life.

E. Eden is perfect harmony living with God.

F. Tree of the knowledge of good and evil and the tree of life.

G. We are called to be responsible stewards.

IV. What does "image of God" mean (Gen 1:26-27)? It is important that the human dignity of each person is intrinsic.

V. What do the following signify?

A. Spirit: life, breath.

B. Eden: mythical place, symbol of complete harmony between humans and God.

    C. Tree of knowledge of good and evil is the power to choose between the two. Adam and Eve did not know the evil of sin.

    D. Tree of life: eternal life.

  VI. The purpose of Sunday is to recover the perfection of Eden at least one day of the week.

 VII. Scientific evolution tells us of God's way of creation—the "how" of creation; Genesis tells us the "why" of creation. God has a purpose and task for each of us. It is our responsibility to find out what our purpose is here on the earth.

VIII. What does our present-day culture say about:

    A. What makes people happy?

    B. What is expected in the areas of rights and responsibilities?

    C. What is a prevailing idea: sin, death, shame or guilt, independence?

  IX. How do the attitudes of present-day culture differ from the Genesis stories?

Discussion

1. Why is it important to understand the creation story?
2. What does it mean to say that the world is good?
3. Does it make a difference whether or not the world is created by God, rather than just happening by cosmic accident?
4. What does it mean to say that human beings are created in God's image?

The Fall

TERENCE NICHOLS

Before Arriving at the Session

Read Notes, the essay "What Does God Tell Us About Sin?" (both below), and Genesis 3–11 in your Bible.

NOTES

I. The Serpent: In Christian interpretation, but not Jewish, Satan is a transpersonal source of evil that exists before humanity. Created as a good angel, Lucifer "fell" from heaven (cf. Job 1). The mystery of evil has a transpersonal aspect that we cannot plumb by reason.

II. Satan

    A. Plants a doubt in Eve's mind: "Did God really say you were not to eat from any of the trees of the garden?"

    B. Lies to Eve: "You will not die."

    C. Incites envy (a deadly sin): "You will be like God" (Gen 3:5). Eve eats the fruit ("apple" is a later conception of painters) and, in doing so, disobeys God. This originates sin. It is due to a free choice. (Not to the "system" or to poverty or genetics or bad upbringing. Although the temptation came from Satan, the choice came from Eve.) Adam chooses sin.

III. Results of the first sin.

    A. Shame and mistrust between man and woman, broken friendship (relationship).

    B. Hide from God: fear of God, broken relationship, broken friendship with God (all sin cuts us off from God and from other people, and even from natural creation).

C. Denial of responsibility: Adam blames Eve; Eve blames the serpent. (First effect of repentance and conversion is acceptance of personal responsibility: "I am responsible, I need forgiveness, redemption, a savior." Repentance reverses the effects of sin.)

D. Serpent is accursed; Satan falls from heaven.

E. Enmity between humankind and nature: a natural process. Childbirth now causes pain and suffering. The soil does not yield fruit but thistles. Farming is hard work, painful, frustrating.

F. Expulsion from Eden, that is, from God's presence.

G. This expulsion causes suffering, alienation, physical death, social breakdown. Genesis 4: first murder is fratricide. All this is the result of sin, which, in breaking our relationship with God, breaks the source of life, goodness, and blessing.

What Does Genesis Tell Us About Sin?

Adam and Eve were told by God not to eat of the fruit of the tree of knowledge of good and evil. But the serpent tempts Eve by saying, "You will be like God, knowing good and evil" (Gen 3:5). The temptation here is to be equal with God and to be able to decide for oneself what is good and what is evil, in other words, to create one's own moral law rather than to submit to God's law (the temptation to be number one is as old as the human race).

People, even children, sometimes ask, "Why was the serpent in the garden?" The serpent, of course, is a symbol. It is a talking serpent, not like an ordinary snake. Like any symbol it carries a richness of meaning that cannot be exhausted in a few sentences. But certainly it points out that there is an evil in the world which exists before humanity, and for which we are not responsible. We are only responsible for our response to its temptations. According to Christian tradition, but not the Genesis text, the serpent is Satan. Satan fell from heaven before humans were created, but God allows Satan to continue in existence, possibly to test human beings (Job 1:6-13).

Thus, although Eve is tempted, she does not have to yield to the temptation. Sin is usually preceded by temptation, but humans always retain the freedom to refuse the temptation. Note also that although Eve is the first to sin, she is neither more nor less guilty than Adam, who also sins.

The results of this first human sin are striking. (1) There is shame and mistrust between Adam and Eve: the perfect relationship that had prevailed between them is broken. (2) Their guilt causes them to hide from God; that relationship is also damaged. (3) They deny responsibility for their sin. Adam blames Eve; she in turn blames the serpent. (4) God curses them, so the harmony that they had experienced with nature is destroyed. (5) They are expelled from Eden, which symbolically means the full presence of God. Henceforth all human generations will be born outside of Eden, that is, in a state of alienation from God. Christian tradition calls this state "original sin."

Theologically, being born in original sin does not mean that we are born evil. Christian couples do not have a baby and say "Yetch! It's evil! It's full of original sin!" Each human person is good because all that God creates is good. But each person (except Jesus and Mary, who were born free of original sin) is also born lacking the full presence and knowledge of God in his or her life. Because of this our human nature, as we experience it in this life, is distorted from what it would be if we lived in the full knowledge and love of God. In particular, our spontaneous desires, such as egotism, selfishness, envy, jealously, rage, hatred, lust, etc., while they seem "natural," are not really natural (they are not the way they were meant to be; they are the result of our maturing apart from God's presence). Such desires are made worse by the "cover story" of the world, which unceasingly tells us that by having money, possessions, sexual pleasure, or power over others, our first priority (our "god"), we will be happy. In fact, this is a lie. Only by turning back to God as our first love can we be made happy. The things of this world are good and are meant to be enjoyed in moderation, but if they become number one in our lives, they block out the presence of God. To return to God, therefore, is a lifelong struggle against the "cover story" of the world and even against parts of ourselves. (Read Gal 5:16-26 on the struggle between the Spirit and the "flesh." But note that what Paul calls the "flesh" is not the body; rather, it is sinful tendencies such as envy, rage, etc.) We cannot make this return without the grace of God, which comes to us through the Church, the Bible, and the sacraments.

After the expulsion of Adam and Eve from paradise, sin gathers force in human history (because human beings are divorced from God), resulting in murder (Cain kills Abel) and violence (Lamech, Gen 4:23), so that by Genesis 6 God "saw that the wickedness of humankind was great in the earth." According to the mythical story, therefore, God cleanses the earth with a flood. But just as sinful behavior among people brought on the flood, the holiness of one man, Noah, is enough to save the human race and the animals from extinction. But after the flood, sin remains on the earth, as is clear from the Tower of Babel story, in which ambitious humans, still trying to be like God, build a huge tower, only to have God scatter them and confuse their languages so that they cannot understand one another. As in Genesis 3, sin brings broken relationships.

In summary, the effect of sin is to break our relationship with God and with each other, and lead us to deny responsibility for our actions. If the relationship with God is never mended, we may be permanently alienated from God, even in the next life. But God's gift of Jesus the Christ was given precisely to heal the broken relationships with God and with other people. That is why Jesus died on the cross, to reconcile us with the Father. That is why the two great commandments of Jesus are to love God with all our heart and to love others as we love ourselves (Matt 22:37-38).

Note that most modern analysis of society's problems blames poverty, broken families, poor education, peer pressure, etc. Almost never is sin said to be the cause. But while poverty, broken families, poor education, and peer pressure can certainly predispose us to sin (they are temptations), we always have a choice. We do not have to follow the crowd and sin. It is important to teach this truth to children.

At the Session

View video "The Fall" on Videocassette 1 (18 minutes), using the outline below as an aid during the video.

After the Video

Discuss one or two of the following issues:

1. What is the main temptation in the garden?
2. What does "sin" mean?
3. The effects of sin are listed below. Continue to fill in the blanks with the meanings of these effects.

   Recognize they are naked means an atmosphere of mistrust; fractured relationship.

   Hide from God means _____

   Blame another means _____

   God curses serpent, woman, and man means _____

   Banished from the Garden of Eden means _____

4. Summary: They do not have full presence of God; they do not have immortality; their relationships (with God, each other, nature) are broken.

5. Describe original sin.

6. Describe personal sin.

7. How did murder, violence, vengeance increase after the first sin? Think of the stories of Cain and Abel, Lamech, the time of the flood, the Tower of Babel. What is the meaning of these stories?

8. How did God reach out in covenant to help restore relationships in Eden and in the lives of Abraham, Moses, and Jesus?

9. In what ways do our present-day cultural attitudes differ from the biblical stories about the Fall?

Further Reflection

1. What is sin and what are its effects?

2. What is the Christian interpretation of original sin?

- The effects of original sin are inherited from our first parents. We wake up in the world selfish and in need of redemption. We do not spontaneously love God and our neighbor; we have to learn this. We struggle to move from "Me-centeredness" to "Thou-centeredness." Even infants are affected by original sin—it is pre-personal. We choose personal sin. Sin does not mean we are "bad"; it means we are disoriented—directed away from God to excessive self-concern. The effect of all sin is to cut us off from God and others. Like a drug addiction, the will is "hooked." We cannot kick the habit alone, but need a redeemer—Jesus. The cover story analyzes evil and explains that problems in society are due to lack of resources, money, the "system," etc. Much of this is true, but the cover story tends to deny personal responsibility. We are all subject to pressure to commit evil (temptation), but in the end it is we who decide and are responsible before God. Repentance acknowledges this fact. Children can understand this. We need to make sure that children hear this message. Our Christian life, from baptism forward, is a growth back to God, to recover the friendship that our first parents had with God.

- Much modern analysis of the importance of psychology, genetics, social upbringing, poverty, etc., is true. But the Christian vision is also true. This vision teaches that the root cause of evil, suffering, and disaster is human sin: lack of friendship with God. For example: Will we solve the drug problem with more money, more prisons, better systems, without a reassertion of personal responsibility before God for our actions?

- Consider the environment as an example. Destruction of the environment, which in part is due to ignorance, poor planning, etc., is mainly due to selfish and short-term behavior.

- A free society can only exist if it is a responsible society. Irresponsible children and adults cannot be given freedom. Hence, the Christian insistence on responsibility, which we find in Genesis and the New Testament, is basic to the preservation of a free society. The cover story's insistence that nothing is anyone's fault leads directly to totalitarianism. Hence, our work as educators is indispensable to the welfare not only of young people but also of the society itself.

Summary

Sin increases fragmentation of relationships. Repentance brings back the life of the Garden of Eden in the beginning.

The story of Noah and the flood in Genesis 6–7 shows that humankind is evil. "The thoughts in his heart fashioned wickedness all day long." (Note: Sin begins in our thought, then is externalized in action. That is why violence on TV and pornography are so bad. Flood is a return to chaos, undoing of creation, and then the remaking of it through Noah.)

The story of the covenant in Gen 8:20-22 shows that creation will not return to chaos. (Note: Humankind now remains sinful. Humans are good, because we were created good, but we are out of tune with God and God's will.) The covenant begins the story of salvation history. Later covenants with Abraham and Moses establish the Jewish People (Old Testament = Old Covenant; New Testament = New Covenant) in Christ, represented in the Mass, reestablishes the original harmony that was, or was to be, ours at creation. The New Covenant is not complete until the resurrection when humanity and creation will be redeemed ("bought back"—a term in finance). We read in Rom 8:18-21:

> I consider that the sufferings of this present time are not worth comparing with the glory about to be revealed to us. For the creation waits with eager longing for the revealing of the children of God; for the creation was subjected to futility, not of its own will but by the will of the one who subjected it, in hope that the creation itself will be set free from its bondage to decay and will obtain the freedom of the glory of the children of God.

This happens in the resurrection.

Providence

TERENCE NICHOLS

Before Arriving at the Session

Read Focal Points and the essay below; refer to glossary for the definition of "providence."

Focal Points

God's providence involves a total and continuous relationship between God and ourselves. An appreciation of the gift of faith enables us to accept the problem of evil in our lives and in the world.

PROVIDENCE

The Christian doctrine of providence means that God provides for and "looks after" the creation and the creatures God has made. This follows from the doctrine of creation. God does not simply create the universe and then stand back, allowing it to run on its own, like a perpetual motion watch or machine. This is a central belief of Deism, but not of Christianity. The God of Christianity, like the God of Judaism, is present and active within the whole history of creation and within the lives of each human creature. This is affirmed in both the Old and New Testaments. Psalms 23 and 91 speak of God's protective care (it might be well to memorize Psalm 23). God intervenes to save God's people at the crossing of the Red Sea (Exodus 14–15) and provides for them in the desert by sending them quail and manna to eat (Exodus 16ff.). In the New Testament God's providential care is expressed in miracles, in the powerful presence of the Spirit within the Christian

community (e.g., Acts 2 and 3), in the guidance given that community
by the Spirit (e.g., Acts 10:3-16; 13:2), and in the experience of grace
and answered prayer. The strongest passage in the New Testament
concerning God's providence is probably Matt 6:25-33. This is so important that it is worth quoting in full.

> Therefore I tell you, do not worry about your life, what you
> will eat or what you will drink, or about your body, what you
> will wear. Is not life more than food and the body more than
> clothing? Look at the birds of the air; they neither sow nor reap
> nor gather into barns, and yet your heavenly father feeds them.
> Are you not of more value than they? And can any of you by
> worrying add a single hour to your span of life? And why do
> you worry about clothing? Consider the lilies of the field, how
> they grow; they neither toil nor spin, yet I tell you, even
> Solomon in all his glory was not clothed like one of these. But
> if God so clothes the grass of the field, which is alive today and
> tomorrow is thrown into the oven, will he not much more
> clothe you—you of little faith? Therefore do not worry, saying,
> "What will we eat?" or "What will we drink?" or "What will
> we wear?" For it is the Gentiles who strive for all these things;
> and indeed your heavenly Father knows that you need all
> these things. But strive first for the kingdom of God and his
> righteousness, and all these things will be given you as well.

According to this passage, if we are holy and righteous, we can
trust ourselves wholly to God's providence (e.g., Mother Teresa's nuns
do not ask for donations nor do they allow others to raise money for
them, yet the money continues to come).

It follows from the doctrine of providence that we can pray to and
trust God for our needs, but not necessarily for luxuries. It is an
ancient Catholic practice to pray for necessities, for healing, for good
weather, for protection, and for any needs we may have.

The Problem of Evil

Even children know that people, including Christians, suffer many
misfortunes. As Harold Kushner puts it in *When Bad Things Happen to
Good People*, the wrong people lose their property, get sick, and die.
Even Jesus and the apostles suffered terrible persecutions. How do we
explain this, while still believing in God's providence?

First, evil is defined by St. Thomas Aquinas as the lack of a good
that ought to be present in order for a person to be fulfilled. Thus, it is
an evil if a person is blind since sight is necessary to human function-
ing and fulfillment, but it is not an evil if a person cannot fly since

flight is not necessary to human fulfillment. Evil can be classed as either moral evil (caused by human free will, such as oppression, exploitation, wars, etc.) or natural evil (not apparently caused by human free will, such as the evil due to natural disasters, diseases, genetic defects, etc.).

The first point to be made about providence and evil is that it is a mistake to assume that God directly wills and causes each event. This would make God directly responsible for evil, such as the evil of an earthquake or a war. Christian theologians therefore distinguish between what God directly wills and what God allows, without directly willing, for the sake of a greater good. Thus God has created human beings with freedom of choice. Without this choice we would be robots, not humans, and we could not come freely to know, worship, and love God. We could not, in a word, be friends or lovers of God, which is what God intends for human creatures. If God were to override human freedom, human beings would have to be destroyed in order to do it. It appears that God does not override human freedom, though he can be active at all times trying to persuade people to act rightly. Thus God did not annihilate the freedom of Hitler, or of those who followed him (a large number of people), for the sake of a greater good, namely, the good of human freedom. This does not mean that God sat back as a disinterested spectator and watched the evil Hitler and his accomplices caused from afar. This would be a Deist view, but not a Christian view. No, God is active in the situation at all times, trying to persuade those committing evil deeds to repent and trying to persuade others to oppose those who are doing the evil. As the great English statesman Edmund Burke said, "It is enough for evil to triumph if good men [sic] do nothing" (Bartlett, 454). Furthermore, God, through Jesus, suffers with the victims of injustice. This is made clear in Matt 25:31-46, a passage so important that it ought to be learned by students, if not verbatim, then in paraphrase.

Thus one explanation for the presence of evil in the world is that God allows human beings the freedom to be human, and to be inhuman, for the sake of a greater good, namely, the existence of human freedom. Perhaps, we might complain, God has given us too much freedom and too much responsibility, but this seems like a childish objection. God wants us to grow into fully responsible beings, worthy of God's friendship, and to do this we have to accept the consequences of our freedom and responsibility.

The appeal to free will, however, does not explain the more difficult problem of natural evil: why people die in natural disasters or suffer from genetic defects and unavoidable diseases. The ancient Christian answer to this problem is that it is due to original sin, that is, to the

fact that humans are individually and communally separated from
God due to the sin of our first parents. If we were in perfect harmony
with God, as God intends, we would not suffer from natural evils.
This seems to be approximately the view of the New Testament: death
and natural evils are due to the power of Satan over the human race,
which in turn is due to the fact that humanity, by turning from God,
put themselves in the power of Satan. Still, there is also a strong New
Testament faith that if we as a community turn back to God, natural
evils will be alleviated or lessened, if not entirely eliminated.

A more modern answer to this problem, coming from scientist-
theologians such as Arthur Peacocke and John Polkinghorne, is that
God has set up creation so that its natural laws are constant. If they
were not constant, we could not rely on them. We know when we get
out of bed in the morning that gravity will still be operating, that the
forces which hold molecules together will still be operating, etc. Were
it not so, if these laws fluctuated, the structures on which we depend
for living, including our bodies, would disintegrate. So the constancy
of the laws of nature is a reflection of God's constant and reliable love.
But sometimes it happens that the operations of nature, in following
its laws, clash with the good of a person or persons who happen to be
in the wrong place at the wrong time. There is nothing wrong per se
with earthquakes, but natural evil is produced when they occur where
people are living. The evil then is the result of a chance intersection of
two lines of causality: that producing the earthquake and that which
places human beings in the vicinity of an earthquake.

Still, the New Testament view, and the view of many modern theologians as well, is that if we trust in God we can be protected from
these things to some extent. Unfortunately, our holiness and faith, not
just individually but as a community, are not deep enough to bring
about the kind of harmony with God which was intended to be present in the beginning. So Christians, as well as other people, do suffer
from natural evil in this life.

The ultimate Christian answer to the problem of evil is to be found
in Christian belief in the afterlife, when God will "make all things
new" and "every tear will be wiped away" (Revelation 21). We cannot
avoid death and suffering in this life. But recompense will be given,
both to the good and to the wicked, in the next life, and, according to
Paul, we will then realize that the sufferings of this life are not worthy
to be compared with the glory which is to come (Rom 8:18). This is the
faith of the New Testament and of the living Christian Church. In the
end, then, our confidence in God's providence will be justified. We
cannot say, in any individual case, why one person suffers or dies prematurely. In this life that is a mystery but in the next life the reasons

may be clearer. This is expressed in a magnificent image at the end of Dante's "Paradiso," the last section of his *Divine Comedy*, where he writes: "I saw all the scattered leaves [i.e., book pages] of the universe bound into one volume" (Ciardi, Canto XXXIII, lines 85–7).

It is important to teach children to realize that they can pray to God and trust in God's providence. Most Christians today seem to think that God exists but is distant and somewhat uninvolved. Hence they do not think that much about God until nearing death. Such a belief effectively is a Deist belief and denies that God is present through the Holy Spirit in every moment of our lives. But for this power to be actualized in anyone's life, that person must be open to God: actively praying to and trusting in God, leading a life of faith and holiness so that the Holy Spirit can truly be a part of his or her life. Sometimes the analogy of radio waves is used (they surround us twenty-four hours a day but we are unaware of their presence unless we have a radio and tune it into the right frequency). This image can apply to our relationship with God. Unless we are tuned into God, which requires seeking God's kingdom and righteousness above all else, God's presence will be unrealized in our lives.

Thus God's providence is really meant to be a cooperation between God and ourselves. God intends to direct and govern his creation in cooperation with human persons, who are the stewards of that creation. To be stewards means we have to be in tune with God—listening, free from sin and selfishness so that we can hear God's direction, experience God's power, and express it in our lives. It is a mistake to think that God directs the creation like a puppet master controlling puppets. Rather, God intends to direct the creation with human cooperation. But if people are not tuned into God, the history of that creation will be less good than God intends.

It is important to note here another Christian belief: that God can bring good out of evil. The classic example is God's bringing good out of the crucifixion and death of Jesus himself. Paul writes that "we know that all things work together for good for those who love God" (Rom 8:28). Thus even evil can be incorporated in God's plan, but it would be better—and entail less suffering—if evil did not occur. We can imagine this as follows: Let us assume that God has a plan A for a given group of people. But some of these people turn against God, forcing God to enact plan B. This plan can still bring about the end God intends but at the cost of greater suffering. Let us consider an example. God, according to Christian belief, sent Jesus to be the Messiah (leader anointed by the Spirit) to the Jews. Many Jews accepted him as the Messiah (the earliest Christian community was a community of converted Jews). In their eyes Jesus brought Judaism to its fulfillment.

If the Jewish leaders, and consequently the mass of the Jewish populace, had accepted Jesus as the Messiah, it would not have meant that Judaism would have been displaced by Christianity. Rather, it would have meant that Judaism achieved the fulfillment promised by the prophets. Jewish followers of Jesus would have gone out and spread the good news of salvation to all the world, as we see Philip doing in Acts 9. This, then, was (apparently) God's plan A. But the Jewish leaders, and following them, most of the Jewish nation, rejected Jesus as the Messiah. Jews are still waiting for the Messiah, or for a Messianic age. So the Holy Spirit went out to the Gentiles (Acts 10), and through the Gentiles spread the good news of salvation to the entire world. This was plan B, but plan B entailed more suffering than plan A, certainly for the Jews but also for the Christians, since it meant hostility, persecution, and war between the Jews and Christians.

The lesson of this is that God works through holy persons (including non-Christians), but must work around evil or ungodly persons. Such persons cannot foil God's plans entirely—God's providence will always prevail—but they can increase the cost of human suffering entailed in the fulfillment of God's plans.

It is important to teach children that even during hard times, God is still present. God has not abandoned us. Somehow, God allows the hard time for the sake of a greater good. If we persevere in faith, we can realize that greater good; often its emergence is directly tied to the difficulty that we must endure. If, however, we give up on God, we probably will not realize the greater good to which God is directing us. In the case of dying persons who are suffering, that greater good may be on the other side of death. Enduring a final illness with patience and faith can bring great purification to a person and to those around a sick person.

What I have given here are, so to speak, abstract theological principles, but most of these ideas are probably best transmitted to children by stories. The story of Joseph in Genesis is a good example of God's providence working through what appears to be great hardship. So is the Exodus cycle of stories, including the crossing of the Red Sea and the wandering in the desert. See also the birth of Samuel (1 Samuel 1). Many of the psalms tell of God's providential care. The New Testament tells the story of Jesus' death and resurrection. There are also many such stories in the lives of past and contemporary saints.

At the Session

Review Focal Points; view video "Providence and the Afterlife" on Videocassette 1 (19 minutes).

After the Video

1. Why is the problem of evil a focal point in this presentation?
2. State the difference between moral evil and natural evil.
3. Form small groups. Each group select one of the five key statements listed below. Then spend a few minutes discussing insights, observations, and points of clarification. After allowing time for discussion have each group summarize key issues.
   - God is actively involved in creation through time.
   - God does not directly allow evil. God allows it in order to bring about a greater good.
   - Our cooperation with God is essential. We are the caretakers of creation.
   - We do not have to be victimized by natural disasters. The greater our relationship with God, the more possibility we have to lessen disasters.
   - We learn through suffering.

Further Reflection

What impact does providence have on your life and on the lives of those with whom you live, work, and socialize?

BIBLIOGRAPHY

Anderson, Bernhard. "Creation in the Bible" and "Creation in the Noachic Covenant." *Cry of the Environment: Rebuilding the Christian Creation Tradition.* Ed. Philip Joranson and Ken Butigan. Santa Fe: Bear and Co., 1984. These pieces are more difficult theologically than Boadt and Vawter.

Bartlett, John. *Bartlett's Familiar Quotations.* 14th ed. Boston: Little Brown and Co., 1968.

Boadt, Lawrence. *Reading the Old Testament.* Ch. 6. New York: Paulist Press, 1984.

Catechism of the Catholic Church. Part One: §1, chs. 1–3; §2, chs. 1–3. Part Two: §2, chs. 1–3. Part Three: §1, ch. 1; §2, chs. 1–2. Part Four: §1, ch. 1; §2, ch. 2, art. 2. Washington, D.C.: United States Catholic Conference, 1994.

Ciardi, John. *The Paradiso.* New York: New American Library, 1970.

Genesis 3–11.

Hawking, Stephen. *A Brief History of Time.* New York: Bantam Books, 1988. A difficult account. In the last half Hawking proposes his own very controversial and speculative theory to the effect that there was no "beginning" to the universe.

Jastrow, Robert. *Until the Sun Dies.* New York: Warner Books, 1977. A simple account for beginners, now out of print but probably available through libraries.

Kramer, William. *Evolution and Creation: A Catholic Understanding.* Huntington, Ind.: Our Sunday Visitor Press, 1986.

Pritchard, James. *The Ancient Near East.* Princeton, N.J.: Princeton University Press, 1969.

Smith, Richard F. "Inspiration and Inerrancy." *Jerome Biblical Commentary.* Ed. Raymond Brown et al. Englewood Cliffs, N.J.: Prentice-Hall, 1968.

Vatican Council II. *Dei verbum* (The Dogmatic Constitution on Divine Revelation). November 18, 1965.

Vawter, Bruce. *A Path Through Genesis.* New York: Sheed and Ward, 1956.

CHAPTER TWO

SCRIPTURE AND SPIRITUALITY

Spirituality of Children

ARTHUR KENNEDY

Before Arriving at the Session

Read Focal Points.

> **Focal Points**
>
> In the first part of the video the presenter recalls incidents when Jesus calls attention to the importance of children. Jesus makes us aware that children, like adults, are persons with a vocation from God. As adults, we have a responsibility to establish trust between ourselves and children so that we may be the instrument through which their gift of faith is strengthened and deepened.
>
> The second part of the tape is an interview with Robert Coles, who describes his experience with six-year-old Ruby Bridges and speaks of the mystery of her spirituality.

At the Session

Discuss the role of adults in a child's Christian formation; view video "Spirituality of Children" on Videocassette 2 (28 minutes).

After the Video

1. How did Ruby incorporate the words of Jesus in her life?

2. What would have been a natural way of reacting to her situation? If Ruby had acted as our culture dictates, how would the outcome be different?

3. How was Ruby able to do this? She did not see things in merely a natural way. She acted in her world of reality that was both natural and supernatural.

Further Reflection

Does my view of everyday life include spirituality?

BIBLIOGRAPHY

Coles, Robert. *The Call of Stories.* Boston: Houghton Mifflin, 1989.

_____. *Harvard Diary.* New York: Crossroads Publishing, 1988.

_____. *Spiritual Life of Children.* Boston: Houghton Mifflin, 1990.

Fitzgerald, Sally, ed. *The Habit of Being: Letters of Flannery O'Connor.* New York: Vintage Books, 1979.

O'Connor, Flannery. "Introduction to a Memoir of Mary Ann." *Mystery and Manners: Occasional Prose.* Sel. and ed. Sally and Robert Fitzgerald. New York: Farrar, Straus and Giroux, 1969.

_____. *Three by Flannery O'Connor.* New York: New American Library, 1983.

Scripture Confronts the Cover Story

ARTHUR KENNEDY

Before Arriving at the Session

Read Focal Points, Notes, and the essay "Scripture Confronts the Cover Story."

Focal Points

In this essay and video we begin to explore thought patterns that cover up and impede our relationship with God. We call these negative patterns of stories "cover stories."

NOTES BY KATHLEEN FOLEY

Apperceptive Mass and Cover Story

Explaining the game of football to a person who knows very little about it and does not really care to learn can be a difficult challenge. The wise explainer would do well to pay attention to both the lack of knowledge and the attitude of disinterest. The learner has a history of experiences stored within that immediately causes a barrier. We call the storehouse of experiences the apperceptive mass of each person.

Parents and teachers are constantly using the gift of apperceptive mass to teach ideas, attitudes, and values to their children or students. Another way to say this is that teachers will go from a known to an unknown idea; from the learned attitude to the reinforced attitude; from a value already there to a more complex value. Apperception means the process of understanding something perceived in terms of previous experience and is the sum total of all our experiences held in our hearts and minds. We understand new ideas or new concepts dependant on our previous experiences. As we continue to live each day, we gain in our hearts and minds not only concepts in the mind, but also attitudes and values in the heart. Building an apperceptive mass is a continual process for each person, and each experience we have helps to reinforce or change what is already there in ideas and attitudes.

Understanding and appreciating the game of football is desirable to some. For others it is a negative to be abhorred or, at least, an activity to be ignored. The cumulative effect of past experiences have created the differences. Religiously speaking, we call the accumulation of experiences that cover up our true relationship with God, others, and all creation a cover story.

Our apperceptive mass includes the images, thoughts, and pictures that we see, hear, and feel from outside ourselves. The images that feed the inner storehouse come from many experiences, at times helpful and at times not helpful. Each experience can help us build a true reality of God in our lives or can reinforce a partial or false notion about God in our lives. We act out of the beliefs and values we inculcate from our experiences. All of us have thoughts and feelings about goodness and evil stored within ourselves. Our apperceptive mass shapes our way of thinking about the realities of life, God, others, ourselves, and all creation.

The cover story is not the image of a magazine cover, but rather like a blanket that enfolds an entire area. We call the experiences that create in us a false or partial "story" about God and other realities of our lives a cover story because they cover up or blanket the true picture of the realities of God in our lives. A cover story describes a distorted or unbalanced look at life. It negates or confuses the relationship among God, human beings, and all creation. Each person has a broad view of life that comes from personal experiences. In a cover story we take a perfectly good idea or attitude and give it too much weight. For example, we might view life as absolutely our own where God has no place or we might carry the good of individual human dignity to the extreme of individualism. In contrast, we can view life as a gift from God who watches over and cares for us, even in tragedy. In the second case our thoughts are governed by the image of Joseph in the Genesis story or one of the saints or Jesus. These views, whether they foster our true relationships or cover them up, slip into our subconsciousness where they are stored in what we call our apperceptive mass as beliefs, attitudes, and ways of acting. For good or ill they come from all the words and images around us.

A cover story is the opposite of the truth that we find in our Scripture. For example, Scripture tells us that God is a loving God and that we have supernatural life. Anything that denies God's action in the world or gives us a partial picture of a full reality can be called a cover story. Some may say that our culture is so bad that there is little hope.

But as we study theology, we see that it is important to distinguish between the good and bad elements in our culture and to make an effort
to avoid the bad and build on the good. We need to think about the
reasons why and how our culture can foster our true relationship with
God, others, and all creation. We also need to think about why and
how a culture can cover up the true story of God living and working
among us.

The reason for using a special term to describe this phenomenon is
that we can learn to name the goodness or evil of our experiences. By
naming our experiences, we have better control over them. Naming a
cover story can show us how a scriptural view of reality differs from a
completely secular view. In this way we begin to describe or define
what keeps us from a closer relationship with God.

Along with individual apperceptive mass, we have group cover
stories believed or taken for granted by a large group of people. When
we call a feature of our society a cover story, we begin to distinquish
the goodness and the evil in it. We need to uncover the true reality as
the people of Israel did and as Ruby Bridges and her family did. Many
people in our day see the world as natural only. Some see nature as
their god. We are going to use "cover story" to mean a merely natural
way of looking at the world, or seeing only part of the truth of reality.
It covers up the story of revelation in the Old and New Testaments.
One cover story in our age is to think that there is only the natural and
to diminish the words of revelation in Scripture. This was not the way
Ruby and her family viewed reality.

Writers have spoken of this cultural reality in various ways. In the
essay, "The Mystery of the Church," we read:

> "Cover stories" are modes of thought which cover up what is
> the full truth of the situation with only partial dimensions of
> reality. By doing this they create distortions which can easily be
> used to replace the reality which it is most important for us to
> know. One of the most common modes of a cover story for
> Christians is to assume that a natural good is the same as a
> supernatural good. This confusion denies the role of grace, the
> mystery of the Church, and missions of the Trinity into our
> world (p. 106).

Robert Coles writes, "The constraints of our culture are often invisible. They coerce us but we don't think of them in connection with our
ideas, our values, our inclinations, our likes or dislikes" (*Harvard
Diary,* 134).

Pope John Paul II says, "Sometimes, witnessing to Christ will
mean drawing out of a culture the full meaning of its noblest inten-

tions, a fullness that is revealed in Christ. At other times, witnessing to Christ means challenging that culture, especially when the truth about the human person is under assault" (1995 speech in Baltimore).

SCRIPTURE CONFRONTS THE COVER STORY

Why Does the Bible Teach in Stories?

It is not surprising that the Bible conveys its message and meaning through stories, because stories are able to engage readers in the concrete details of daily life. Such details are shown as the way in which God is present to people. In the Old Testament the Bible provides unveiling (revelation) of God's presence to different persons in history; in the New Testament it tells the events and meanings of the life of Christ and of those who followed him by seeking to live their lives according to his teaching. That teaching of God's love for those who have been created is given to us in the stories of the Bible. These stories invite readers to accept that love so they can shape their own stories and lives according to what those original stories reveal.

Such stories have the power to draw our attention to events that we might otherwise ignore, or they can point us toward the meanings of our lives, which can be missed. Sometimes they give us an example of how God's grace provides strength for turning away from conflicting stories which may enchant readers and lead toward dangerous or damaging understanding and actions. These latter stories can easily tempt us toward personal and public disasters. Certainly history is filled with examples of events and lives that have been shaped and informed by stories which have drawn people into collaborating in their own destruction. One of the important helps of the stories of the Bible is that they can rescue readers from those other stories, which lead them toward destruction. The biblical narratives provide a new orientation for understanding human origins and human goals; and they provide some food for the journey from the one to the other.

What Is Unique about the Stories in the Bible?

Bible stories most frequently speak to us from within a very interesting assumption, namely that people have already accepted another story onto which they have grafted their lives. Usually biblical stories counter this first story so as to confront their visions and images about the place of humans in the cosmos. Very often, these first stories proceed from the point of view of a hostile world in which evil abounds and so is leading everyone toward a spiritual and physical death. Of course, these stories never reveal that they are themselves leading readers toward death; they always promise some good or delight. Because of this deception, these stories, which the Bible always assumes are working in people, are called cover stories because they cover up the true matters with confusion and illusion, and they hide the true realities which alone can provide us with a mysterious, full humanity.

Bible stories then reveal the truth by showing us how the cover stories are leading those who accept them to become contributors to the evil or death which is in need of being overcome or redeemed. Bible stories invite hearers to grow in belief—belief in the truth of the stories when they talk about the relationship between God and the people to whom God's presence is first revealed. Bible stories also invite hearers to grow in faith—faith that God gives us a new story out of an absolute love. The lover's first gift is to invite us out of the cover stories we have unwittingly and unsuspectedly accepted. For these reasons it is very important for children to hear the biblical stories; they help them listen to the deeper rhythms the story carries. These deeper rhythms are the mysteries of the divine life in the text. While these may be very deep indeed, they must be such in order to engage and confront the cover story. These narratives call children to a first recognition of the divine mystery in which they participate.

How Can We Discover the Tension between the
Cover Story and the Bible Story?

Bible stories reveal some of the fundamental elements of God's purpose of giving freedom. We will consider a major confrontation in the Old Testament where the gift of God's truth confronts a cover story and, because God's story is accepted, all matters of living are changed. This moment of confrontation and freedom is found in the story of Abraham, the father of faith. Abram, like his ancestors before him, had his life informed and shaped by a story that he accepted. However, Abram had the grace to call into question what his life was really about. The cover story that permeated the private and public life of his ancient world, which shaped all its images and rituals, we will call the cosmogonic myth because its scope was cosmic.

This myth, in its many varieties, identified the cosmos as the deity. Nature, in its many elements, was the god; humans came from the hatreds and wars of the cosmic gods; thus human existence was fated and determined by limits of its evil origin. With their lives fated, persons had no freedom; rather, all were determined to live out the evils and envies of the hostile cosmic deities. Humans have evil and death as their origin, goal, and purpose; they have no significance.

This powerful cover story is broken in the fullest way only by the Judeo-Christian revelation in the Bible. Abram becomes Abraham only when he accepts the gift that moves his soul to wonder about his life as something more than what this cover story has proclaimed it to be. A gift that is accepted opens up this wonder to the fact that one is not first evil, but good, that one is beloved, and that one has a certain kind of freedom. The very reality of highlighting Abraham's faith is to highlight that he is not determined and that God is not some dominant ogre. Perhaps one's first act of freedom must be to follow this grace and seek more of it and to seek the source of such a great gift!

That Abrahamic moment is the foundation of the Bible's stories about the gifts that flow from God. God has called into being those who will eventually be named the people of Israel. They will be the first ones to carry in their daily lives and routines the story that will confront and reverse the cover story of death and doom.

If that is the larger context, there is now a need to turn to one major specific story which reveals how people of the Old Covenant, in the first wild and long confrontation with the cover stories, both receive the grace of liberation and suffer its consequences. So we turn to the story of Joseph and his brothers in Genesis 37–50.

Why Is Confronting a Cover Story a Difficult Matter?

Before we reach this story we have had many revealing stories and their confrontation with the prevailing cover stories of the age. For example, we have learned from the Bible that gifts are not equal (Cain and Abel). We have learned that people are not specifically graced because of where they come in family, and that those who are not really seeking blessings will be left behind if not out (Jacob and Esau). Now we come to the sons of Jacob, who himself once sought out, plotted, and sacrificed so that he could participate in the mystery of truth and the blessing of his father, Isaac.

Jacob is blessed by the God of Abraham and Isaac. More and more children are being born to this small clan and are being taught the stories that oppose all the stories they would otherwise have heard. But as the biblical stories proceed we learn something of great interest and importance, namely, that even the people who are given God's story accept and live out some aspects of the cosmogonic cover story of determinism and death.

At the Session

Begin a discussion on cover story: What is it? Can you describe it? View video "Scripture Confronts the Cover Story" on Videocassette 2 (10 minutes).

After the Video

The gospel shows us the Christian way of living but there is an opposing way that surrounds us. We call the opposing way the cover story or the cover-up story. How is this apparent in the following options?

Option 1 (respond to each paragraph below):

1. Ruby's way of thinking about people who were mean to her was like that of Jesus. She learned Jesus' way of living from her parents and her pastor in church. Many of us learned this way of acting also but have not lived out forgiveness and prayer for others as Ruby did. If this is true of us, what is the cover story?

2. Before the Israelites were a people, humans had different beliefs about the origin of life on earth. These belief stories had human beings formed in the battle between gods who were made to be their slaves. The prevailing story about the origin of life was a cover story (or cover-up story) believed by all the people until God revealed differently to the Israelites. The true reality is that a loving God makes us free. What was the cover story of the ancient peoples?

Option 2:

The following is a quotation from Archbishop Harry J. Flynn's article in *The Catholic Spirit.* Can you identify a cover story in each of the following?

In 1988, Monsignor John Tracy Ellis, that esteemed church historian, in a splendid commencement address at the Catholic University of America, shared what he called five homely truths, his advice to the graduates. They were as follows:

1. Hold tenaciously to the enduring principle that there is a right and a wrong in human affairs, regardless of how much a hedonistic society seeks to eradicate that truth from your lives.

2. Resist with all the force at your command the pervasive tendency to succumb to the herd instinct and to follow the majority wherever it may lead, recalling the solitary axiom of Archbishop John Ireland,

"The timid move in the crowds, the brave in single file." Thus you will resist one of the most menacing aspects influencing human conduct in our time.

3. Learn to live with mystery, and to accept with serenity the truth embodied in the oft-quoted remark of Adrian Van Kaam to the effect that "life is a mystery to be lived, not a problem to be solved."

4. Trust the church to answer more questions than any other institution about life's baffling problems, but do not expect her to answer them all, for there are questions to which there is no answer this side of eternity.

5. Finally, at intervals give thoughtful consideration to the end of life knowing you cannot foretell its time or circumstance, yet fully reconciled to its inevitability and in that regard make your own the prayer of that noble lay man, St. Thomas More. He said, "Good Lord, give me the grace so to spend my life that when the day of my death shall come, though I feel pain in my body, I may feel comfort in soul and with faithful hope of thy mercy, in due love towards thee and charity towards the world, I may, through thy grace, part hence into thy glory. Amen" (*The Catholic Spirit*, 2).

BIBLIOGRAPHY

Coles, Robert. *Harvard Diary.* New York: Crossroads Publishing, 1988.

John Paul II. "Homily of Pope John Paul at the Papal Mass at Oriole Park at Camden Yard." 8 October 1995. <http://www.popevisit. com/history/pope/Homily Camden Yards.htm> (28 January 1999).

The Catholic Spirit. St. Paul: Archdiocese of St. Paul and Minneapolis, August 7, 1997.

Joseph and Gifts

ARTHUR KENNEDY

Before Arriving at the Session

Read Focal Points and the essay below; read Genesis 37; 39–47; 50 in your Bible.

Focal Points

The essay begins with an introduction to ways in which we can interpret Scripture.

The author points out the gifts of Joseph, his faithfulness to his gifts, and the contribution he made to his people because of his faithfulness. Joseph's faithfulness to his gifts caused him suffering that worked for the good of the community. Joseph's life shows how he was true to the mystery of God's way of love and gifts.

JOSEPH AND GIFTS

In this bible story we hear about Joseph and his brothers and how the cover story infected their lives.

Joseph's father separates him from his brothers. He has been given a lovely tunic, a coat of many colors, and the elder brothers are not pleased. Indeed they resent such singling out of Joseph. Their anger grows when they hear this adolescent announce that he has been having strange dreams. Unashamedly, though still unsure, he tells them first one and then another dream—about being in the field, harvesting wheat, when the sheaves of the others bent down, while his remained upright and standing. Interestingly, Joseph did not interpret his dreams; he simply announced them. His brothers interpreted them, however. They asked, "Are you indeed to reign over us?" (Gen 37:8).

His father, who knew mystery, wondered what this was all about. At this point Joseph is separated from his brothers not only by his father's gift of a coat, but by a dream, which has created a furious resentment in his brothers and confusion for his father. The resentment of the brothers reveals one constant aspect of the cover story; it interprets gifts in others as a threat of domination and a fear that all is not equal, and that they may be thought worthless because they do not have the same gift.

There is considerable pathos in Joseph's innocent search for his brothers who are out in the fields. When they see him coming, the brothers act according to the cosmogonic cover story. They want to kill him so that he will not lord it over them. They connive; they plan; they turn on their own father; they determine themselves as better, or more worthy, because they are older or more intelligent. One of the elder brothers participates in enough of the ongoing revelation of God so that he can resist the cover story's call for death, with the suggestion that they simply get rid of him by selling him as a slave. Then they can take his tunic, cover it in animal blood, and tell Jacob (Israel) that a wild beast had destroyed his son. Such minimal but important resistance to the full cover story is accepted by the other brothers. So Joseph is sold to their enemies, or those whose lives are driven by cover story (Gen 37:14-28).

Joseph's gifts are now transformed in that he is deprived of his father's gift of the coat; it is destroyed, bloodied, and brought to Jacob. The gift of the dream—the wonder and fidelity without understanding—grows. The wife of the Egyptian master Potiphar, to whom Joseph has been sold, seduces him. Refusing this cosmogonic trivialization of love and sexuality, he is imprisoned because the Egyptians accept the cover story of the seductress. His truth seems useless and his freedom is further removed from him. Fidelity to his gift of authentic love and freedom brings him to jail. There he suffers his gift. As he suffers the gift, it increases and takes on new forms. Now he is not the dreamer, but the one to whom others come for some assistance in making sense of their dreams. He knows well the experience of not understanding one's dreams. He interprets two fellow prisoners' dreams and asks only that if there should be an occasion to recall his gift that they rightly do so (Gen 39:6-23).

When the Pharaoh has a dream that no one in the cover story context can understand, the court baker recalls the truth, that there was one fellow in prison who had correctly interpreted his dreams; perhaps he could help the Pharaoh as well. Joseph is called out of prison to interpret dreams about fat and skinny cattle and about nature in its unpredictable inequality. Joseph, now well aware of the experience of an abundant presence and gift and then an unexpected loss and suffering at the removal of gifts, interprets the Pharaoh's dream. It is about years of abundant harvests and years of famine; there will be enough to get the people through the drought as long as the gift of abundance is properly treated and stored and measured out justly. Joseph is appointed to the court to plan the agricultural policy of the cosmogonic empire (Gen 41:1-45).

In this context he meets his brothers, who come to Egypt in the midst of the drought to purchase grain. Joseph instantly recognizes them. They, however, do not recognize him and assume that they will be able to arrange some equal exchange because they have money to buy the grain that they need. Suddenly they are caught up defending themselves against Joseph's charge against them: that they are strangers and spies. They assure him they are not and explain their journey, revealing that they have left an aged father and younger brother (Benjamin) at home. Joseph demands that they verify their claims by bringing their youngest brother with them when they return. On their journey back to Jacob they find that the money they thought had liberated them from any connection to this fellow is back in their sacks. They have received an inexplicable gift (Gen 42:6-28).

On their second journey they bring their younger brother, the money needed to buy food, and the silver that had been placed in their sacks during the first journey. They are assured that their account is paid. They have also brought gifts to Joseph; when he arrives to meet them, they bow before him. Asking for their father, he sees Benjamin and is so affected that he leaves the room and weeps (Gen 43:11-30).

When he returns he has the meal served to them, always giving Benjamin more than the others, though each one eats his fill. Finally, there comes the test he devises to examine his brothers. Have they changed? Would they do to Benjamin what they had done to him? But the test is also a test for Joseph. Would he in fact become, as his brothers had feared, someone who oppresses them?

After having his own cup placed in Benjamin's sack, he sends his steward to apprehend the men and accuses them of stealing. They argue that should the cup be discovered among them, the one who has it shall die! Then it is found in Benjamin's sack. Judah pleads with Joseph to let him stand in for Benjamin, but Joseph refuses the offer. Judah pleads again, asking Joseph to consider this in the light of the question, "Have you a father, or a brother?" Imagine the effect of that question on Joseph! Judah goes on to recall the loss of another brother (Joseph himself) who is always remembered by Jacob and also by the brothers who sold him. Judah says that unless Benjamin goes back, their father will die. Judah could not bear to think of the depth of Jacob's loss (Gen 43:31–44:34).

The test is finished and now Joseph must respond. He reveals himself to them by saying, "I am your brother Joseph whom you sold into Egypt" (Gen 45:4). And even here the gift grows in him as he extends not domination but forgiveness; he finds a new interpretation of the meaning of history in the light of God's love and presence:

> And now do not be distressed, or angry with yourselves, because you sold me here; for God sent me before you to preserve life. . . . God sent me before you to preserve for you a remnant on earth, and to keep alive for you many survivors. So it was not you who sent me here, but God; he has made me a father to Pharaoh, and lord of all his house and ruler over all the land of Egypt (Gen 45:5-8).

This is how Israel comes to be in Egypt.

There remains the final consequence of Joseph's coat and dream. It is Joseph's interpretation of God's gift of forgiveness that is different from his own act of forgiveness. Afraid that Joseph would finally turn against them after Jacob's death, his brothers appealed to him for forgiveness once again. Joseph in turn says to them, "Do not be afraid! Am I in the place of God? Even though you intended to do harm to me, God intended it for good, in order to preserve a numerous people, as he is doing today" (Gen 50:19-20). Thus does Joseph acknowledge that it is not his forgiveness that has the power to overcome evil with good but rather God's forgiveness that fully heals and restores humans to God.

There are many larger historical and theological issues in this narrative that children cannot yet engage; but it can be of great help to them in hearing how the biblical narratives face the cover stories of any age, and redefine the meaning of human life and of history.

At the Session

Review Focal Points; view video "Joseph and Gifts" on Videocassette 2 (13 minutes), using the Notes below as a guide.

Notes

1. Notice:
   • The coat symbolized Joseph's father's special love.

- The coat brought out the jealousy of Joseph's brothers.
- The coat caused suffering.
- How is the coat a gift?

2. The ancient (cosmogonic) reality of creation and life imposed slavery on humanity.

3. Joseph's gifts increased as he continued to live faithfully. His gifts ascend in the following order:
   a) Joseph only presents his dream to his family (private).
   b) He interprets dreams of others (public).
   c) He interprets a nature dream for Pharaoh (cosmic).
   d) He interprets history for his family by saying, "God sent me here" (historical).
   e) He interprets God's forgiveness as the cause of overcoming evil with good (theological).

After the Video

1. How, in the Joseph story, are the following statements true?
   - Gifts are unequal, unclear, and mysterious.
   - Gifts demand suffering if one is to be faithful to them.
   - Gifts increase and deepen through suffering.
   - Gifts cannot be purchased.

2. How did Joseph overcome the following cover stories?
   - All gifts are equal.
   - The oldest son gets the blessing.
   - Gifts cause a threat of domination and fear.
   - The threat of domination and fear may call for death.
   - Love and sexuality are trivialized.
   - A person can buy what is desired.

Further Reflection

1. What are the positive and negative aspects of suffering? See Gen 50:19-21.

2. Have you experienced a time when "there is always enough if the gift is in the world of mystery"?

3. In what way do you see your life mirrored in the story of Joseph?

BIBLIOGRAPHY

Catechism of the Catholic Church. Part One: §1, ch. 2, art. 3; §2, ch. 1, art. 1, para. 4. Part Two: §2, ch. 1, art. 2. Washington, D.C.: United States Catholic Conference, 1994.

CHAPTER THREE

GOSPELS

Approaches to the Gospels

KATHLEEN FOLEY, C.S.J.

Before Arriving at the Session

Read Focal Points and the essay below.

Focal Points

Awareness of major patterns in the Bible can help one interpret particular passages of the Bible. One Bible pattern is the interaction between God and individuals. The pattern of God calling and a person responding is seen from Adam through the New Testament. Notice especially the interaction between Jesus and his Father.

This essay addresses the pattern of call and response in the Gospels. The video will address other helps in reading the Gospels using the two blind man stories in Mark 8:22 and 10:46. All Scripture references are at the end of this section.

APPROACHES TO THE GOSPELS

Introduction

Many stories of the Old and New Testaments tell of calls by God and the response of the individual. The call of Jesus by his Father and his response show us perfect human faithfulness throughout a lifetime. The call of Jesus and his response to his Father are a model for us. Each person has a particular calling. The challenge is to develop a vocation and contribute to the good of others. One way to interpret the New Testament is to reflect on Jesus' response to his Father. Another way is to reflect on the people's response to Jesus. What is the calling and what is the response?

The call and response of a person today is often as difficult as the ones we read about. Christians have the human Jesus as a model of possibilities and the divine Jesus to give us the power to live faithful to the call of God. Scripture stories show how God calls individuals to share in the work of redemption.

Call and Response in the Old Testament

In the beginning Adam and Eve were invited to enjoy a life in complete harmony with God. In their positive response to God, they lived in intimate communion with God and were clothed with resplendent grace and justice (CCC, 54). They knew that their relationship with God was one of love, freedom, and obedience to be lived within certain parameters. However, when tempted they abused their freedom and love by responding negatively to God.

In God's plan to reconcile all to himself, God continued to call Adam and Eve's descendants. Abraham and Sarah, Joseph, and the tribe of Jacob are among those we know from our study of the Old Testament. In Abraham's day people believed that human beings were the pawns of the gods by whom their lives were determined. But Abraham learned that God wanted him to be truly liberated. Abraham and Sarah were not to be pawns but were called to cooperate in their freedom to full humanity. They sometimes failed in their attempts to live in God's love, but they also remain examples of faithfulness to us (Genesis 12–25).

Joseph grew up learning the true story about God's invitation and the promise of his people always to be faithful. Joseph lived out his faithfulness to the God of his ancestors in spite of hardship and temptation and in the end explained to his brothers that God was watching over and caring for them unceasingly (Genesis 37–50).

Although the Old Testament characters did not always live up to their beliefs, they were faithful in their life-long attempts to carry out their special vocation. The New Testament finds examples of the same patterns of responses with one exception: Jesus was always faithful to his Father's calling.

The Call of Jesus by His Father and Jesus' Response

We read of the faithful response of Jesus to his call as shown in his complete love and obedience to his Father. The vocation to sonship became clarified at Jesus' baptism. We see his calling as beloved Son by God when the Holy Spirit descends upon him:

> And when Jesus had been baptized, just as he came up from
> the water, suddenly the heavens were opened to him and he
> saw the Spirit of God descending like a dove and alighting on
> him. And a voice from heaven said, "This is my Son, the
> Beloved, with whom I am well pleased" (Matt 3:16-17).

In Jesus' baptism the Son presents himself to be baptized as a sign
of his representation of humanity. The Father's voice responds to the
Son's acceptance, proclaiming absolute delight in the Son. Jesus is im-
mersed in water and the Spirit and he will be the source of the Spirit
for all humanity (CCC, 536). We recognize Jesus' initial vocation in his
baptism as we hear his calling by God as beloved Son when the Holy
Spirit descends upon him.

The response of God's beloved Son, Jesus of Nazareth, was complete and loving. The Father called Jesus to reconcile to himself all that
he did through word and deed. Jesus' response shows that he was
clear about his vocation and true to it to his death.

Gospel stories tell us that throughout Jesus' life he remained true
to the mystery of God's way of love. Jesus understood that the most
important way of showing sonship is to listen attentively to his
Father's word and live his life accordingly. Keeping in mind Jesus'
loving attention to his Father is an important help in interpreting the
stories and sayings in the Gospels.

Response to God in the Face of Obstacles

Jesus met with obstacles that he had to overcome in order to be
faithful. Immediately after his baptism Jesus is led by the Spirit into
the desert where he is tempted by Satan. The all-encompassing gift
that Jesus received was that of the vocation of sonship, which involved obedience to his Father. Even in spite of opposition that caused
him suffering, Jesus remained faithful to his Father and the life he was
called to lead. "The temptation in the desert shows Jesus, the humble
Messiah, who triumphs over Satan by his total adherence to the plan
of salvation willed by the Father" (CCC, 566). Notice Jesus' attention
to his Father in the following passages.

In preparation for the obstacles to come, Jesus fasted forty days
and forty nights. He was very hungry when the tempter came asking
him to make the stones turn into bread "if you are the Son of God"
(Matt 4:3). Jesus responded that there is more to life than eating; that
every word that comes from God is important.

The devil took him high on the pinnacle of the Temple to tempt
him in another way. Satan challenged Jesus' claim to be the Son of

God by saying that Jesus could easily prove his sonship by throwing himself down. God would protect his own by sending angels to bear them up and not allow them to be harmed. Jesus took up the challenge by saying that Scripture also says that it is not right to test God. Spectacularly throwing himself off the Temple to show his greatness was not the way Jesus would honor his vocation as Son.

Next Satan said plainly enough that he was the one that Jesus should worship. Jesus could be powerful if he would worship Satan. Jesus would have no part of such blasphemy. He would worship and serve only God. Taking power at any cost and from anyone was not a way to worship and serve God, so Jesus said, "Away with you, Satan."

As the Catechism says, "Scripture witnesses to the disastrous influence of the one Jesus calls 'a murderer from the beginning,' who would even try to divert Jesus from the mission received from his Father" (CCC, 394). Through his actions and words in the temptation story, Jesus says that humility and obedience are greater than food and pride and power. Jesus establishes his superiority over the devil by denouncing several cover stories that linger with us today. He says that personal need is not the highest priority, that the pride of showing one's own greatness is not a sign of worshiping and serving God, and that worshiping a false god is not to be compared with the worship of the true God.

Jesus is faithful to his call even to death. In the crucifixion we see God's continuing call for the beloved Son's obedience and faithfulness. He is the suffering Servant as he allows himself to be numbered among sinners. Mark tells us that those who passed by Jesus on the cross derided him. The chief priests and the scribes mocked him and those who were crucified with him also taunted him. In this atmosphere of condemnation, the Roman centurion confirms the vocation of Jesus as he says, "Truly this man was God's Son" (Mark 15:39).

In the stories of Jesus in the New Testament we see Jesus living true obedience to God, that is, faithfulness to God's invitation of love. Followers of Jesus are also challenged to live out a loving obedient response to God's call. God gathers us to his son Jesus Christ, who stands at the heart of this gathering of men and women in the family of God (CCC, 541–2). Jesus has forty days of solitude in the desert after his baptism. Three times Satan tempts him to reject or compromise his attitude of sonship toward God. He does not succumb as did Adam and Eve and the Israelites in the desert. Christ reveals himself as God's servant, totally obedient to the divine will. This victory over Satan anticipates his victory through the Passion, which is the supreme act of obedience of his filial love for the Father (CCC, 538). To this we are also called.

The Call and Response of the Christian

The story of God's love and the peoples' response continues to the present day. God calls us, inviting us to life in relationship with God. This is an invitation to full humanity and to a liberation of ourselves. Christians respond to the call by participating in the life of Christ through the Holy Spirit. Christ Jesus lived in perfect communion with God, his Father. Christ's disciples are invited to live in the sight of the Father in order to be in communion with God. All the faithful, each in his or her own way, are called by the Lord to the perfection of sanctity (CCC, 1693–4).

Obstacles to Faithfulness in the Life of a Christian

Like Christ in the desert, temptations and attractions in life often conflict with spiritual life and cover up the truth of God's magnanimous invitation. The situations that challenge the true possibilities of God's closeness to humanity can be pervasive in one's society.

In a world of complexity and contradiction the good of culture is apparent in many fields such as technology, medicine, and astronomy. In other ways, we see examples of selfishness, greed, exploitation of the person, and glorification of glamour. The challenges or temptations to pull away from our true vocation are constantly before the Christian who needs to uncover what faith teaches and live alertly and creatively in regard to the allurements of culture. Because each person is a part of culture, it is often difficult to discern what is a help to follow a vocation and what is a denial.

The way of life in society can be a help to a Christian vocation but it can also be a deterrent that leads away from a holy life in union with God. However, baptism is an immersion in water in the name of the Father, and of the Son, and of the Holy Spirit. The Christian believes and responds totally by plunging into the life of Christ and the Spirit.

The vocation of Jesus frames the gospel story from his baptism to his death. We can read about Jesus' call and his faithful response in the stories of the gospel. Faithful response to God also frames the life of a Christian from baptism to death. On the pages of life is written the response to the divine invitation to love.

At the Session

Briefly discuss the baptismal call of God. Do you have helps to get meaning when you read or listen to a gospel passage? View video "Approaches to Interpretation" on Videocassette 2 (19 minutes; Scripture passages used are at the end of this session).

After the Video

Choose from among the following for discussion:

1. How do words and images convey deeper meanings for us as we read Scripture?

2. Blind Man Stories:

   • Interpret one of the blind man stories.

   • Tell how it refers to present-day Christians.

   • Consider the challenge in the question, "What would you like me to do for you?"

   • Contrast the response of James and John to the response of blind Bartimaeus.

3. Discuss the Baptism of Jesus.

Further Reflection

1. How do the Gospels show Jesus, faithful to his vocation, acting completely in tune with his Father's will?

2. In daily life what are the conflicting attractions or situations that lead us, baptized Christians, toward life in Christ or away from life in Christ?

3. Study the CCC, 1846–76, to review our teaching on sin. How does this relate to a cover story?

4. We have many distractions and attractions that counter the Christian message we teach. What is it in our lives that we need to recognize and confront? Are the experiences that cover up the gospel stories the same today as in Jesus' time?

5. How do the Scripture stories of Jesus' baptism and temptations help us to understand our gifts of vocation? How do these stories help us understand the obstacles that hinder our faithfulness?

6. Interpret the following passage about the call of the disciples (remember the key elements in interpretation).

   • The pattern in this story is obviously call and response. How does this help interpretation?

   • The type of literature is a narrative between Jesus and the disciples. What do we learn about Jesus and about his disciples from this incident?

   • Study the literal text carefully.

- What words, phrases, or images can you see as metaphors for today's people, places, or activities?
- What is a spiritual interpretation of this short passage?

7. What would be my response to Jesus' question, "What do you want me to do for you?"

SCRIPTURE REFERENCES

Call of the Disciples (Mark 1:16-20)

As Jesus passed along the Sea of Galilee, he saw Simon and his brother Andrew casting a net into the sea—for they were fishermen. And Jesus said to them, "Follow me and I will make you fish for people." And immediately they left their nets and followed him. As he went a little farther, he saw James son of Zebedee and his brother John, who were in their boat mending the nets. Immediately he called them; and they left their father Zebedee in the boat with the hired men, and followed him.

First Blind Man Story (Mark 8:22-26)

They came to Bethsaida. Some people brought a blind man to him and begged him to touch him. He took the blind man by the hand and led him out of the village; and when he had put saliva on his eyes and laid his hands on him, he asked him, "Can you see anything?" And the man looked up and said, "I can see people, but they look like trees, walking." Then Jesus laid his hands on his eyes again; and he looked intently and his sight was restored, and he saw everything clearly. Then he sent him away to his home, saying, "Do not even go into the village."

First Passion Prediction (Mark 8:31–9:1)

[Prediction] Then he began to teach them that the Son of Man must undergo great suffering, and be rejected by the elders, the chief priests, and the scribes, and be killed, and after three days rise again. He said all this quite openly. [Lack of understanding] And Peter took him aside and began to rebuke him. [Instruction] But turning and looking at his disciples, he rebuked Peter and said, "Get behind me, Satan! For you are setting your mind not on divine things but on human things."

Second Passion Prediction (Mark 9:30-37)

[Prediction] They went on from there and passed through Galilee. He did not want anyone to know it; for he was teaching his disciples, saying to them, "The Son of Man is to be betrayed into human hands, and they will kill him, and three days after being killed, he will rise again." [Lack of understanding] But they did not understand what he was saying and were afraid to ask him.

Then they came to Capernaum; and when he was in the house he asked them, "What were you arguing about on the way?" But they were silent, for on the way they had argued with one another who was the greatest. [Instruction] He sat down, called the twelve, and said to them, "Whoever wants to be first must be last of all and servant of all." Then he took a little child and put it among them; and taking it in his arms he said to them, "Whoever welcomes one such child in my name welcomes me, and whoever welcomes me welcomes not me but the one who sent me."

Third Passion Prediction (Mark 10:32-45)

[Prediction] They were on the road, going up to Jerusalem, and Jesus was walking ahead of them; they were amazed, and those who followed were afraid. He took the twelve aside again and began to tell them what was to happen to him, saying, "See, we are going up to Jerusalem, and the Son of Man will be handed over to the chief priests and the scribes, and they will condemn him to death; then they will hand him over to the Gentiles; they will mock him, and spit upon him, and flog him, and kill him; and after three days he will rise again."

[Lack of understanding] James and John, the sons of Zebedee, came forward to him and said to him, "Teacher, we want you to do for us whatever we ask of you." And he said to them, "What is it you want me to do for you?" And they said to him, "Grant us to sit, one at your right hand and one at your left, in your glory." But Jesus said to them, "You do not know what you are asking. Are you able to drink the cup that I drink, or be baptized with the baptism that I am baptized with?" They replied, "We are able." Then Jesus said to them, "The cup that I drink you will drink; and with the baptism with which I am baptized, you will be baptized; but to sit at my right hand or at my left is not mine to grant, but it is for those for whom it has been prepared."

When the ten heard this, they began to be angry with James and John. [Instruction] So Jesus called them and said to them, "You know that among the Gentiles those whom they recognize as their rulers lord it over them, and their great ones are tyrants over them. But it is not so among you; but whoever wishes to become great among you must be your servant, and whoever wishes to be first among you must be slave of all. For the Son of Man came not to be served but to serve, and to give his life as a ransom for many."

Blind Bartimaeus (Mark 10:46-52)

They came to Jericho. As he and his disciples and a large crowd were leaving Jericho, Bartimaeus son of Timaeus, a blind beggar, was sitting by the roadside. When he heard that it was Jesus of Nazareth, he began to shout out and say, "Jesus, Son of David, have mercy on me!" Many sternly ordered him to be quiet, but he cried out even more loudly, "Son of David, have mercy on me!" Jesus stood still and said, "Call him here." And they called the blind man, saying to him, "Take heart; get up, he is calling you." So throwing off his cloak, he sprang up and came to Jesus. Then Jesus said to him, "What do you want me to do for you?" The blind man said to him, "My teacher, let me see again." Jesus said to him, "Go; your faith has made you well." Immediately he regained his sight and followed him on the way.

BIBLIOGRAPHY

Catechism of the Catholic Church. Part One: §1, ch. 1; §2, chs. 1, 2. Part Three: §1, chs. 1, 8. Washington, D.C.: United States Catholic Conference, 1994.

Parables

KATHLEEN FOLEY, C.S.J.

Before Arriving at the Session

Read the Focal Points and the essay below.

Focal Points

The parables challenge our habitual response to life. Forces of culture can cloud the mind and weaken resolve to live in response to God's continuing call. A parable can alert us to a more spiritual meaning of God's call and the possibilities of response. They help us to question our experiences beyond our present mind set.

This essay lays out the steps to interpret a parable in the spiritual sense. The parable story calls us to see our daily relationship with God and the opposite demands that our culture makes on us. We have given the name "cover story" to the interweaving aspects of our culture that blanket over or cover up the possibilities of our lives in relationship to God. We will demonstrate the use of the two levels of interpretation.

PARABLES

How Do Parables Challenge One's Response to Life?

A parable offers the opportunity to enter the mystery of God. Parables challenge ordinary ways of seeing that strike us as strange at first. We express surprise that God thinks and acts differently from the systems of justice or love that we live by. As we reflect on these stories, we learn about the continuing mystery of God. Parables challenge us to see reality as Jesus describes it.

As we continue to form questions about our lives, the answers are often unclear and elusive. We may ask, "Is this relationship fruitful?"

"Why did my child die?" "Is my life going in the right direction?" "What is the meaning of the accident?" A parable speaks to us in different ways depending on our current questions. The challenge of a parable can help us see the mystery of our lives and the mystery of God.

Parables help us to see that the kingdom is the reality taught by Jesus. The parables invite us to enter the kingdom of God by applying the meaning to our own situation. Jesus and the presence of the kingdom in this world are at the heart of the parables. One must enter the kingdom, in order to "know the secrets of the kingdom of heaven. For those who stay 'outside,' everything remains enigmatic" (CCC, 546).

What Are Stories of Everyday Life
That Cover Up the Meaning of a Parable?

Revelation liberates us from the cover story. Parables, in a special way, keep us alert to the stories in our culture that oppose Scriptures. Parables call into question what we take for granted in everyday life and, for this reason, are often rejected or diminished in meaning. They challenge us to accept the invitation of Jesus to be willing to give up everything. They challenge us to recognize God's activity in our lives in ways different from what we normally take for granted.

We communicate to others the promises in our culture that we take for granted. They seem good but we fail to call them into question against gospel standards. We promise our children that they will be happy if they work hard enough; that those who work hard will control their own lives; that those who please others will succeed in life; that hard work, control of life, and success will assure the good life. We tell others that salvation depends on their innocence. We indicate that those who are innocent do not suffer and that persons are good because they are victims. Sometimes we question these statements but often they are a part of our own thinking. Jesus' life and stories teach us otherwise.

Before we turn now to the parable of the sower to gain insights into Jesus' invitation to the kingdom, we need to review the four levels that help to interpret a parable.

The Senses of Scripture

The literal sense is the meaning conveyed by the words. All interpretations of Scripture are based on the literal level.

In the allegorical sense we understand Scripture stories by recognizing their significance in Christ; thus the crossing of the Red Sea is a sign or type of Christ's victory and also of Christian baptism. The words and images of one story relate to other events in Scripture or in our own lives.

In the moral sense the stories reported in Scripture lead us to act justly, that is, in a moral way.

In the anagogical sense we see our experiences in light of their deepest life-meaning significance leading to eternal life (CCC, 116–7).

The Sower in Matthew 13

THE LITERAL LEVEL

We know that learning takes us from the known to the unknown. The literal level speaks to what is known. Because it is the area of which we know the most, we tend to take the literal level for granted. However, this level needs to be learned from as many points of view as possible. This is the level that remains in our memories to grow in unexpected ways as we mature and as situations in life change.

APPLICATION OF THE LITERAL LEVEL

In the sower parable, we need to become as familiar as possible with the literal elements of the story: sower, sowing, seed, path, rocky ground, thorns, and good ground. The discussion will revolve around the interaction among the parts of the story: the work and delights of a sower, the pattern of sowing, the relationship of the sower to the ground in which the seed is sown, and the possibility of growth on rocky ground. Time and attention must be given to the story in its literal sense.

THE ALLEGORICAL LEVEL

The next level of interpretation in a parable is the allegorical level. In an uncomplicated way, we understand that one thing or activity can stand for something else. The story can have significance other than the literal description.

THE MORAL LEVEL

The moral level tells us that the stories and events in Scripture should cause us to act accordingly.

THE ANAGOGICAL LEVEL

The deepest level of interpretation is the anagogical or life meaning. This level is a key to unlocking a deeper meaning of life. We find questions about the nature of our lives and the nature of God. For each parable we look for a contradiction or something that seems strange; a part of the story that does not fit the way we would act or think. We are unsettled because the parable says it fits. Is this our God who acts like this? Are these expectations for those who live in the kingdom? It seems that God has a peculiar way of acting or thinking and challenges our way of thinking. If we allow this strangeness to work in us, we find new possibilities in our lives. It allows us to think, "What if . . .?"

APPLICATION OF THE ANAGOGICAL LEVEL

In the sower parable we concentrate on the sower, seed, ground, sowing, and growing. We seek to discover what these stand for on a deeper level than farming. One possible interpretation is (1) I am the sower, (2) the seed is the word of God that I sow among others, (3) the different kinds of ground represent the receptivity of the people I reach, and (4) the fruit means the goodness that people do upon hearing the word of God.

At first in the sower parable we say, "I am the sower." Later in chapter 13 we have a surprise, a twist to the story that we did not think of at first. I am not the sower as I first thought. I am the ground. This evokes a number of questions.

What if I am the ground? What kind of ground am I? Who is the sower? What is being sown? If I am good ground (which I think I am), what is my yield? Does everyone get the same kind of seed and the same amount of seed? Will the seed be taken from me? What if the ground I am becomes hardened or overgrown with thorns? What if the seed is God's promise and my hope of salvation? With this interpretation, instead of thinking that I am cooperating with God in challenging others to hear God's word, I am challenged to hear and accept my utter dependence upon God for everything in this life and eternal life.

Our culture exemplifies many cover stories. The cover story for the sower is a non-gospel way of thinking about God and the gifts of God.

The parable of the sower challenges us to realize that life is truly measured by God's goodness and the gifts given. The parable says that hope is in God. God's presence is the promise for which we can truly hope.

The message of the parable will contradict the messages heard and seen on a daily basis. The vocation of the Christian is to clarify the truth about the promise of salvation and the promise of the cover story. The parables invite readers to accept God's love so that they can shape their own stories and lives according to the parable stories.

At the Session

View video "Parables" on Videocassette 2 (21 minutes; the Scripture references used are at the end of this session).

After the Video

1. Choose one or two of the following questions for discussion and writing:
   - Describe a person whom you think of as "path" (rocky ground, etc.).
   - Do the persons you describe as "path" know that they are in this group?
   - Do you think a person changes from one kind of ground to another?
   - What difference does it make whether I am the sower or the ground?
   - How is God active in our lives?
2. Individually, then with one another, interpret the parable of the treasure.

Further Reflection

1. What is the challenge in the words "Listen" and "Let anyone with ears listen"?
2. Ponder this question: "What if God were never active in my life?"
3. Give examples of persons who respond to God's gifts as a pathway, rocky ground, thorny ground, or thirty, sixty, or a hundredfold good ground.

SCRIPTURE REFERENCES

Matthew 13:1-9

That same day Jesus went out of the house and sat beside the sea. Such great crowds gathered around him that he got into a boat and sat there, while the whole crowd stood on the beach. And he told them many things in parables, saying: "Listen! A sower went out to sow. And as he sowed, some seed fell on the path, and the birds came and ate them up. Other seeds fell on rocky ground, where they did not

have much soil, and they sprang up quickly, since they had no depth
of soil. But when the sun rose, they were scorched; and since they had
no root, they withered away. Other seeds fell among thorns, and the
thorns grew up and choked them. Other seeds fell on good soil and
brought forth grain, some a hundredfold, some sixty, some thirty. Let
anyone with ears listen!"

Matthew 13:18-23

Hear then the parable of the sower. When anyone hears the word
of the kingdom and does not understand it, the evil one comes and
snatches away what is sown in the heart; this is what was sown on the
path. As for what was sown on rocky ground, this is the one who
hears the word and immediately receives it with joy; yet such a person
has no root, but endures only for a while, and when trouble or persecution arises on account of the word, that person immediately falls
away. As for what was sown among thorns, this is the one who hears
the word, but the cares of the world and the lure of wealth choke the
word, and it yields nothing. But as for what was sown on good soil,
this is the one who hears the word and understands it, who indeed
bears fruit and yields, in one case a hundredfold, in another sixty, and
in another thirty.

The Parable of the Treasure from Matthew 13:44-45

The kingdom of heaven is like treasure hidden in a field, which
someone found and hid; then in his joy he goes and sells all that he
has and buys that field.

BIBLIOGRAPHY

Catechism of the Catholic Church. Part One: §1, ch. 2; §2, ch. 2. Washington, D.C.:
United States Catholic Conference, 1994.

CHAPTER FOUR

OUR BELIEFS

We Believe in Jesus Christ, the Only Son of God

ARTHUR KENNEDY

Before Arriving at the Session

Read the following essay and the essay "Redemption" on p. 72; these essays serve together as an initiation to our beliefs about Christ. Both essays act as a preparation for the next videos: Redemption, Development of Doctrine, Mystery of the Church, and the Mission of the Church. There is no videotape for this essay.

WE BELIEVE IN JESUS CHRIST

Most children first hear about Jesus Christ through the faith of the Church. The central commission of Jesus to his disciples is to preach and testify to his redemption and presence in the world. When the Church teaches about Christ it does so not just by telling us about Jesus' life two thousand years ago, but also about the fact that he is God with us now.

The believing Church brings us to learn about Jesus from what he has disclosed about his presence in Scripture. When we learn what he does and says about himself, we learn several important things.

First, we find that Jesus speaks to all of us, and all peoples, through the Hebrew world of faith and the promise made to Israel by God's covenant. He teaches all nations, including us, through the long history and through the life and prayer of the Jewish people. In order to know about Jesus and his mission, we enter into the world of Jewish history and life. We learn the stories that tell us about the action of God in the lives of Abraham and Sarah, Joseph and his brothers, Moses, Ruth, David, and the prophets. Jesus fulfills and completes what they had been, because he is God acting in history. Therefore, he elevates and draws the early grace of those faithful to Yahweh into the mystery of his life as the Messiah. God sends this Savior to overcome the division between God and humans that resulted from Adam's fall. By his presence Jesus creates a new covenant with us, a new bond with God and humans, in which he, as both priest and victim, offers his life for us.

We also learn that Jesus prays and how he prays. His life is lived so as not to take any glory for himself, but to give glory to his Father by being true to the divine love that the Father has for human creatures. He prays to the Father with the intimacy of a son. While we are told about Jesus' prayers and learn of them in all the Gospels, it is especially in John 17 that we are allowed to listen to Jesus' prayer as part of the infinite conversation of God. That special prayer teaches us about the mystery of the Trinity as the foundation of all life, of God's infinite love of for us which Jesus reveals by his death and resurrection, and of his constant presence with us. This also discloses to us the importance of prayer in our lives, the importance of bringing our lives into God's life by allowing our words to say again Jesus' words that elevate and transform our own hearts, minds, and affections.

It can be very helpful to follow the pedagogy of the Scriptures and the Church in the way in which we meet and learn from Jesus. First Jesus calls people to him both by his presence and by his witness to the Father, as we see a group of disciples forming around him. They begin to call him rabbi and teacher. In addition, he calls some, those named apostles, to come closer to him. In both instances those who seek him and answer him begin to undergo a conversion, a turning toward him and away from some other interests or commitments. He teaches this conversion explicitly, of course, when he says that we must leave some things behind to follow him—indeed, finally, leave everything to follow him.

He teaches us that his life is the model and standard for us; that he takes up the cross for us and that we are to take up our crosses and unite our suffering with his.

In the New Testament, Jesus is named by seven different titles. These refer to some task that Jesus undertakes or fulfills and to the reality that he is. While "Messiah" is the most common one, for it names the anticipation of Israel that God will send the promised servant to heal Israel, the title that is used consistently by Church doctrines is "Son of God." This title holds within it the fullness of all the other titles, even while acknowledging the need and value of these others.

It seems that the manner of Jesus' calling of his disciples, the apostles and us, to turn toward him in conversion fits our human situation quite precisely. Notice how in the Gospels of Matthew (16:13-23), Mark (8:27-33), and Luke (9:18-22) he asks them to name who he is. First he asks his followers that parable-like question, not the usual

"what" do people think about him, but "who do people say I am?"
Some say that he is really an advance on preparing Israel for the coming of the promised Messiah. He then asks them "who" they say he is.
Peter answers with the words of faith and conversion, "You are the
Messiah, the Son of the living God." In other words, you are the One
we have been waiting for. Jesus responds to Peter with his confirmation of blessing and testimony that his very answer of faith is a gift
from the Father.

Peter's testimony of faith holds within it not only the call and gift
of conversion, but also the need for this conversion to penetrate more
deeply into the human soul. After blessing Peter, Jesus begins to define the "what" or the nature of the Messiah. When teaching them that
he must go to Jerusalem to "suffer, die and be raised up on the third
day," Peter objects. He and all the others with Jesus already have a
definition of the Messiah; the Messiah is one who will overthrow the
Romans and return to Israel its land. What good is a defeated Messiah? Jesus warns Peter in the clearest terms, "Get behind me, Satan."
Peter's conversion of faith will need to guide his understanding and
knowledge. Peter will have to turn away from his human definitions
and accept the teaching from the one that he acknowledges is the
Messiah, the one he has named in faith as his savior.

Jesus also teaches us the way faith leads us to who he is, and allows us to know what he is. We can create cover stories about Jesus,
and so destroy the mystery that he invites us to participate in, just as
Peter attempted to do. The Church is always attentive to the danger of
human trivializing of the mystery of the person Jesus is. That is why
the creeds include statements of doctrine about the mystery of Christ
as both human and divine. He is the *logos,* or the Word, the second
person of the Trinity, born of the Virgin Mary, who suffers, dies, and
rises; he is the judge of the living and the dead and the One who will
come again to save us. Jesus Christ is God incarnate. Jesus Christ is
true God and true man. The infinite God has come to dwell with us
and open our finitude to divine infinity.

These doctrines of faith and the Church restate in a succinct way
what the Church has learned from what Jesus reveals in "who" he is.
They seek to invite conversions of faith to grow into conversions of
knowledge and even of understanding. These doctrines, or Church
teachings about Christ, are named dogmas to indicate the permanence
of their truth as formally and explicitly revealed. They remain true no
matter what other developments occur in the Church's understanding. As Flannery O' Connor once put it, ". . . dogma is an instrument
for penetrating reality. Christian dogma is about the only thing left in
the world that surely guards and protects mystery" (O'Connor, 178).

Doctrines treat the "what" question so that we who did not know Jesus in his historical time can know the true "who," the person he is. Doctrines express truth about what was originally taught in and to the world of ancient Israel. So in the process of our conversions, and of children in the beginnings of their being called through the Church and the Holy Spirit, we often move from who Christ is in his person, to what Christ is in his being, and always back to who, to his presence.

This is important then in thinking about Christian life today when there is much dialogue with other world religions. Jesus is not the founder of a religion. He is not comparable to the Buddha or to Mohammed or to John Calvin or Mary Baker Eddy or Joseph Smith. He is the Son of God sent to us in the incarnation, and he alone redeems human creatures from sin and death. There is no human quest more important than that of finding God. Catholics therefore give due honor and respect to those in the world's religions. While doing so they give witness to the Cross and resurrection of Jesus Christ.

BIBLIOGRAPHY

Catechism of the Catholic Church. Part One: §2, ch. 2. Washington, D.C.: United States Catholic Conference, 1994.

O'Connor, Flannery. *Mystery and Manners: Occasional Prose.* Sel. and ed. Sally and Robert Fitzgerald. New York: Farrar, Straus, and Giroux, 1970.

Redemption

ARTHUR KENNEDY

Before Arriving at the Session

Read Focal Points and the essay below.

Focal Points

Redemption is the reality at the heart of all Scripture and Christian tradition and is at the heart of the Church. Flannery O'Connor and Christopher Dawson help us reflect on the gift of Christ's redemptive act.

REDEMPTION

Introduction

Redemption is the reality at the heart of all Scripture and the Christian tradition; it is the way in which God's will is shown as offering the gift that is needed by all humanity. Redemption is the practical unfolding of the mystery of the Trinity, whose life is given in such a manner that humans can share in that life. It is made available to us through the action of Christ Jesus, the second person of the Trinity, in his becoming flesh, in his suffering and death on the cross, in his resurrection from the dead, and in his giving to the Church the sacraments that bring into human life the graces we need to grow into the redemptive process by becoming like him. Redemption is at the heart of the Church.

The Cover Story Denies the Need for Redemption

God's revelation of redemption points to the human need for redemption, and the surest way for a cover story to destroy the very center of Christian teaching in the Bible and tradition is to convince people that there is nothing from which they need to be redeemed. If such a cover story were to be developed it would be telling us that we are able to bestow on ourselves the necessary sense of self-esteem, which for Christians comes only with the gift of justification given in baptism. A redemption cover story would also need to train us into the notion that we are able to forgive ourselves rather than seek out God's forgiveness that is given to us through the Church. In addition, such a cover story would point to the foolishness, imperfection, and arrogance of any "institution" which claims that it has been given the mission of announcing and being the vessel of redemption for humanity. Catching a glimpse of this, in one of her diagnoses of the tension of faith and cover stories, Flannery O'Connor remarked:

> The universe of the Catholic fiction writer is one that is founded on the theological truths of the Faith, but particularly on three of them which are basic—the Fall, Redemption and the Judgment. These are doctrines that the modern secular world does not believe in. It does not believe in sin, or in the value that suffering can have, or in eternal responsibility. Since we live in a world that has been increasingly dominated by secular thought, the Catholic writer often finds himself writing in and for a world that is unprepared and unwilling to see the meaning of life as he sees it (O'Connor, 185).

In 1931 Christopher Dawson wrote an essay on the universal quest for salvation entitled "Stages in Mankind's Religious Experience." He compared different world religions in their understanding about God, the rituals of worship, the moral and spiritual transformations that they announced and called forth, and the effect they had on the cultures in which they flourished. He refers to a universal aspect of the human condition, a desire for liberation from physical and moral evils. He remarks, *"Libera nos a malo* (Deliver us from evil) is a universal prayer that answers to one of the oldest needs of human nature" (Dawson, 175). He goes on to indicate the radical difference in the process of such liberation in the lived events and teachings of Christ. Among other things he notes how "the Incarnation of the Divine Word . . . is brought into vital and sensible contact with the life of the believer" (Dawson, 185). It is the sacramental unity of humans with God that engages the individual and the community in a sensible, intelligent, moral, and religious bond that incorporates humanity into the mystery of the healing of creation.

Christians learn about the mystery of evil and sin and the mystery of redemption from the whole of the Bible. In the Old Testament the experiences of redemption are tied to economic acts of payment of a ransom or liberation by power from some captivity or oppression. The first-born male in every Jewish family was ordered to be consecrated to Yahweh and had to be bought back for the price of five shekels (Num 18:16). All other persons could be consecrated to Yahweh through a personal vow and payments that varied by gender and age (Lev 27:2-8). In the Mosaic Law the first-born male animal was sacred and, if it was from those designated clean animals, it was to be sacrificed to Yahweh. If it was from those designated unclean animals it had to be redeemed, or ransomed, with a price paid to the priest of the Temple (Lev 27:11-13).

New Testament Teachings

In the New Testament redemption is from the fall of Adam, which affects the totality of our nature, and from the sin by which we, within our own freedom and responsibility, live out the consequences of that fall. In this condition of our nature, humans separate themselves from God and place themselves under the servitude of evil and Satan. Redemption refers to the recovered unity between God and humanity. It is named by St. Paul (1 Cor 6:20) as "the great price" that Christ paid for our liberation from sin and slavery and which "elevated" human nature into such condition that it is identified as being "adopted" into the Trinitarian life. So the New Testament presupposes that humans have fallen out of their original and rightful union with God and that human nature must be transformed. It tells us that the transformation (elevation) of human nature occurs only with reconciliation with God in which God's honor is restored and a repentance is undertaken. It gives ample testimony that only one who has a nature not deformed by the rejection of God's presence and gifts can initiate and accomplish this reconciliation. This one must be of human nature so that in the reconciliation the transformation can be effected, opening our lives to allowing God's will to be accomplished. In Christ we have been offered the gift of God's life, not just God's mind or intention, and this gift is presented in the mystery of agapic, or self-sacrificing, love in the details of the sensible world of our feelings and imagination. In him, the New Testament reveals the embodiment of God's solution to the reality of evil.

There are certain New Testament teachings, or doctrines, that are essential for us if we are to be able to identify different aspects of the central mystery that Christians are called to live. First, Christ paid a price (Matt 20:28; Mark 10:45; 1 Cor 6:15-20; Gal 3:13; 1 Tim 2:5-6). Second, Christ's passion and death were undertaken for us sinners.

Christ himself is sinless, so his death is vicarious, for it is others' sins that he bore (1 Pet 2:24; 2 Cor 5:21). Third, Christ's sacrifice was related to his representation as High Priest who offers his own blood as a way of atoning for human sinfulness and for reconciling human and divine nature. His death is not an accident but is intended as the recreative divine act that changes human destiny and reveals the divine self-sacrificing love which pays the cost. Christ is the eternal high priest who continually intercedes for us (Heb 7:25; 8:1ff.; Rom 8:34; 1 John 2:1). Finally, Christ's suffering and death are identified as an act of obedience (Mark 14:36; John 10:17-18; Phil 2:8).

The Church

Specific Church doctrines on the mystery of the redemption are not to be found, although the reality is referred to in any number of doctrines related to other aspects of Christian mystery, such as in the Nicene Creed.

Origen

There are three major theological doctrines that should be noted because they provide some assistance in our efforts to find a deeper understanding of this mystery of redemption that is at the heart of the Church. An early effort at an integral understanding of all the different aspects of the redemption given in the scriptural testimony had been proposed by Origen (185–253) in his theory of "apocatastasis," a theory for understanding how Christ will reconcile all of creation. But this effort was very much influenced by a Gnostic reduction of redemption to acts of knowledge and it was weak in relating it to the historical concreteness of human living.

St. Anselm of Canterbury

In the Middle Ages, a second and more systematic effort to understand the full complexity of the mystery of redemption was undertaken by St. Anselm of Canterbury (1024–1109) and is a theological explanation formulated under the notion of "Christ's Satisfaction." It is this understanding that underlies the interpretations given above. The mystery of redemption includes the reality of the Fall as an offense against God, the need for reparation, the nature or mode of being of the One who would undertake such a restoration, the need for God's justice and mercy to be held together by an understanding of satisfaction, the vicarious nature of satisfaction in which the sinners are redeemed by the sinless One, and the fact that satisfaction has an infinite and eternal effect.

One danger that existed in this understanding was that the context of the Church which was needed to carry out the Counter-Reformation was that of legal distinctions. From this context Christians read Anselm's theory in the context of laws and crimes. In such a context much emphasis would be placed on God's proportionate punishment for the Fall as the way in which divine justice was accounted for, while the testimonies of God's mercy were considerably weakened.

Lonergan

A third and different context for thinking about "satisfaction" is that the Scriptures teach how Christ names those entering into the process of redemption as friends. In this context the divine friendship is central and it is most evidently manifested in the Cross. As it is developed in the christology of Bernard Lonergan, S.J. (1904—84), the Cross of Christ is the sign, symbol, and effective act for the Christian which carries the whole of redemption. The Cross mediates the full reality of redemption with the Fall and sin on one side, and resurrection and glory on the other side. When redemption is recognized as grounded in the law of the Cross it is connected with the fuller manifestation of the self-sacrificing love that is to be found everywhere in the New Testament. It affects redemption by drawing persons to become collaborators in the work of God in and through their lives. The law of the Cross is not just found in the Cross itself but in the whole life of Christ and in the lives of those who follow him. This law reveals infinite self-sacrifice in a vast manifestation of sensible images. These images are important not only for children but also for adults in being able to find the encouragement needed for being obedient to this law and undertaking the self-sacrifice that also shares in the glory of God's life. The Cross is important not only, but especially, because children require sensible images of what can be known only through faith. Christians need their Lord and the communion of saints in order to know the effect of self-sacrificing love in the transformation of evil. The Cross is also needed to find a way into the meaning of the suffering of Christ. For Catholic Christians it is especially the crucifix that presents the mystery of redemption as the self-sacrificing love of Christ. Today some Catholics object to the crucifix, perhaps because they read it through the legalistic tinge mentioned above. There remains, however, a reading through the law of the Cross as it opens the mind and heart, by means of a God-given historical image, to the principal gift that re-orders and re-establishes the soul in friendship with God.

At the Session

Discuss briefly why the mystery of the redemption is so important in the life of a Christian. View video "Christ and Redemption" on Videocassette 3 (12 minutes).

After the Video

What is the meaning of the statement, "Redemption is grounded in the law of the Cross"?

Further Reflection

1. Discuss the meaning of the statement, "Redemption is at the heart of the Church."
2. Reflect on the importance of redemption in relation to sacramental life and the life of virtue.
3. Read "An Introduction to the Memoir of Mary Ann" by Flannery O'Connor (see bibliography).
   How did Mary Ann become an "active participant in a mystery"? [Refer to the glossary for the meaning of "passive diminishment."] To not only endure suffering but to accept it is an act of redemption. This is not a submission but rather a taking hold of the gift.
4. Discuss how a person can be an active participant in a mystery.

Further Thoughts to Consider

1. Biblical stories help us to understand a "hunger for redemption" and how people were interrupted by the power of cover story. When cover stories are redeemed, they bring about changes in the world. In reading biblical stories remember the idea of a person looking for redemption and the obstacles encountered in the search for redemption.
2. Jesus is the "new" Joseph and the "new" Moses overcoming the evil of sin. The acceptance of suffering brings about the saving gift of redemption. The acceptance of suffering is through self-sacrifice, not self-pity. All people can share in overcoming evil with good.
3. The Cross becomes for the Christian the symbol or sign of hope. It is an image of divine love that is unlimited love, and it is an invitation to us to imitate that love. A proper understanding of this is the test

for Christians. It is the ability to accept suffering (overcoming evil with good) in the light of the love that Christ showed us (self-sacrifice), rather than the cover story (self-pity).

4. What is Abraham's cover story?

Abraham believed that the first-born male must be sacrificed in order to pacify the gods and that he must act upon this belief in his own life. Abraham overcame the cover story by believing and acting on the true God telling him not to sacrifice his son. The outcome was a son for Abraham and Sarah and posterity for their line.

5. Interpret the Moses' story of killing the Egyptian. What is the cover story?

BIBLIOGRAPHY

Dawson, Christopher. *The Dynamics of World History*. Ed. John J. Mulloy. New York: Sheed and Ward, 1956.

Catechism of the Catholic Church. Part One: §2, ch. 2, art. 4. Part Two: §1, ch. 1. Washington, D.C.: United States Catholic Conference, 1994.

O'Connor, Flannery. *Mystery and Manners: Occasional Prose*. Sel. and ed. Sally and Robert Fitzgerald. New York: Farrar, Straus, and Giroux, 1970.

Redemption Today

DON BRIEL

Before Arriving at the Session

Read Focal Points and "Other Plans: Journal of an Illness."

Focal Points

Redemption is a central mystery in the life of the Christian. God's revelation of redemption points to the human need for being redeemed. This session will illustrate and accent the meaning of redemption through the story of James Miller, who found this reality in his own experience of suffering.

OTHER PLANS: JOURNAL OF AN ILLNESS
JAMES ANDREW MILLER

I had spent most of Saturday, February 29, 1992, Leap Year Day, working through a stack of books and notes I was using for a major paper on transcendentalism, due in draft at Cleveland State University in the Graduate English program. Sunday afternoon, too, was reserved for this endeavor. Sunday morning, my wife and I were planning to begin the first of a series of membership classes at a church in the greater Cleveland area that we had been attending since the fall. We had as well—and I mention this only to indicate priorities set for the weekend—declined coveted orchestra tickets at Severance Hall offered to us by a friend, and had asked to postpone dinner with another couple. There were other plans.

In my study, midnight Saturday approached. I suddenly woke up in my chair: I had fallen asleep. And now, being the only one up, I went through the half dreamlike routine of shutting down the house, brushing my teeth, and dropping into islands of proper sleep. There was a no less exacting day arriving in the morning and, with the end of the quarter approaching in the next several weeks, an assuredly even more taxing half-month on the horizon. Sleep, as it almost always came to me, should be sweet and nearly immediate.

Only the sleep did not come. It didn't come by twelve-thirty, nor by two, nor by three. Instead, a glittering kind of pain was shooting across the lower stretches of my abdomen. It came in spasms; continued for periods of ten to fifteen seconds, then abated, only to return at intervals just short enough to prevent sleep. By four, my wife sensed something was amiss: we thought it might be the flu she had had two days before, or the Mexican meal we had eaten with such relish earlier in the evening. Whatever it was, it was no doubt sure to go away if several hours of sleep could be found.

That sleep finally came hours later. I awoke shortly after noon feeling wan but, on the whole, better. Twitches played less frequently across my lower abdomen. I split a grapefruit with my wife and drank a glass of cranberry juice. Perhaps that was all there was to it. Sleeping it—whatever it was—off, and then some fruit. I proceeded to my study. *On to transcendentalism.*

Emerson, Thoreau, and Theodore Parker came along, surely enough, but then the spasms came too. Not continuously, but at twenty-to-thirty minute intervals; everything was normal between them. But they too, those burning jags across the stomach, would no doubt pass, I believed, as the night ones had. Around four in the afternoon, my wife prepared a steaming cup of universal medicine, chicken noodle soup, and brought it to my room. I managed a quarter of it, but my taste was gone. And the spasms now came on with even greater intensity. Their duration barely varied: ten to fifteen seconds of back-arching lower abdominal pain, then nothing. As if all were normal.

So the day progressed: I would read for fifteen to thirty minutes, then suffer a ten-to-fifteen-second spasm, until nearly eight o'clock, when I finally stumbled into the next room to my wife. "Do you think it could be ulcers?" I asked. I had been toughing it out. She was more concerned; as a nurse, she was afraid of obstruction somewhere in my abdomen. "I'm calling the doctor," she said.

Meanwhile nausea came, then vomiting. After, I felt much better. Perhaps that was all there was to it. When the doctor returned the call my wife explained my symptoms. Dr. Kent from our health plan wanted us to go immediately to the Green Road Urgent Care facility. They could decide from there if we should continue on to the University Hospitals' ER. My wife packed a small overnight bag, just in case.

At the Urgent Care, my appendix came under immediate suspicion: nothing suggested itself more clearly by way of diagnosis. There would have to be further tests, the doctor there told me, "and you are obviously ill." I was sent to University Hospitals to be admitted.

The spasms continued, though with less frequency. Shortly after 1 A.M. I was a patient for only the second time in my life: the first, a two-night stay in 1981 for naturally passing kidney stones. But now a fierce hiccuping began. Nausea and vomiting recurred: the hiccuping ended. I felt better. Perhaps I was cured. I fell asleep.

Monday morning dawned as test day. There was so very little transcendental, that is, viewing life as if from the stance of a god, about it. There seemed everything of the human and reality—batteries of X-rays, EKGs, body fluid analyses. The organism as laboratory. By the end of the day the attending surgeon, Dr. Joseph Crowe, reported that all the early diagnoses had been cleared. The day's X-rays did show some kind of blockage in the colon that only a more intrusive picture of the area could fully reveal. Those tests were scheduled for the next day, Tuesday.

Release that afternoon was thus foreclosed, but I still held out hope that I would perhaps be discharged the following day. For the first time, however, we called my family: it was not going to be a one-day wonder we could best tell about some days later. We informed them that there was only discomfort and tests involved at this hour. I called my editor at the newspaper where a story of mine I still needed to attend to was in production; he told me it would surely appear but that my health was the highest priority. And I had called the university earlier in the day to let my professors know I would not be in class that evening, and perhaps not Tuesday, depending on release and how I felt, but I was hopeful about the rest of the week.

These things happen, I reminded myself. It was odd and disconcerting, but normality would return soon enough, we, or at least I, was confident.

At just past 4 P.M. on Tuesday, March 3, 1992, Dr. Crowe and four residents came into the room. There was an added measure of seriousness in the air. The doctor had the findings of the past several days, and specifically this day's test results. He had a paper for me to sign. He explained. They had found a tumor. A large one. High up on the left side just below the rib cage, the colon had become constricted by the growth to perhaps (he showed with his fingers separated) an eighth of an inch. Surgery was imperative. Tomorrow. The paper—the release form—included exploratory surgery, a possible spleenectomy (the spleen was just above the site), a possible colostomy. There were other possibilities, too, some listed. The gravest, however, though not listed, seemed most in mind even as I, somewhat numbly, signed. It somehow didn't seem real.

I had cancer. Cancer!

Several days, several hours ago I had a future. T. S. Eliot's lines seemed to fill the room in a kind of aural antiphony, "Pray for us now and at the hour of our death, pray for us now at the hour of our death."

                              * * *

I heard the somehow spectral voices of family outside the hospital room even as they were being turned away from the door, asked to wait several minutes down the hall. I was being prepped for surgery, and I was now fully in the grip of an institution: not just of a massive urban hospital but of hundreds of years of medicine. I was relating to the world and to those closest to me from a most unexpected distance, I, among creation's most uninstitutional of creatures.

Throughout the evening members from the surgical team, nurses, doctors, anesthesiologists, stopped by my bedside to introduce themselves, asking if there were questions. (Was this now standard procedure, I wondered, those opening up the inside chatting with the one opened up?) They were, it seemed irrefutable, uniformly sympathetic and friendly. Before the procession ended a half-dozen gowned and soft spoken people—people I was not, however, to recognize in the shadowy operation room (only the medical student who held my hands in hers as I sat waiting on the table's edge registered)—passed by my bedside like emissaries of another world, a world I was even now in the vestibule of, pressing inwards.

A more familiar, almost ancient, world was still waiting down the hall to see me. They had begun their eighty-mile journey to Cleveland almost on hearing the news of the afternoon. I realized yet again that I was in the grip of an institution; my emotions were somehow annealed to its corporate matter-of-factness, the incremental, inevitable, necessary next thing: I was unprepared for the emotion—my wife and others had been talking to them—as my siblings finally approached bedside, restrained though they sought to hold themselves: a brother's tremulous voice, a sister's tear-streaked face.

For the first time something broke loose in me, and I wept. But my tears were, odd perhaps, tears of sympathy. My suffering seemed less than theirs, somehow, I wished to comfort them; I sorrowed with them. It was they, I somehow felt, who were most in need of consoling.

But there was barely time for anything. I was soon being sent downstairs once more for a last round of pre-op X-rays. A hapless kind of processional formed in the hallways as siblings and several friends whispered encouragement and waved as the wheelchair entered the elevator then disappeared inside. Several promised to return again early in the morning. My wife, having barely left my side since entering the hospital, stayed to see them off.

Now alone and waiting in the hallway by the X-ray room in the bowels of the quiet nighttime hospital, I was joined by another. A second porter wheeled a chair near to me. Seeing the human being set beside me I was shamed, and for the first time somehow, frightened. The middle-aged patient's taut nose and mouth were fully masked; his head was glistening almost iridescently bald, no doubt from un-told radiation; his eyes were tightly shut to the world. Upwards to ten assorted bags and packs rode above him like a vast multi-sac bladder and fed into his body through tangled capillaries of tubes. He seemed almost an appendage of them. Regal, preternatural still, he appeared like a barely breathing mummy. His porter, I observed then, was wear-ing latex gloves.

Compared to this woeful seemingly skinless man I was, I felt, even in my extremity, in the pink of health. Here was not The Boy Inside the Bubble, but The Man Outside. He seemed to be sleeping, or rather, in a trance. I searched for something to say: a word of comfort, cama-raderie. I was somehow there too, now, I thought. I should acknowl-edge him. I searched for words, but no words came. I failed. His silence silenced me. I felt a peasant near majesty in the court of suffer-ing. His fierce, clenched eyes followed me into the X-ray room, down the hall when leaving, and then to my last night's sleep before the knife.

Early next morning, my eldest sister and sister-in-law followed my wife and the transport lady on the long ride from University Hospi-tals' Hanna House to the portals of the operating room. Their whis-pered, aching, fierce endearments as the doors opened to me and closed on them again brought tears to my eyes. Their fear, their help-lessness, cut me with grief. *I alone,* I told myself at the time though now know it to be less than true, *am made of sterner stuff.*

I am, however, most certainly made of a human body that all too easily can be opened up with a cut extending vertically from below the belly button to the very peak of the sternum—all without know-ing. Sitting on the operating table's edge I breathed deeply a small black muzzle fitting just over the nose and mouth. Five, then fifteen inhalations, then nothing, nowhere (that is, the dictionary definition of utopia), which, you later discover, lasts for four and one half hours. Until the voices—far-off, somehow unearthly, insistent voices—and the tattoo of pinpricks along the thigh and sides: "Can you feel this? Can you feel this?"

My own surreal voice echoed from some ether in the present: "Ygeke. Ygeke. [Yes. Yes.]"

This is now present tense, things are happening now: when I wake up, sliver by sliver of consciousness, in my private room (recovery room entirely lost to me), my first lucid if muffled question to the voice I recognized, my wife's: "A colostomy?"

"No."

"Oh thank goodness! Oh . . . ! I'm living?"

"Very much so."

"Able to go home?"

"Of course. Of course. Soon enough."

The more compelling question, however, is: Will I be able to handle the larger findings of the surgery I've just passed through? What—in the doctor's jargon: adenocarcinoma, colon resection with direct anastomosis—has changed my life forever, if not prematurely ended it?

Soon enough, soon enough.

By late afternoon of March 4, 1992, I essentially know in outline what has since been fully revealed: that upwards to 50 percent of the total cancer still remains even with the softball-size tumor removed, that it has broken through the abdominal walls, that some lymph nodes are enveloped, and the liver has been encroached upon.

It is all rather serious business, the furthest removed from illusion, as the transcendentalists would have it; sickness, death, or their prospects.

Life is no joke.

If my inauspicious birthday to this mortal coil was Christmas Eve of 1951, my worst day then was the evening of Leap Year Day 1992, onset of a second endlessly problematic round of life. Life quite unlike any I would ever have imagined for myself, though all too, even brutally real.

Life, in a sense—my life—is starting all over again.

Even as it is threatening to end.

To coin a phrase, and even to praise: life—but another one—goes on.

* * *

I would be healed.

Or at least, barring that, heal as quickly as my condition allows. On Wednesday evening, hours after surgery, I stand upright beside the bed, supported by my wife and her sister. The day after, I take some steps within the room. The following day, I venture some feet up and down the hall. By Saturday, I circumambulate on my own among the chairs set at the end of each long hallway on the tripartite floor. I have become quite the traveler.

Sunday afternoon we invite the nearly twenty-five nieces and nephews in my family up to the hospital. In a family with eight children, where I am the youngest of five boys and have three younger sisters, nothing quite like this has ever happened. We are a family where, until my now-aged father's ailment of several years' standing, no serious illness or accident to speak of has visited. This had been true even in my childhood and youth, and now that run of almost uninterrupted health and a shielding from adversity has extended into yet another generation. My siblings tell my wife and me that their children seem quite bewildered, stunned even, by this turn of events and barely know what to make of things. An uncle gravely ill is almost fully outside their register of life.

So, we'll have a meeting.

As we are a singing family, on Sunday afternoon, March 8, 1992, the dining arboretum known as the Atrium at University Hospitals in Cleveland is filled with the lifted voices of children eight to eighteen and their parents. They surround their uncle who, still with a nasogastric tube inserted and a morphine pump in place for pain at the push of a button, listens: they sing like cherubs. Forty minutes later, I ask to speak. The children gather as if circling a camp fire, their parents scattered behind them like sentries. They are very quiet.

I start by telling them that I think I understand. They are in the position I was in at their age—all of their ages. Apart from an Amish grandmother who died when I was six and a grandfather who died when I was twenty-eight, there was no death or serious illness or accident in the family I know. (We are now a clan of over forty.) The full range of suffering, reversals, calamity, and death common to the lot of all families was somehow through God's mercies temporarily suspended for us. I have no better reason why, I say, apart from mercy.

So if I couldn't fully answer their—or my—questions about the run of good fortune, then I could assure them that I too, through my own years, had felt that dearth of experience with close-up sorrow and loss I knew intellectually was as fundamental to life itself as—life. I knew, as we all knew if we thought about it, and sometimes we did, the time was coming when the run would be over. Only I hadn't, I confessed, exactly pictured myself as the one to end it.

No matter; here it was, the run was definitely over. What I could assure and reassure them of with no reservations was that what they saw before them in myself was not somehow abnormal or out of this world or unreal, but very real, natural, and normal in the affairs of people and families.

Women and men are born, they live, they enjoy, they suffer slings and arrows of both banal and outrageous fortune, they, at last, die. This is the natural rhythm of life, I tell them. Realizing the boundaries of the mortal coil is important even in understanding ourselves, knowing who we truly are. We are not little gods. We are humans, and since the Fall every last mother's daughter and son have been subject, indeed captive, to sickness and death. Thus they truly should not be worried overmuch about my ailing body. Like theirs, like every other person's, I tell them, it has obsolescence built into it. It is made to wear down and out. And early or late, it does.

The soul, however, is another matter. It's more than mortal clay. It's made not merely for time but for eternity. That, I tell them, is the sum of things. And how we mortal humans born with immortal souls respond to who breathed life into us—and, later, died to restore us, alienated, back to himself—makes all the difference.

The indisputable cancer I have, I tell them, bears only on my body. My soul, my spirit, has no out-of-control cells to speak of. On that they can rest assured. I am truly in good hands, medically and every other way. Every human effort, they can be sure, is being made to fight the disease (I tell them I plan on making presidential contender Paul Tsongas, who fought off lymphoma, look like a malingerer), but the disease—disease itself—should not be thought of as anything out of this world.

It has everything to do with this world. It is so very important for them to understand and remember that. Life, one way or other, goes on—including mine. Including theirs. Let's—I end my peroration— keep looking upward, shall we?

Whereas earlier, before the singing began, the children had been warily edging around me, unsure how to approach or what to say and catching themselves staring, the ice appears to be broken between us. I seem to have lost my dread, totemic aspect; here again is someone they know. Five of them walk with my wife and me on the long trek back from the Atrium to Hanna House to see the way the room has been decorated and the many flowers. Before they leave to join their parents, I conduct a mock interview with each of them concerning strategies for eats on the ride back, and then their goals for the rest of the evening when they get home, playing it all back to them from a microcassette player. We record much laughter.

By now I am quite tired. My wife is walking the children downstairs. I hadn't even known I was going to be giving, and certainly hadn't prepared beforehand, a speech today. My thoughts are racing even as I'm dozing off . . . when suddenly an imposing figure sweeps into the room, followed by someone unfamiliar. It's my editor. He introduces the second man as a doctor friend brought along "to make sure they're treating you right." They are, mostly. An hour later the publisher of the newspaper stops by, and we end up walking together, he, my wife, and I, down to the Atrium again and back, discussing news of the day and business.

It's almost as if there has been no illness. It's almost possible to imagine a time when there won't be any.

It's also true that I am about to fall into a twelve-hour sleep and, when I awaken, be four days from even leaving the hospital still, no question, a cancer patient.

Or, *im*patient.

It makes no difference. The reality remains the same. Even as W. B. Yeats resonates of everything having changed, changed utterly. We must wait to see if a terrible beauty has been born.

We are pilgrims and strangers in a new land. Cancer does that to you. When I am released from the hospital on March 12, 1992, a week after surgery, the world no longer looks the same. There has been a transformation: nothing will ever be as it was either within the world of men and nature or within myself. Still leafless, skeletal trees stand as sentinels along the street; bee-like traffic has taken on a different rhythm; the atmosphere itself somehow seems as if of a different substance. The diaphragm consciously takes in air and breathes out. The earth is drenched with mortality.

My wife's sister drives the car that takes us home. The two have spent some portion of the past several days making, to their satisfaction, "the house ready." It does indeed look like a new home. Yet everything, though burnished, remains much as it's always been. The new hue seems to rise both from human hands and from sources beyond. Had a house ever felt so much like a home and yet like a transit station?

In the evening, while I am resting, my wife calls to Connecticut to let her aunt and uncle know. He, a much-honored Ivy League historian, has been abroad, guest of Aberdeen University in Scotland through much of February and March as lecturer in a long-standing series. His wife, it turns out, is flying to join him in the morning; she will bear the news.

Daily, the mail brings a cache of letters and cards; flowers are dropped off. I do not, as yet, have the wherewithal to do any writing or giving out. It is others who give; I receive. I am not just a patient, but a debtor.

The thoughts and words received are humbling, restorative, and even disconcerting. I hear from expected and unexpected quarters. A two-year-younger fellow alum who "always looked up to you as a role model in my high school years" writes from Illinois "shocked to hear the news of your cancer," and with "sadness knowing I will probably never see you again in this life." A colleague who begins, "During the years we worked together I have come to love and respect you as a brother," assures me that "He told us, when we go through the waters He would be with us." A Liberian emigre also from the same institution writes, "I ask myself, why did this happen to good people like you, when all these wicked people are walking around town?"

These are metaphysical questions, and one discovers soon enough that with a grave illness or accident the depths are plumbed by nearly everyone; we ask ourselves, and others, the most fundamental questions. If it is indeed true that there are no atheists in foxholes (a somewhat doubtful proposition), perhaps even more true is the certainty of the metaphysician by every sick bed.

Why do we suffer? And to what ends?

Friends of ours from Cleveland make a cottage they own in the country of my birth available to us for the last ten days of March— vacation days, as it happens, for my wife, and we plan for going there. We want to think. We want to separate ourselves from everyone. We want to spend time with people. We want to be alone. We want to be with family. We are at times unsure of what we want.

We do know that the cottage is lovely, set back in a craggy woods all to itself. Here the skeletal trees mass like an endless thicket. Deer venture up to the wooden patio where corn has been laid to entice them. (My eldest brother arrives one morning straight from the feed mill with bulging sacks.) A menagerie of birds live their bird lives just outside the wall of glass the lodge is enclosed by. Snow limns land and tree in a gauzy hush early in the week; warm spring breaks out several days later. When we arrive home, somehow having managed to live with all our contradictory hopes for the vacation, an air mail letter, among others, awaits us. It reads like the sum of humanity and yet is suffused with the divine. It breaks my heart.

> Dear James and Lynne, Sylvia arrived from the USA over the weekend, but our delight at being back together after too long a separation was marred by the news she brought about the cross that has been laid upon you. I cannot even attempt to explain such things, and one of the reasons I did such an unsatisfactory job when I used to try to do pastoral work is my inability to get much past the boundaries of "past finding out" and "incomprehensible" that the New Testament has placed against our scrutinizing what is inscrutable.
>
> But of this I am sure: that the same mystery from which such trials come shows itself to be as well a source of strength and patience, even of joy, far beyond anything we ever dreamed of. And that is, I suppose, the ultimate meaning of the suffering, death, and resurrection of Christ.
>
> It is, I'm sure, no secret to anyone that the two of you hold a special place in our hearts, as though you were our own chil-

dren. With that bond between us comes, the privilege also of suffering with you and weeping with you, but of sharing consolation and peace with you as you face the future.

As a professional, Lynne, you know far better than I what can be done to battle against this disease and why it is so important not to surrender hope.

You will both be in our thoughts and prayers. We leave for Czechoslovakia on Friday, and I'll be back in the States on the evening of the 31st. With our abiding love.

And so we begin the second life, not surrendering hope.

Dr. James K. V. Willson and his fellow, Dr. James Sabiers, direct the treatment program I begin at University Hospitals' Ireland Cancer Center. By March 31 I am healed enough from the surgery that a CAT scan can be taken to reveal what cancer yet remains. There are two tumors perched like lethal leeches on the liver. However, these tumors do allow for important monitoring. We will be able to assume that the treatment will affect smaller tumors "seeding" the area the same way it affects these larger, more visible tumors.

After an initial five-day hospital stay, I maintain a regimen that continues to this day: a weekly round of chemotherapy (of 5-Fluorouracil, or 5-FU) as an out-patient, together with three weekly shots of Alpha-Interferon, a biological agent, at home. And so it will be through late June. A second CAT scan will then reveal if the leech-like forms on the liver have grown, remained the same, reduced, or, *mirabile dictu*, disappeared.

The treatment will be considered a success if the forms remain the same size. I would then continue the same treatment. If the forms have grown, more experimental therapies would be considered.

If the latter, the time of my end will be that much nearer, even if hope, the blessed hope, is never surrendered.

* * *

You never get over the needles.

The probing, the pinching, the sense of violation.

But then, cancer is a violation. And life is a matter of scale: we tolerate things that would otherwise repulse us if we did not know that worse things, in this case mortal illness, await us.

Still, you never get over the needles. Each week at the chemotherapy sessions a butterfly needle is inserted into a vein at the crook of my arm. No doubt I am a timid soul, but it has yet to become easy; I blanch at each entry. I try, however, to put up a brave front. Each insertion, I know only too well, is a sluice both for drawing out the body's most vital data and for sending in its most vital treatment.

Once a vial of blood is drawn through this means, it's quickly sent to the lab. The needles remain in place, as does a large syringe. Usually within five minutes the report comes back on this week's counts of platelets, red blood cells, and, most importantly, white blood cells (the disease fighters). The combination of chemotherapy and Alpha Interferon is an equal opportunity destroyer of fast (and far-too-fast) growing cells. That includes blood cells, with a ten-day life cycle, as well as the cancerous cells.

Each week becomes a kind of medical minuet between the compromising effects of the cancer treatment on the blood counts—consistently lowering them, and hence increasing vulnerability to a wide range of infections—and the favorable effects on the fastest growing cells of all, the cancerous ones: killing them.

The protocols are elaborate. If the blood counts are below a specified number, I am sent home without that week's treatment (this has happened several times). The risks are too great, my defenses too low.

Otherwise, the giant syringe still attached to the butterfly needle becomes the modem through which this week's portion of liquid chemotherapy is slowly pushed into my veins. (A sobering thought: nurses wear gloves in defense against what I'm ingesting.) The killer chemo goes in search of the killer cells that have given me Dukes D colon cancer, the most advanced of four stages of cancer. My doctors tell me that although it is not curable, it may perhaps be controllable.

Think of it, they tell me, like a chronic disease. Asthma, diabetes, arthritis, high blood pressure, for example. These and other maladies are never really cured, but, with patience and medication, can be controlled, managed. There is the potential for this even for my illness, advanced though it may be. If the tumors remaining after surgery can at least be kept from growing—their natural life—their lethality can be arrested, for however long. With treatment, my life can go on.

The first evidence of success—and hope—for this modest ambition came in late June and again in late August. A CAT scan each time showed that two inch-length tumors perched on the liver, the furthest advance of the mass, had not grown at all since this treatment began. *Gloria Deo.* To be sure, the tumors had neither shrunk nor disappeared, but even to check their growth placed me in a minority of patients with my diagnosis; this was success, they told me. Treatment should continue.

And so it shall. Life will go on. Even if knowing there is no real end to treatment in sight, both of the chemotherapy at the hospital and the Interferon shots (needles again!) I administer to myself at home. Even if knowing, as I've been told by my doctors, that checked tumors can, over time, build up an immunity to ongoing treatment and resume growing.

Perhaps they will. Perhaps, they won't.

Meanwhile, I can resume living. Not just as before—that will never be; my cancer will always exist—but much like before, only, with the added measure of mortality weighing, *much more so.*

My ambitions have been few, even singular: I have felt impelled since youth to write; scribble, scribble. Little else has motivated me.

That urge continues. These pages reflect, and have reflected, one part of my interest.

And sitting in a desk drawer I too have that no-doubt-less-than-great American novel that every self-respecting journalist is said to have, which I would like to return to between assignments. I fancy it the best thing I've done, perhaps will do.

Finally, perhaps at this late hour a straightforward statement will be permitted me: I love my wife. She has been the hero.

God has been merciful.

To appropriate Beckett in *Waiting for Godot,* I will go on.

* * *

There is a state, twilit but real, somewhere between life and death.

Those with terminal disease inhabit it. They are, for want of a better term, emigrants of the spirit. What citizenship they possess subtly shifts; the air about them somehow changes. They become alien in their own residency.

Having a terminal illness places one on a febrile Ellis Island of a new and undiscovered country from whose bourn, as doleful Hamlet observes, no traveler returns.

But sail has been set, unquestionably, from the Old World; the New World awaits.

Yet this gradual, ongoing estrangement holds a profound paradox, one it might be hard to imagine short of being drawn in oneself. It comes as a point of wonder and surprise. It makes one marvel anew at the quality of mystery in life. For even as the threads weaving one to the native country of health unravel, the ties that bind to all we know and love—family, friends, coworkers, even strangers—tighten.

Or if not tighten, transform: they take on a fresh heightened character; a nuanced dynamic quality enters every relation, from the most intimate to the marginal; complacency is effectively banished; *carpe diem,* seize the day, does not so much become an anthem of hedonism as a reminder that only the day, not the year or the decade or the life, is vouchsafed.

Never have tears been so near to laughter. Never the profusion of both. And never has loss and gain, longevity for depth, seemed so much of a piece, so exquisitely inextricable the one from the other.

This paradoxical, perhaps transcendent, emigre status was borne home anew by a recent CAT scan, the third set of computer pictures since March, monitoring my hereto checked tumors. Giving me the report, my doctor's voice faltered slightly on the word "unfortunately." Unfortunately, the treatment I have been on has now failed.

For five glorious months and two scans the treatment held; growth was checked. The odds, medically, had never been very long for even this.

But hope builds on hope—and success. Why shouldn't a third view of the two inch-length malignant eels on a vital organ show the same assessment as earlier views? Why? Why not?

The treatment, now beginning in early October, has been altered. The concern all along about the chemotherapy (5-FU) has been the unavoidable effects it has had on the blood counts, seriously depressing them. These lowered counts over time forced a correspondingly reduced volume of the chemotherapy itself; these past several months, less and less has been taken.

The new regimen, if still 5-FU based, begun this week after a two-week hiatus allowing the counts to rise has a new biological agent enhancer thought to be less punishing on the bone marrow than the one to date. Much higher doses of the chemotherapy are now within hope—the first full treatment has already begun.

Time will tell, certainly enough, as will the bi-monthly computer pictures monitoring.

Yet all of this, including (perhaps especially) the medical minutiae, is occurring on a somewhat surreal terrain.

The New World does take getting used to.

There is, for example, no illusion of old age. No thought of decades between now and whatever terminus might give me, and life itself, meaning. Either the meaning is now or it no doubt never will be.

There is no, or certainly a fading, illusion of ever fully holding on to things. Things: not to denigrate their due place in living, but not a single item, not a book from my library, not a Mozart CD, not my gift of a lap-top computer or the vintage fountain pen made mine one Christmas morning can accompany. It all, every single blessed thing, stays behind, like me, to founder eventually in the dust.

There is no illusion of hanging on to any person, even the closest. We all, in the end, become separated: we had best cherish those who are near us (a gift, after all) before we do.

The night comes soon enough, in the words of One who rose from the dead, when no man can work or love.

As I believe in the One who conquered death, who promised the like to all believing in him, the prospect of my own departure from this mortal coil does not fill me with terror.

I have hope. To be sure, I hope for more days. I love life—I've positively thrilled in it throughout this year, never cherishing it more deeply.

But our human life is a being trapped in time. And time, for every single one of us, ends: sooner for some, later for others.

But ends. For all of us. Eternity extends: where and how we board is everything.

We are all of us, then, to that extent somewhere on an unfolding continuum between life and death.

Terminal. Between countries. Emigres.

I'm simply, perhaps mercifully, reminded (Miller, 26–33).

At the Session

Review Focal Points; view video " Redemption Today" on Videocassette 3 (9 minutes).

After the Video

1. Discuss one or more of the following statements or questions.
   - James Miller's illness was a great mercy for him and for his family. How can this be the case?
   - "We are pilgrims, not at home in this world. We have some other destiny." What does this mean for the Christian?
   - How did cancer allow James Miller to look differently upon life and death? How does he counteract the cover story in his acceptance of suffering?
2. Following are several excerpts from a letter Miller received from an aunt and uncle after they heard about his cancer. In small groups, choose one excerpt and discuss in terms of: (1) What is the meaning for a Christian? (2) What is the cover story to be overcome?
   - "But of this I am sure: that the same mystery from which such trials come shows itself to be as well a source of strength and patience, even of joy far beyond anything we ever dreamed of. And that is, I suppose, the ultimate meaning of the suffering, death, and resurrection of Christ."

- "You hold a special place in our hearts. . . . With that bond between us comes the privilege also of suffering with you and weeping with you . . . as you face the future."
- "You know why it is so important not to surrender hope."

3. List the key ideas from each group's responses. Add to your notepages.

BIBLIOGRAPHY

DeVinck, Christopher. *The Power of the Powerless.* 9–14. New York: Doubleday, 1988.

Miller, James Andrew. "Other Plans: Journal of an Illness." *First Things* (March 1993) 26–33. James Andrew Miller was a correspondent with *City Reports*, a Cleveland, Ohio, newspaper, where portions of this journal first appeared. Permission for use granted by *First Things*.

Vocation

DON BRIEL

Before Arriving at the Session

Read Focal Points and the essay below.

Focal Points

Vocation is important in establishing a foundation for study of the Catholic tradition. We will examine the value of human existence and fulfillment and the role that each of us plays in the light of Christian hope. Each person has a personal responsibility to participate in the total mission of the Church.

Current pervasive thinking often opposes the messages that we find in vocation, the Old and New Testaments, spiritual life, and redemption.

VOCATION

The term vocation has always implied not merely a calling but also a calling forth to a particular task or good; it is perhaps useful today to reconsider the distinctiveness of the particular good that the Christian teacher is called to serve. In *Easter in Ordinary* Nicholas Lash has reminded us of Baron von Hugel's penetrating insight that the essence of Christianity is to be found in "the revelation of personality," most directly the personality of Christ, who discloses in himself the fullness of divine invitation and the pattern of human response. For von Hugel, reflection on this mysterious revelation of personality also establishes a school for the fostering and production of persons, that is, we become persons, we develop personality, precisely in an engagement with the incarnate Christ who disclosed to us the unexpected possibility of fullness of life. It is in this sense that the Church is the materialization of Christ in history and that as Christian teachers we are called to share in the Church's life by a participation in this epiphany or uncovering to the world of the "personality" of God. And so in *Gaudium et spes*, the council affirmed that "The Lord is the goal of human history, the focal point of the desires of history and civilization, the center of mankind, the joy of all hearts and the fulfillment of all aspirations."

We can say that one of the primary ends of teaching in a Catholic context is not merely the uncovering of some veiled secret but the achievement of the condition of "persons" living in relation to a vital truth. Nevertheless the conditions of personhood are not self-evident and there is in any particular age considerable confusion about what its achievement would require. In our own time the attainment of personal identity is often confused with the achievement of success or power or autonomy and it is, therefore, difficult in an individualistic culture to provide alternative accounts and images of the nature and goals of life, for at the heart of human experience is a profound ambiguity. We have two basic convictions about our condition that appear to be absolutely irreconcilable. On the one hand we have a clear sense of the value of human existence, indeed that we are called to a certain fullness of life, to immortality. On the other hand, we know that we are born to die, that we are really, not merely metaphorically, food for worms. How can both be true at once, and more immediately for our purposes, what does Christianity tell us? How can we illuminate this, our existential human dilemma? Clearly the vocation for the Christian teacher is to introduce learners to this complex ambiguity and to provide resources through which children might be able to realize their lives in hope and in truth in relation to it.

One perennial response to this two-fold awareness of the promise and despair of the human situation is repression. Some of the stories in one's culture cover over the awareness of the apparent tragedy of the fact that we are born to die, and instead claim our lives as our own. This is in sharp contrast to the Christian tradition's emphasis on remembrance and representation of the transforming events of Christ's life, death, and resurrection and active anticipation of the fulfillment of Christian hope. Here we confirm the Christian paradox: to gain our lives is to lose them; to lose them for the sake of Christ is to gain them. Unlike the acts of repression which enable us to claim our lives as our own by denying the reality both of death and immortality, Christians gain their lives by an act of surrender to God who has sustained and created them and who has, in the person of Christ, intervened in history to secure their freedom and fullness of life. So the

Christian begins in grateful memory and is called to a life of conversion to the will of God.

But we are often undone by this consciousness of ambiguity and our tendency is to deny it. Fear of death manifests itself as a fear of life. In trying to free ourselves from the apparent tragedy of the human situation, it is not clear that there is anything worth living for, much less worth dying for. We find we cannot act at all. Our lives are flat, stale, and dispersed, and the chronic complaint is of boredom. This is not a uniquely modern problem, although Walker Percy reminds us that the English word "boredom" did not exist until the seventeenth century.

Christians acknowledge all the sources of despair but refuse to give them the last word. Rather, the last word is God's creation of and superintending providence for the world. As human persons we are called to be co-creators of this creative act of love, and it is in the co-creation that we achieve our freedom. This is why, in the Christian tradition, there has always been the insistence that freedom is at the heart of the human person, as indeed it is in the mutual, consubstantial love of Father, Son, and Spirit in the Trinity. Of course, as John Paul II recently stated, we are most free when we are most responsible. This is in sharp contrast to an American emphasis on autonomy in which we are most free when we are least dependent on anything outside ourselves. But if we understand life as a gift, then responsibility goes hand in hand with our exercise of freedom. It is for this reason that sin is central in the Christian tradition. This is not because sin is a source of guilt and anxiety, but rather that it presupposes genuine freedom and responsibility. However, it is interesting to note that Jewish thinkers such as Buber and Christian thinkers such as Kierkegaard are united in their assertion that those who lack a capacity for guilt and anxiety also lack humanity. Kierkegaard argued that at the heart of the human situation is a certain dread, and in contrast to modern therapeutic claims that we are most healthy when we are least anxious, he argued that we are most sane when we are most conscious that our lives are not in our control, a source of anxiety if there ever was one.

How would this traditional Christian emphasis affect the way we invite our students to the fulfillment of personhood? We live in an age in which there is real concern about the psychological well-being of many of our learners and there have been a number of efforts to develop programs which emphasize the goodness and self-esteem of individual learners from a number of cultures and economic situations. As Christians we too support the goodness of creation, but a difficulty is that too often such programs tend to seek to reassure students, either through an unconditional acceptance of themselves as good or through an unrealistic emphasis on their unlimited capacity for achievement. The problem is that students know their own guilt, know that they are often accomplices to their own moral failures. From a Christian perspective, self-discovery or self-esteem will depend upon creatureliness, that is, that to be ourselves is not merely to be true to our present condition, but to be true to the God who created us. We cannot simply raise ourselves up to meet the challenge and destiny of our existence or to support our own adequacy. Those we teach are very honest about this. They know their present inadequacy and need permission to acknowledge it. They will continue in many ways to be inadequate. Their hope is not in themselves alone. They are not going to resolve the problems of human life by their own goodness and decency because they will never fully achieve that goodness. And not only they, but also others, will suffer for their failure. It seems wrong to tell our learners not to feel guilty, that it does not really matter. It does matter. It matters a lot.

We have to acknowledge our failures very honestly and not say that they don't matter. People suffer for them, not only our wives or husbands, our children, our students, but also people we will never know. In this sense our vocation is not simply that of teacher but also as witness to the essential mystery of Christian freedom and responsibility.

As teachers we have three primary resources on which we can draw in order to participate in the materialization of Christ in the world: revelation, liturgy, and tradition. (I am thinking principally of an intellectual tradition here, both in the formal teaching of bishops and the critical reflection of theologians, but also central is the experience of daily Christian living, the saints.) Of course these elements are not discrete and ought to interact with one another in a fruitful tension.

To some degree these three resources also correspond to a threefold process which according to von Hugel accomplishes this schooling of persons. In childhood, one encounters facts; in adolescence, one develops critical reflection and theory; and in adulthood, one is called to a life of mature action. In such a scheme no one stage is fully matured. What adult can claim to have left childhood behind? Nonetheless, there is a kind of natural progression in the development of understanding and of personality that can be described in these three stages.

In the first stage children respond to the directives and immediacy of facts and it is here that the child wonders at the essential individuality of persons, things, and events. Children do not see things whole; they learn in units and so the task of the religion teacher is to present images and stories which reveal and disclose Christ not only in his person but in his saving action in history. These facts include not only biblical narratives and other stories from the tradition, but also teachings of the Church which children may first encounter in a fairly stark and declarative form (much like the periodic table in chemistry) but which are enfleshed and rediscovered in worship, narrative, and moral life, much in the same way that a child understands chemical compounds both through chemical "doctrines" and immediate experience.

At the adolescent stage the phase of immediacy is called into question as a demand for differentiation emerges. In religion we need now to confront issues of metaphor, history, and myth and pay new attention to the complex interaction of human nature and divine purpose. The facts of childhood experience now require new contexts and more explicit relations to one another, for the adolescent feels that these unit experiences bump against one another and no longer fit.

In the last analysis, von Hugel, like Cardinal Newman, argued that this schooling of persons is an education for action and not merely reflection, for we are called to a certain heroism even in ordinary acts of life. We are called to sanctity, to make Christ present in and to the world. Again this mature life of action leaves behind neither the childhood immediacy of knowledge of facts (of which our dreams continually supply pressing images) nor the critical reflection of adolescent awareness of the ambiguity and tension of our situation and our claims. But it translates and at least partly resolves them in action.

Of course, as teachers we do not often see in the lives of our learners these phases in their fruitful interaction, but we need to be mindful of them and the larger end they serve as we participate in the Church's larger vocation of the revelation of personality and the transformation of experience.

At the Session

Review Focal Points; view video "Vocation" on Videocassette 3 (20 minutes).

After the Video

1. How does our culture think about "vocation"?
2. What is the mystery of being called by God?
3. Summarize the main understandings presented in the video and discussion.

Further Reflection

How do I respond to the statement: "Our vocation is not simply a job but is also a witness to the essential mystery of Christian freedom and responsibility"?

BIBLIOGRAPHY

Catechism of the Catholic Church. Part One: §2, ch. 1, art. 1, paras. 6, 7. Part Three: §1, ch. 1, arts. 1, 8. Washington, D.C.: United States Catholic Conference, 1994.

Newman, John Henry. *An Essay on the Development of Christian Doctrine.* London: Longmans, Green, 1920.

Vatican Council II. *Gaudium et spes* (On the Church in the Modern World), no. 24. December 7, 1965.

PART TWO

THE CHURCH

CHAPTER FIVE

MYSTERY AND MISSION

Mystery of the Church

ARTHUR KENNEDY

Before Arriving at the Session

Read Focal Points and essay below.

Focal Points

The essay begins with definitions of the Church and then looks at the aspect of mystery. The mystery of the Church leads one to consider the mysteries of Trinity and of Christ in the Old Testament and the New Testament.

Membership in the Church is begun and continued through the sacraments.

Cover stories of the Church are examined.

MYSTERY OF THE CHURCH

Some have called this century "the century of the Church." And the label has a proper fit considering all of the documents, discussions, and dialogues that have focused on the Church. During this time there has been a valuable recovery of the multiple symbols and images used in the Scriptures to convey the mystery of the Church. Thus we have been focused at different times on the mystical body, the people of God, the community, and the sacrament of God. Most certainly, one major recovery that has been important in these four decades has been the role of the laity in the mission of the Church in the world. In order to understand something of the mystery of the Church, we need to consider some of the fundamental aspects that make it what it is.

Mystery of the Church and Mystery of Christ

In the first place, the Church has its origin in the mystery of Christ. It is created to reflect and bring about one essential part of the mystery of God—to overcome evil with good and to guide and bring people into the reign of God. In the plainest language the Church has been created by God to get people into heaven or to bring them into the intimacy of God's holiness and infinite love. Since this cannot be done by any natural achievement, this is one of God's most important works, and it requires certain divine actions on behalf of us humans. Because of the revelation in both the Old Testament and in the person of Christ in the New Testament we have been enlightened with certain aspects of this mystery.

Mystery of the Church and Mystery of the Trinity

When Christ teaches us about his own ministry in the world, he teaches us that what he does is coincident with the divine plan for our lives. His mission is to show us how, and to give us the gifts and aids we need, to effect the Trinitarian life for us so that we can bring our own wills into attunement with the divine will. That is certainly one of the important parts of the prayer which Christ has taught us to say again and again, "thy kingdom come, thy will be done on earth as it is in heaven" (Matt 6:10).

To put it another way, the Church is revealed to us as the reality, intended by the Trinity, as the way in which we can come to be with God as we live out our journeys and our daily lives. The Church is instituted by the mission of the Son, the second person of the Holy Trinity, who manifests, teaches, and effects that reality in all that he does. The Church is manifested to us as the way that God is with us through the mission of the Holy Spirit. This mission, which we celebrate at Pentecost, not only reveals the divine life, but provides the Church with the gifts it needs for its journey in history.

Characteristics of the Church

When the community named itself in relationship to the way it knew itself through the Trinitarian missions, it came to know itself as one, holy, catholic and apostolic.

As one it has been given the gift and the task of reflecting the divine unity that grounds the Trinitarian life. The Church, as constituted by this character, needs to accept, to find, and to live by the one absolute gift God makes of his Body.

As holy its members have been given the divine task of collaborating in the gift of redemption, and so they must strive to collaborate with those graces which call people to be as God is—to live in sanctity. Such a life of sanctity requires a proper balance between the physical and spiritual aspects of daily human life. Thus such sanctity knows the balanced need of education and learning, of liberty and the authority of traditions, of the individual and the common good, of affection and discipline, of imagination, intelligence, morality, and faith.

As catholic its members must be able to know the common graces in people of every place and time, every race and culture, and every nation and tongue. As catholic the Church is the fullness of the truth of revelation and it means that the members treat one another as Christ treats each one of us. As universal, the members of the Church are called to be of service to each other in preaching the mystery of redemption through the mission of the Son and in supporting each other in material as well as spiritual needs.

As apostolic its members acknowledge their dependence on the leadership of Christ that has been handed on to those who were with him (the apostles) and to whom he taught the mystery of his life and mission. The Church is thus tied into a detailed and concrete history of mediators (bishops) and representatives, or vicars, of Christ (popes). The Church has an order for fulfilling the authentic mission that was given by Christ. This order is guided by the image of Christ, the Good Shepherd, and the new shepherds require the same graces that every member requires.

The Church and the Sacraments

We become and continue as members of the Church through the sacraments. The first is baptism, which incorporates us into the life, suffering, and death of Christ. This incorporation is through an absolutely gratuitous gift of God. We are justified by Christ. It is God's love that brings us into the Church.

The other sacraments continue to provide various forms of growth or of recovery in living out what God gives to us. This is very important because at the present time the Church is in need of addressing the fact that some of its members are accepting two destructive cover stories.

Cover Stories Regarding the Church

Cover stories are modes of thought which cover up what is the full truth of the situation with only partial dimensions of reality. By doing this they create distortions that can easily be used to replace the reality which it is most important for us to know. One of the most common modes of cover story for Christians is to assume that a natural good is the same as a supernatural good. This confusion denies the role of grace, the mystery of the Church, and missions of the Trinity into our world.

The first cover story in our time is that the Church is a free voluntary association. Such associations are like clubs that form around some common purpose which members identify as having a value to themselves or to the community. The concerns of such associations are to improve some natural human end that might include fixing the park, developing the transportation system, raising monies for the school library, and helping those who are abused. These are all good things and they are natural goods. The Church's mission is related to those goods but from an altogether different foundation, because the proper end of the Church is bringing people into the life of God. So that when Christians perform tasks that are natural goods, they may do so from the framework of the mission of redemption and through the virtue of charity—the love of neighbor grounded in the love of God. Or they may just undertake some ordinary natural good.

But the Church is not a free voluntary association created by persons interested in the improvement of the natural world with members who commonly decide its proper purpose. Its mission is given to it by Christ. The proper exercise of that mission will make people more properly concerned about the conditions of the common good. Thus the cover story of American civil religion would teach us that we should be tolerant of others. The Church teaches that we should have charity toward our neighbors and that we strive to love them as God loves them. When charity is rightly understood it makes tolerance a pale and weak imitation of Christian virtue. The mission for Christians is to love the sinner while affirming the evil of the sin. Thus we know the need to grow in sanctity rather than living by the illusion that we are already perfect.

The second cover story seeks to undercut the mystery of the Church, namely that Christians are supposed to be already perfect. This cover story says that we have a natural utopia here on earth. This is a type of secular puritanism that denies the very purpose of the Church in bringing God's grace into the concrete lives of sinful people who need the grace of the sacraments in order to be transformed. This cover story proclaims that the Church, in its sinfulness, is a hypocritical club that needs to learn the proper therapies for human improvement. However, the Church must find its perfection in God. We are to "be perfect, therefore, as your heavenly Father is perfect" (Matt 5:48). That is quite a different, demanding, and liberating story than accepting the modern therapies as normative. Therapies have their place, but they are not replacements for the mystery of God's mercy and healing redemption.

These cover stories are encountered in both the personal and public dimensions of the Church.

The Imperfection of the Church

The Church unifies the visible and invisible, the physical and the spiritual, and it has sin within its members that calls out for redemption. That is part of what Flannery O'Connor had in mind when she wrote her first letter to her friend "A" in July 1955. She explained her belief in the Church and its role in history and her own life. She noted:

> I think that the Church is the only thing that is going to make the terrible world we are coming to endurable; the only thing that makes the Church endurable is that it is somehow the body of Christ and that on this we are fed. It seems to be a fact that you have to suffer as much from the Church, as for it, but if you believe in the divinity of Christ, you have to cherish the world at the same time that you struggle to endure it . . . there is nothing harder or less sentimental than Christian realism (O'Connor, 90).

At the Session

Review Focal Points; list the reasons why the Church is important for you; list some difficulties you encounter in the Church; view video "Mystery of the Church" on Videocassette 3 (16 minutes).

After the Video

Re-read the paragraphs on cover story in the essay above. Give examples from your own experience.

Further Reflection

How do I see the Church as a mystery? How do I respond to the mystery?

BIBLIOGRAPHY

Catechism of the Catholic Church. Part One: §2, ch. 3, art. 9. Washington, D.C.: United States Catholic Conference, 1994.

O'Connor, Flannery. *The Habit of Being: Letters of Flannery O' Connor.* Ed. Sally Fitzgerald, 80. New York: Vintage Books, 1980.

Vatican Council II. *Gaudium et spes* (On the Church in the Modern World). December 7, 1965.

Mission of the Church

JAN MICHAEL JONCAS

Before Arriving at the Session

Read the Focal Points and the essay below.

Focal Points

The mission of Jesus is fivefold: preaching, teaching, praying, community-building, and direct service. The author says, "The primary task of the Apostles is to proclaim Jesus of Nazareth risen from the dead as the Christ of God." The apostles appoint others to sustain the Christian life locally. The apostle is commissioned to proclaim God's message to the people. The mission of the Church follows on the five-fold mission of Jesus grounded in the witness of the Twelve.

MISSION OF THE CHURCH

Earlier essays in this series have addressed the topics of "Vocations" and "The Mystery of the Church." We were reminded that "vocation has always implied not merely a calling but also a calling forth to a particular task or good" (see p. 95, above) and that the mystery of the Church is a communion of persons sharing the life of the Triune God. Following the scholastic axiom *"agere sequitur esse"* ("action follows being"), this essay will sketch the mission of the Church as an interlocking series of activities grounded in its nature. Insofar as the Father through Christ in the Spirit has called and empowered people for union with the divine persons and one another, they have received a calling, a vocation, to be Church. Insofar as the Father has sent Christ and the Spirit for human and cosmic transformation, so people who share the life of the Trinity share the divine activity, having received a calling forth to particular tasks and goods that can be identified as the mission of the Church.

This essay assembles some elements for writing a "mission state-ment" for the Roman Catholic Church. It examines biblical notions of "mission," the "mission" of Jesus, and the "apostolic mission" con-fided by Jesus to his disciples. All of these elements should assist cate-chists in identifying the self-understanding and appropriate activities of the contemporary Church. At worst such an essay might constrict our appreciation for how the Spirit may be transforming the Church in our day; at best it may convict us of distortions in our ecclesial living and provide us with a renewed focus for our energies.

How Does the Bible Talk about "Mission"?

The English word "mission" comes from a Latin root *missio/mitto*, meaning "to send out, to dispatch." This linguistic root suggests that a mission is something dynamic, active, energy-filled. In addition a mis-sion seems to be given by one in authority or with power to another who will act with that authority and/or power. Being sent by some-one also implies that recipients of the mission exist, that these people may or may not receive the message and the person empowered or authorized by the sender to deliver it.

The biblical background (H. Rengstorf, *"apostolos"*) to the Latin/English term is found in the Greek root *apostolos/apostellein* (clearly re-lated to the English term "apostle"). Some biblical scholars have seen the origin of the New Testament apostolate in the rabbinic institution of the *sheluhim/sheluhin* ("commissioned emissaries"), but evidence for such rabbinic ambassadors stems from the late first century C.E. At that time certain Palestinian authorities commissioned or sent out rabbis to represent them and act for them with full power to conduct financial business, collect tithes or Temple taxes, to act with religious authority ("to bind and loose"), or to proclaim religious truths. Those sent were sometimes ritually commissioned by the laying on of hands. Most importantly, when acting within the limits of their commission, the *sheluhim* had all the authority of the sender.

What Is the Mission of Jesus?

The author of the letter to the Hebrews employs the term *"apostolos"* to designate the relationship of Jesus to his Abba-God and to the members of the Christian community. After a lengthy comparison of the respective positions of Jesus and the angels in relation to the Father, the author begins his comparison of Jesus and Moses by writ-ing: "Therefore, brothers, holy partners in a heavenly calling, consider that Jesus, the apostle and high priest of our confession, was faithful to the one who appointed him" (Heb 3:1-2a).

Some have found in the double title in this passage a two-fold mission statement for Jesus: he is absolutely authorized by God for word ("apostle") and deed ("high priest"). Others have claimed that Jesus is the One uniquely sent by God in contrast to Moses ("apostle"), the bearer of God's revelation, and Aaron ("high priest"), the leading priestly mediator. In any case this sacred author's theology affirms that Jesus' mission involves his authoritative representation of God in a conjunction of proclamation and priestly office. This appears to be the only time in which Jesus is directly presented as God's *apostolos/ shaliah,* but five further elements of his "mission statement" can be gleaned from other New Testament passages.

PREACHING

Contemporary Scripture scholars seem agreed that the central activity of Jesus' earthly ministry was preaching (Gerhard Friedrich, *"kêryx, [hierokêryx,] kêrussô, kêrygma, prokêrussô"*) the proclamation of the "reign/kingdom of God" (Mark 1:14-15). Jesus can thus be described as the herald of God's in-breaking reign. Impelled by his authoritative commission he announces what God is doing in human history, much as the prophets of the Old Testament and John the Baptizer had done. Unlike the Old Testament prophets and John the Baptizer, however, Jesus' proclamation is the event: what he declares occurs in the very fact of its declaration. He does not debate the truth or the plausibility of his message, nor does he detail the implications of its acceptance. He simply declares it and moves on to the next group. He does call people to the appropriate response to God's in-breaking reign: repentance *(metanoia).* What is distinctive about Jesus' kingdom-preaching is that three things have to be held together: (1) God's kingdom is a present event, actualized in the preaching and person of Jesus; (2) God's kingdom is a future event, still to be brought to fulfillment by God in human history; and (3) God's kingdom is connected with Jesus' ministry, so that a decision for/against him is a decision for/against God's reign. It should also be noted that the Gospels present Jesus' proclamation of the kingdom as involving certain characteristic rhetorical forms: (1) similitudes, (2) parables, and (3) exemplary stories.

TEACHING

Although Jesus appears in the New Testament witness primarily as a herald of the in-breaking reign of God, the Gospel records also image him as a teacher (*didaskalos*/rabbi). Similar to a scribe both in the form and content of his teaching (i.e., authoritative commentary on Torah), nevertheless Jesus does not act like a scribe when he gathers around himself disciples *(mathêtai)* who, having been seized by his proclamation, are apprenticed to his message, his way of life, and his person. Jesus' teaching is sometimes addressed to the crowds as a whole (e.g., Matt 5:1–7:29 = Sermon on the Mount; Luke 6:17-49 = Sermon on the Plain) and sometimes just to his disciples (e.g., Matt 10:5-42 = instructions to the Twelve; John 13:31–17:26 = Last Supper discourse). This teaching inculcates a particular vision of life. Particular behaviors are commanded or forbidden as embodying or perverting the vision taught.

Praying

Although Luke especially presents Jesus as a man of prayer, relatively little of the written material about him gives direct commands about praying. He does offer his disciples a prayer-outline to mark their fellowship (Matt 6:7-15; Luke 11:1-4), commands them to celebrate the Lord's Supper "in memory of him," and commissions them to "baptize all nations in the name of the Father and of the Son and of the Holy Spirit" (Matt 28:19). Though the letter to the Hebrews strongly attempts to interpret Jesus' life, death, deeds, and destiny in terms of priestly cultic activity, as far as we know Jesus was a layman who most probably shared the religious practices of first-century Jewish laity: Temple sacrifice when in Jerusalem (especially for the great pilgrimage festivals of Passover/Unleavened Bread, Pentecost, and Booths), attendance at synagogue services when outside of Jerusalem, and various forms of individual and domestic prayer (e.g., the twice daily recitation of the *Shema;* the thrice-daily praying of the *Tefillah;* blessing prayers when eating meals, rising, or resting).

Community-building

Jesus seems to have spent relatively little time in direct community building. As a wandering charismatic preacher, he does not settle or "found" churches (as the later apostles will). He calls people to discipleship; from the pool of disciples he calls some to serve as apostles or as "the Twelve." Once when he is called to arbitrate a dispute he refuses. One form of "community-building" might be his table-fellowship with outcasts and sinners.

Direct Service

The New Testament presents evidence that Jesus performed various acts of direct service to people in need, most often scripturally recorded as miracles *(dynameis,* "acts of power," in the Synoptics; *semeia,* "signs," in the Johannine literature). These can be conveniently divided into three groups: (1) exorcisms, (2) healings, and (3) nature miracles. The miracles are to be seen in the context of his preaching ministry, as confirmations of his message, and as concrete demonstrations that God's reign is in-breaking in the ministry of Jesus.

Overarching and subsuming all these functions is Jesus' radical obedience to his Abba-God manifest especially in his passion, crucifixion, and death: the "paschal mystery." It is here that God's reign is definitively accepted and manifest, here that humans are challenged to offer themselves in self-sacrificing love, here that sacramental life finds its source and confirmation (symbolically from the blood [i.e., eucharist] and water [i.e., baptism] flowing from the wounded heart of Christ), here that a community of Christian believers is born, here that right relationships are established between God and humanity and among people.

These multiple elements of Jesus' "mission statement" appear yoked in a famous passage from the Gospel of Luke:

> When he came to Nazareth, where he had been brought up, he went to the synagogue on the sabbath day, as was his custom. He stood up to read, and the scroll of the prophet Isaiah was given to him. He unrolled the scroll and found the place where it was written:
>
> > "The Spirit of the Lord is upon me,
> > because he has anointed me
> > to bring good news to the poor.
> > He has sent me to proclaim release to the captives
> > and recovery of sight to the blind,
> > to let the oppressed go free,
> > to proclaim the year of the Lord's favor."
>
> And he rolled up the scroll, gave it back to the attendant, and sat down. The eyes of all in the synagogue were fixed on him. Then he began to say to them "Today this scripture has been fulfilled in your hearing" (Luke 4:16-21).

What Is the Apostolic Mission?

Before discussing a "mission statement" for the apostles, we should distinguish among disciples, apostles, and the Twelve. Disciples [*mathêtai*] form the largest group of Jesus' followers. Though Roman Catholics traditionally refer to the "twelve apostles," the New Testament designates many people in addition to the Twelve as apostles: James the "brother of the Lord" (Gal 1:19), Paul (1 Cor 1:1), Barnabas (Acts 14:14; 1 Cor 9:6 with 4:9; Gal 2:9), probably Andronicus and

Junias (Rom 16:7; is the latter a woman?), Silvanus and Timothy (1 Thess 2:6; Acts 17:4, 14), Apollos (1 Cor 4:6, 9). The Twelve thus signifies the innermost circle of Jesus' disciples, sometimes called "the twelve disciples" (Matt 10:1) or "the twelve apostles" (Matt 10:2; Luke 22:14), but very frequently simply "the Twelve" (Matt 26:14). The New Testament lists of the Twelve offer both common and varying names: Peter and Andrew, James and John always appear in first place, while Judas "the Betrayer" usually appears last.

MISSION OF "THE TWELVE"

Three passages in the Synoptic Gospels give "mission statements" for the Twelve. In Mark 3:13-19 Jesus appoints the Twelve as his companions and commissions them to preach with authority to cast out demons (as a confirmation of their preaching?). Matt 10:1-42 modifies this commission; Jesus gives this group only a share in his healing ministry: they are authorized to cast out unclean spirits (exorcism) and to cure diseases, but no mention is made of kingdom-preaching. Luke 9:1-6 reads as a summary of all the functions found in the parallel passages in Mark and Matthew: the Twelve are to preach God's reign, to hold power and authority over demonic forces, and to heal and cure diseases.

Scripture scholars suggest that the number twelve probably refers to the traditional numbering of the tribes of Israel; thus the Twelve represented in symbolic form the restoration of Israel as God's reign is fulfilled. The ministry of the Twelve seems limited to Jesus' earthly life and the period immediately after the resurrection: although we read of the election of Matthias to replace Judas in Acts 1:15-26, there is no record of a similar election after the death of James, the son of Zebedee, in Acts 12:2, thus suggesting that as an institution the Twelve did not outlast the first generation of Palestinian Christians.

It should be noted that the Gospel of Luke also records a "mission statement" for a group of seventy/seventy-two disciples, distinct from the Twelve. According to Luke 10:1-20, their fundamental task, performed in groups of two, is to prepare towns along Jesus' route for his visitation; however, they are also commissioned to preach that God's reign is impending, to heal the sick, to demonstrate power over demonic forces, and to enact a symbolic gesture of eschatological judgment.

MISSION OF "APOSTLES"

As we have already noted, the term "apostle" designates a wider group than simply the Twelve. Their primary task is to proclaim Jesus of Nazareth risen from the dead as the Christ of God: if the earthly

Jesus preached God's reign as imminent, the apostles preach Jesus as the fulfillment of God's reign. An apostle is also one who authoritatively bears the authentic tradition concerning Jesus as the Christ, thus only those who personally know Jesus (whether "in the flesh" or, as in the case of Paul, only as risen Lord) and have been personally called by him to apostleship can assume this office. While apostolic preaching may found particular churches, the apostle's concern is for the Church as a whole, not simply local communities. The apostle appoints other officers to sustain the Christian life of local communities, but it should be noted that no apostle appoints other apostles: the call to be an apostle is the sovereign act of Christ, not a commission by a community or one of its officers. From the foregoing it should be clear that some elements of this office could only be fulfilled by first-century Christians, while other elements are so essential for the life of the Church that the apostolic office is a constitutive dimension of any authentic Christian community.

This understanding of what constitutes apostleship shows a resemblance between the Old Testament prophet *(nabi')* and the New Testament apostle. Where the Old Testament prophet did not assume his task on his own authority but began his career by being introduced in vision into the heavenly court before God and then sent to preach God's will to the people, the New Testament apostle likewise does not assume the office on his own authority, but is commissioned by God in Christ to proclaim God's message to the people.

MISSION OF "DISCIPLES"

Greek civilization knew of a teacher-student relationship and Jewish civilization knew of a rabbi-follower relationship, but the master-disciple relationship developed between Jesus and certain individuals took some elements from these models and transformed them in others. The biblical record does not suggest that Jesus made a career out of imparting knowledge or charging tuition for his teaching. A rabbi's followers could hope to master his teaching, to repeat by memory what they had heard the rabbi teach, and to "graduate" to become rabbis in turn. In contrast, Jesus' disciples can never hope to master his teaching or "graduate" from his school: they remain his disciples forever. They did not attempt to reproduce his teaching verbatim but proclaimed the salvific import of his life, passion, death, and resurrection. Scholars are divided on whether or not a personal invitation from Jesus was needed in order to become his disciple, but it is clear that Jesus' demands on his disciples were greater than those proffered by philosophers or rabbis: the disciple must be willing to cut family ties, take up a cross, and lose life in following Jesus.

Thus the mission of the Twelve seems to be to serve as the symbolic manifestation of the Israel saved by God and brought to fulfillment. The mission of the apostles seems to be to witness authoritatively to the risen Christ, founding communities of disciples brought to faith by their preaching. The mission of the disciple seems first and foremost to maintain a personal relationship with Jesus in the context of the community of fellow-followers of the Lord.

What Is the Mission of the Church?

In the light of our examination of Jesus' mission and the mission of his first followers, we are now in a position to sketch the ongoing mission of the Church, a community of Jesus' disciples, "one, holy, Catholic and apostolic," grounded in the witness of the Twelve.

Kerygma

First, the Church has a message to proclaim *(kerygma):* the Good News that God exists, loves us more than we can imagine, has entered into our history, became human in Jesus of Nazareth, and has empowered us with the Spirit of Jesus. In a world that often seems pitched on the edge of despair and self-destruction, such a message is frequently perceived as too good to be true, but proclaiming this message "in season and out of season" is fundamental to the Church's mission. Traditionally the proclamation of this message is called "evangelization." Its goal is to give birth to an internalized faith-trust relationship to the Lord in those who have not yet been converted to Jesus and his way of life.

Didache

Second, Christians have to think through the consequences of their teaching *(didache).* Teaching and learning together we discern the practical implications of the message we proclaim, both for ourselves as Christian believers and for other human beings.

Traditionally, this "thinking through" is called "catechesis." Its goal is to disclose how Christian faith is embodied in the traditions, customs, practices, and doctrines of the believing community. One major component of catechesis is reflection on sacramental experience; believers are challenged to a deeper appreciation of their liturgical worship. A second component of catechesis is growth in Christian decision making; believers are led to make moral decisions congruent with their belief-system and to nurture their spiritual lives.

LEITOURGIA

Third, Christians engage special forms of prayer by which God encounters them and sustains their lives and vision of reality *(leitourgia):* we praise and thank, petition and intercede, confess and worship God both individually and as a community since, as Peter says, "You are a chosen race, a royal priesthood, a holy nation, God's own people, in order that you may proclaim the mighty acts of him who called you out of darkness into his marvelous light" (1 Pet 2:9). Some liturgical prayer will involve the sanctification of life: birth, maturation, vocation, reconciliation, sickness, and death all provide opportunities for Christians to acknowledge God at work in their individual and communal existences. Other liturgical prayer will focus on the sanctification of time: daily (Liturgy of the Hours), weekly (Lord's Day Eucharist), and yearly (Liturgical Year) cycles of prayer shape Christians' responses to God's activity in history. Some liturgical prayer will mark the sanctification of space: the gestures performed, the postures taken, the clothing worn, the buildings erected, the sites visited, enshrine Christians' encounters with God.

KOINONIA

Fourth, Christians have a responsibility to care for each other's physical, mental, emotional, and spiritual welfare *(koinonia):* the "new commandment" that Jesus gives his disciples at the Last Supper discourse in the Gospel of John demands that we "love one another" as Jesus has loved us (John 15:12). One of the more intriguing insights stemming from the names of the Twelve recorded in the New Testament is the fact that they represented fiercely opposing ideologies in first-century Judaism. Simon the Zealot and Judas "the dagger-man" (one interpretation of "Iscariot") seemed to have been sworn to execute any Jews who collaborated with the occupying Roman forces; Matthew/Levi "the tax collector" made his living from just such a collaboration. Somehow these ideological enemies were able to live in some level of amity due to their relationship to Jesus. The implication is clear: membership in the Church is not a gathering of the like-minded but a school in which Jesus teaches us how to love one another.

DIAKONIA

Finally, Christians have a responsibility to care for the non-Christian world *(diakonia):* as Jesus spent himself in humble service without concern for the social and religious boundaries that marked his world, so must Christians respond to human need wherever it appears. They are called to charitable deeds and action to promote justice and peace in the world. This may involve direct social service: feeding the hungry, clothing the naked, visiting the sick and those imprisoned. It may also involve advocacy on behalf of the marginalized. It may even involve critique and transformation of social structures insofar as they impede the values of the gospel.

The stirring words of the fathers of the Second Vatican Council in the Dogmatic Constitution on the Church, *Lumen gentium,* form a fitting conclusion to this essay on the mission of the Church:

> The Church, "like a stranger in a foreign land, presses forward amid the persecutions of the world and the consolations of God," announcing the cross and death of the Lord until he comes (cf. 1 Cor 11:26). But by the power of the risen Lord she is given strength to overcome, in patience and in love, her sorrows and her difficulties, both those that are from within and those that are from without, so that she may reveal to the world, faithfully, however darkly, the mystery of her Lord until, in the consummation, it shall be manifested in full light.

At the Session

Briefly discuss how the media portrays the mission of the Church; view video "Mission of the Church" on Videocassette 3 (30 minutes), listening for the following:

1. What is the mission of Jesus?

    a. *kerygma* (preaching/heralding)

    b. *didache* (teaching)

    c. *leitourgia* (liturgy, prayer)

    d. *koinonia* (community building—comes from first three)

    e. *diakonia* (service)

2. What is the mission of the apostles?

3. What is the mission of the Church?

After the Video

1. Compare the mission of Jesus, the mission of the apostles, and the mission of the Church.

2. Compare the mission of the Church as seen here and the mission of the Church as seen by the media.

Further Discussion

1. Clarify the scriptural meaning of the term "mission."
2. Summarize the fundamental elements of Jesus' mission based on the New Testament accounts and subsequent ecclesial reflection.
3. Distinguish the categories of "disciples," "apostles," and "the Twelve" and indicate the distinctive missions conferred on each.
4. Suggest how the missions of Jesus, conferred on disciples, apostles, and the Twelve, continue through time in the activities of the Church.

Further Reflection

1. What is my self-understanding as a disciple of Jesus?
2. How, by what, or by whom was I called to discipleship?
3. What range of activities is appropriate for me as a disciple?
4. What is the history of discipleship that I can identify in my family? Parish? Religious community?
5. Who are my heroes/heroines that make discipleship look not only possible but attractive?
6. How, by what, or by whom have I been called to serve the Church's mission?
7. Who has formed the history of catechesis in my family? Parish? Religious community?
8. To whom am I sent?

BIBLIOGRAPHY

Catechism of the Catholic Church. Part One: §§1–2. Part Two: §§1–2. Part Three: §§1–2. Part Four: §1. Washington, D.C.: United States Catholic Conference, 1994.

Friedrich, Gerhard. *"Kêryx, [hierokêryx,] kêrussô, kêrygma, prokêrussô."* *Theological Dictionary of the New Testament.* Ed. Gerhard Kittel, trans. and ed. Geoffrey W. Bromiley, 3:683–718. Grand Rapids, Mich.: Eerdmans, 1965.

Rengstorf, H. *"Apostolos."* *Theological Dictionary of the New Testament.* Ed. Gerhard Kittel, trans. and ed. Geoffrey W. Bromiley, 1:407–45. Grand Rapids, Mich.: Eerdmans, 1964.

Development of Doctrine

DON BRIEL

Before Arriving at the Session

Read Focal Points, the essay below, and the essay "The Church's Teaching Mission" on p. 123.

Focal Points

To appreciate the history of revealed doctrine; to recognize our responsibility to live the revealed truth and transmit it to others; to understand the role of the Magisterium.

DEVELOPMENT OF DOCTRINE

In his 1845 essay on the development of doctrine, Newman wrote the now often cited sentence, "In a higher world it is otherwise, but here below to live is to change, and to be perfect is to have changed often" (Newman, 40). The statement was certainly more startling in 1845 than it is now, for we have come to accept the historical character of human thought and experience in ways that were not easily foreseen in the mid nineteenth century. Nonetheless, the statement remains somewhat problematic at least in the terms in which it is frequently interpreted in contemporary culture. For although it seems necessarily the case that perfection requires change, it is certainly not self-evident that all change leads to perfection. And this is, of course, the difficulty. How does one distinguish between an authentic development that unfolds and "perfects" an earlier statement and a corruption which betrays or contradicts an earlier teaching? For it is often the case that what appears to be a very different reality is in fact merely a new expression of the earlier form and that what may seem to be a clear development of an earlier teaching is, in fact, fundamentally inconsistent with it. Newman himself uses the example of the butterfly which succeeds the grub. It would appear to be a contradiction to suggest that one arises out of or develops from the other, but in fact it does and this biological example provides a helpful reminder of the fact that external consistency alone is no real guarantee of continuity in development.

Newman wrote his essay in the course of his conversion to Roman Catholicism. While in the Church of England he had argued in favor of a principle of antiquity, claiming that Anglicanism had protected the primitive simplicity of the Church of the first centuries from two contradictory temptations. Protestantism, he argued, reduced the Church to a scriptural fundamentalism whereas Catholicism had added so freely to the doctrinal claims of the Church that it had lost its original purity. He was ultimately led to the conclusion that the Catholic principle alone could explain the process of development and continuity in Church teaching. He argued that only Catholicism could articulate how Christianity, like any living idea, could both influence and be influenced by history and yet retain a coherent and continuous set of beliefs. This would lead him to employ another analogy. Some would argue he said that the stream is purest nearest its source, before its contamination with foreign elements, but, in fact, the stream is clearest when it develops its power and direction most fully and it separates out contaminants and purifies itself.

Such confidence in historical development does not reduce the problem of distinguishing between authentic and inauthentic developments. It seems clear that if revelation were given for the purpose of salvation, if it were providential that the good news was offered to the human race, then there must be some authority to which one could appeal to resolve this problem. For many Christians, the Bible has served as such an authority, but as Newman pointed out, the appeal to Scripture has rarely resolved theological disputes because proponents of competing views will cite scriptural passages that seem to support their conclusions. The problem has always been one of interpretation. The answer to these disputes cannot be "found" in Scripture. This problem ultimately led Newman to argue that the authority required to make such distinctions would, of necessity, have to be a living authority capable of interpreting the complex relations between truths and their historical and cultural expression. In fact, he argued, the authority would have to be infallible if we were to have any confidence that the truth claims of Christianity were not merely provisional projections of historical needs. This is why he placed emphasis on the complementarity of Scripture and tradition communicating, safeguarding, and elaborating the deposit of faith. This emphasis is at the heart of the *Catechism*'s assertion that

> both of them, flowing out from the same divine well-spring, come together in some fashion to form one thing and move towards the same goal. Each of them makes present and fruitful in the Church the mystery of Christ, who promised to remain with his own "always to the close of the age" (CCC, 80).

In 1973 the Congregation for the Doctrine of the Faith issued a declaration *Mysterium Ecclesiae* in which it acknowledged four specific types of historical conditioning of doctrine. Faith statements are influenced by the presuppositions, concerns, thought categories, and available vocabulary of the culture in which they were composed. The acknowledgment of this specific character of the historical conditioning of doctrine does not in itself undermine the claim that the Church has always taught one truth throughout human history, but it does highlight the problem of criteria to differentiate an authentic development from a corruption. Newman insisted that great ideas are grown into; they cannot be learned by heart. This is true not only for individuals but also for the Church as a whole, which helps to explain Newman's image of Mary as the first theologian, pondering in her heart the mysteries of faith. Such reflection requires patience and humility as well as sustained and complex theological reflection.

At the Session

Review Focal Points; view video "Development of Doctrine" on Videocassette 3 (12 minutes). NOTE: Because of its relevance to "Fulfilling the Kingdom," the session and lecture on the development of doctrine could also be used in Chapter 8; therefore, the lecture also appears on Videocassette 6.

After the Video

Discuss the following:

1. What is the purpose of doctrines? Why care?

2. Can doctrines change and yet remain the same?

Further Reflection

Have I changed my understanding of doctrine? If yes, how? If no, why not?

BIBLIOGRAPHY

Catechism of the Catholic Church. Washington, D.C.: United States Catholic Conference, 1994.

Congregation for the Doctrine of the Faith. *Mysterium Ecclesiae.* Rome: 1973.

Newman, John Henry. *An Essay on the Development of Christian Doctrine.* London: Longmans, Green, 1920.

The Church's Teaching Mission

ARTHUR KENNEDY

The Teaching Office of the Church is called the Magisterium. The Magisterium is a gift to the Church to present what Christ taught to the apostles, namely that which gives hope to every generation. Christ gave to the Church the gift to teach infallibly what he had taught regarding human life in its origin, purpose, and destiny.

The Church's teacher is Christ. Its principle teaching is about Jesus Christ and his self-disclosure about the mystery of the Trinity, our relationship to God, and God's relationship to all that is. As faith accepts the reality of God, it also accepts what Christ, who teaches about God, has given to the Church. The purpose of this is to bring the Church into the first stage of its union with the Father, Son, and Holy Spirit, the life of infinite truth, goodness, and love. Its purpose is to prepare humans to be in God's eternal presence in the kingdom.

It is difficult for many moderns to accept the authority of Christ and the Church because our culture teaches us that the only authority comes from people reaching a free and common consent. It is not surprising that many find the claims of the Church's spiritual authority opposed to the individualism of the age.

In Vatican II the Church spoke of its life as having a "hierarchy of the truths of faith." In this way the Church affirms that there is both a progression of the knowledge of faith and that there is an inner coherence of everything that is taught. Often members of the Church only realize the inner coherence of the mystery of God's revelation and presence centuries after some aspect of the mystery has been identified. This fact helps us to understand that there is both a development of doctrine or teaching and a development of the understanding of what the Church has taught.

Over the centuries the Church has identified levels of the "hierarchy of truths." These levels have been specified in their classical form as follows:

> (1) Scriptural (from faith, *de fide*). The clear teaching of the Scripture as in the mystery of the Trinity, the incarnation, salvation

through Christ's death and resurrection, etc. We accept this as a truth based on the authority of God's own testimony and self-disclosure in both the Old and New Testaments.

(2) Church defined *(de fide definita)*. The second dimension pertains to the teaching of the Church as defined infallibly as she reflects on Scripture. Examples of this are the mystery of the Immaculate Conception of Our Lady, the effects of God's grace, the seven sacraments of the Church, and the infallibility of the papal office. We accept these as true based on the authority that God has given to the Church to teach the mystery bestowed on it (Matt 16:15-19; Rom 10:17; 2 Cor 4:13; 2 Tim 1:13-14).

The teachings of the first two levels of doctrines are called dogmas. These are the teachings that one finds for example in the Nicene Creed, although the creed does not include all dogmas. As the *Catechism* notes, "Dogmas are lights along the path of faith; they illuminate it and make it secure" (89). Dogmas are permanent truths about Christian reality. They would be analogical to statements in the natural world such as, "Thomas Jefferson was the third president of the United States," but dogmas are truths about the supernatural life, God's divine being, presence, and action in our midst.

(3) Theological knowledge (taught in the developing theological tradition of the Church over long periods of time). The third level teaches about basic matters such as the unity of faith and reason, the relationships of the divine persons to each other, the moral teachings that flow from the commandments and the beatitudes.

(4) Opinions. The fourth level contains individual or group opinions on various questions such as the Church teachings on the meaning of work, economy, and society as these issues appear in various cultures and times.

BIBLIOGRAPHY

Catechism of the Catholic Church. Part One: §2, ch. 3, art. 9, para. 4. Part Three: §1, ch. 3, art. 3.

Congregation for the Doctrine of Faith. Note on *Ad Tuendam Fidem* (To Defend the Faith). Rome: 1998.

John Paul II. *Ad Tuendam Fidem* (To Defend the Faith). Rome: 1998.

_____. *Apostolos Suos* (On the Theological and Juridical Nature of Episcopal Conferences), issued *motu proprio* May 21, 1998.

CHAPTER SIX

SACRAMENTAL LIFE

Sacramental Life

JAN MICHAEL JONCAS

Before Arriving at the Session

Read Focal Points and the essay below.

Focal Points

The essay allows the reader to reflect on sacramentality, which is the humanity of Jesus as sacrament of God, the Church as sacrament of Jesus, and the "seven sacraments'" as sacraments of the Church. Sacramental worship is grounded in the activity of the Triune God.

The author unpacks the definition of the "seven sacraments" as in the CCC. He explores the people, actions, times, and places of the sacraments.

SACRAMENTAL LIFE

A major theological, pastoral, and even aesthetical characteristic of Catholicism is its commitment to the sacramental principle. Catholicism has never hesitated to affirm the "mysterious" dimension of all reality: the cosmos, nature, history, events, persons, objects, rituals, words. Everything is, in principle, capable of embodying and communicating the divine. God is at once everywhere and all-powerful. There is no finite instrument that God cannot put to use. On the other hand, we humans have nothing apart from finite instruments to express our own response to God's self-communication. Just as the divine reaches us through the finite, so we reach the divine through the finite. The point at which this "divine commerce" occurs is the point of sacramental encounter. For Christians, the point of a sacramental encounter with God is Jesus Christ (McBrien, 2:731).

So Richard McBrien presents the centrality of sacramental life to the Roman Catholic vision of Christianity.

Many contemporary theologians use the notion of "sacrament" as sign and instrument of God's encounter with humanity as a foundational concept uniting christology, ecclesiology, and sacramental theology. The humanity of Jesus is presented as the "primordial sacrament" of the encounter with God: in Jesus, the mysterious presence of God is disclosed and made effectively present in human history. The Church is then presented as the "foundational sacrament" of Christ: in the Church, the mysterious presence of Christ is disclosed and made effectively present in human history. The seven ritual actions traditionally designated "sacraments" are the privileged means by which this happens. Thus discussing Roman Catholic sacramental life must involve considering the Triune God (since no consideration of Jesus can prescind from his divine character), the Church, and the Church's sacramental worship in creative interaction.

The following essay will explore how the CCC treats sacramental life. The first section sketches a theological foundation for sacramental life in the work of the Holy Trinity. The second section turns to a consideration of the sacraments in general under various headings. The final section comments on the fundamental characteristics of sacramental celebration: who, how, when, and where the Church celebrates the sacraments.

Sacramental Life as the Work of the Holy Trinity

The CCC wisely founds all sacramental life in the work of the Holy Trinity. God the Father acts as the source and goal of all liturgical worship, a worship that is fundamentally *blessing:*

> 1110. In the liturgy of the church God the Father is blessed and adored as the source of all the blessings of creation and of salvation, through which he has blessed us in his Son, giving us the Spirit of filial adoption (cf. Schmemann, 113).

Grounded in the Jewish *berakah* (a prayer form by which life, time, and space are all referred back to their source), Christian blessing has a dual dimension. On the one hand the Church united to Christ and under the impetus of the Spirit blesses the Father in adoration, praise, and thanksgiving for his manifold gifts. On the other hand, the Church offers the Father its own gifts, asking the Father to send the Holy Spirit upon them, upon the Church itself, upon the faithful, and upon the entire world.

According to the CCC the work of Christ in liturgical worship is threefold:

> 1111. The work of Christ in the liturgy is sacramental because his mystery of salvation is rendered present there through the power of his Holy Spirit; because his body, which is the church, is like a sacrament (sign and instrument) in which the Holy Spirit dispenses the mystery of salvation; [and] because through its liturgical actions the church in pilgrimage participates already as a fore-taste in the heavenly liturgy.

The actions of the earthly Jesus (preaching, teaching, healing, exorcizing, performing miracles, calling people to discipleship) all reveal and embody the reign of God; these actions are brought to perfection in the paschal mystery of his death and resurrection. The risen Christ confides the saving power of his actions to the Church where he is present in a variety of modes: in the sacrifice of the Mass, in the person of the minister, in the eucharistic species, in sacramental actions, in the proclamation and preaching of his word, and in the Church gathered, praying, and singing (cf. SC 7). Christ's salvation of the world, accomplished once for all in his sacrificial death on the cross, is made effectively present in the sacramental life.

The CCC also specifies the proper missions of the Holy Spirit in the Church's liturgical worship:

> 1112. The mission of the Holy Spirit in the liturgy of the church is to prepare the assembly to encounter Christ; to summon up and manifest Christ to the faith of the assembly; to make present and actualize the saving work of Christ through his transforming power; and to make fruitful the gift of communion in the church.

The Spirit prepares the assembly to encounter Christ by illuminating their understanding of the Old Testament. In reading these Scriptures, praying the psalms, and remembering God's saving events (the promise of a covenant, the Passover and Exodus, the kingdom and the Temple, the Exile and the Return from Exile) the mystery which will be fully revealed in Christ is anticipated. The Spirit is the living memory of the Church, assisting proclaimers and readers of the New Testament to receive it as powerful witness and not as a "dead letter"; in the Spirit liturgical memorial *(anamnesis)* is not so much simple recollection of past events as encounter with a living presence. The transforming power of the Spirit is invoked *(epiclesis)* upon sacramental signs and symbols, the Church and its members, as well as the world, in order to extend the saving power of Christ's work. Finally, the Spirit's mission is to bring all into genuine communion as members of Christ's body, an organic union of life and activity.

Thus sacramental life is a genuine sharing, under a complex ordering of signs and symbols, in the very life of the Trinity.

The Sacraments in General

In a paragraph highly reminiscent of the definition of a sacrament in the *Baltimore Catechism*, the CCC states:

> 1131. The sacraments are efficacious signs of grace, instituted by Christ and confided to the church, through which divine life is dispensed to us. The visible rites under which the sacraments are celebrated signify and actualize the graces proper to each sacrament. They bear fruit in those who receive them with the proper dispositions.

The CCC clarifies the meaning of this rather dense definition of the sacraments in general under five headings: these ritual actions are sacraments (1) of Christ, (2) of the Church, (3) of faith, (4) of salvation, and (5) of life eternal.

SACRAMENTS OF CHRIST

Under the heading "sacraments of Christ," the CCC affirms that the sacraments have been instituted by Christ. "Institution" in contemporary theological thought does not mean that Christ intended the specific matter and form for each of the seven sacraments, but that the salvific words and actions of Christ—his "mysteries"—are foundational and irreplaceable for the Church's sacramental life in the power of the Holy Spirit. As St. Leo the Great asserted in his Sermon 74: "That which was visible in our Savior has passed over into his sacraments."

SACRAMENTS OF THE CHURCH

Instituted by Christ, sacraments have been confided to the Church in the dual sense that they are "from the Church" and "for the Church." They are from the Church because the Church itself is the sacrament of Christ at work in it through the Holy Spirit; they are for the Church because the sacraments (especially the Eucharist) manifest and communicate to human beings the mystery of communion in divine love, the very life of the Trinity.

SACRAMENTS OF FAITH

The sacraments presuppose faith. In fact, according to the definition quoted above, faith is one of the "dispositions" required in the
recipient in order that the sacrament be "fruitful." Yet celebrating the
sacraments also nourishes, strengthens, and expresses faith.

It should be noted that the faith of the Church is prior to the faith
of the individual; the individual is invited to adhere to the Church's
faith, received from the apostles and proclaimed in sacramental worship. This intimate connection between the Church's faith and its worship is expressed in an adage ascribed to Prosper of Aquitaine in the
fifth century: "The law of praying establishes the law of believing"
(legem credendi lex statuat supplicandi). Thus, participating in and reflecting upon sacramental experience should lead the individual
Christian to deeper and richer faith.

SACRAMENTS OF SALVATION

Instituted by Christ and confided to the Church, these sacraments
of faith are *efficacious,* that is, they confer the grace that they signify.
They are effective because in them Christ is at work: in the sacrament
of baptism it is Christ who baptizes, in penance it is Christ who recon-
ciles, in orders it is Christ who permanently configures members of
the faithful for particular ministry. A traditional Catholic understanding of this sacramental efficacy was expressed in the phrase *ex opere
operato,* i.e., that the sacraments brought about what they signified not
because of the merits of the minister or the recipient but because of
Christ who was at work in them. The Church goes so far as to state
that for believers the sacraments of the New Law are necessary for
salvation, since they are the principal means by which the Holy Spirit
conforms human beings to Christ. The ultimate result of the sacramental life is that the Holy Spirit "deifies" the faithful by uniting them
totally to the Only-Begotten, the Savior.

SACRAMENTS OF LIFE ETERNAL

Finally, celebrating the sacraments gives a foretaste in the present
of the life of the world to come. Sacramental life is the pledge and
down payment of the life of the reign of God, a contemporary participation in the end of history. St. Thomas Aquinas highlighted the
eschatological dimension of the sacramental life in a formulation that
has become classic:

> A sacrament is a sign which recalls what has preceded, i.e., the
> passion of Christ; which places in evidence that which is oper-

ating in us through the passion of Christ, i.e., grace; and which
predicts, that is to say, that proclaims the advent of the glory
that is to come (*Summa Theologiae* III, q. 60, a. 3).

Sacramental Celebration

Presuming the foregoing exploration of the "sacramental economy,"
the CCC then calls attention to "sacramental celebration" under four
headings: (1) Who celebrates? (2) How do they celebrate? (3) When do
they celebrate? and (4) Where do they celebrate?

THOSE WHO CELEBRATE SACRAMENTALLY

A strong conviction of Roman Catholic Christianity is that the
liturgy is celebrated by "the entire Christ—Head and members" (cf. SC
7). Thus Christ is the principal agent of sacramental worship, the
Church through the power of the Holy Spirit joining in the worship
offered to the Father by Christ. In considering the sacramental
worship offered by the "members of Christ," the CCC distinguishes
between the celebrants of the heavenly liturgy (the angels and saints
as well as the transformed created order) and the celebrants of the
earthly liturgy (the community of the baptized hierarchically ordered):

> 1187. The liturgy is the work of the entire Christ, Head and
> Body. Our High Priest celebrates it unendingly in the heavenly
> liturgy, with the holy Mother of God, the apostles, all the saints
> and the multitude of humans who have already entered into
> the Kingdom.
>
> 1188. In a liturgical celebration, the entire Assembly is "litur-
> gist," each according to his or her own function. Baptismal
> priesthood is that of the entire Body of Christ. But certain
> members of the faithful are ordained by the sacrament of
> Order to represent Christ as Head of the Body.

THE MEANS OF SACRAMENTAL CELEBRATION

Sacramental celebration takes place by means of signs and symbols.
Since human beings unite corporeal and spiritual dimensions of existence, they perceive and express spiritual realities through material
elements. Some signs/symbols are taken from nature (e.g., day and
night, wind and fire, water and earth, trees and fruit), while others
arise from human social life (e.g., washing, massaging with oil, sharing a meal). Some signs/symbols developed in the religious culture of
Judaism (e.g., circumcision, consecration of kings and priests, imposi-
tion of hands, sacrifices, the Passover), some of which Jesus employed

and transformed. Both words and gestures can have sacramental import, the actions signifying what the words express. Music and singing, sacred art, and artifacts all furnish important elements in sacramental celebration. As the CCC summarizes:

> 1189. Liturgical celebration admits signs and symbols that refer to creation, . . . to human life, . . . and to the history of salvation. . . . Inserted into the world of faith and assumed by the power of the Holy Spirit, these cosmic elements, these human rites, and these gestures of recollection of God can become entryways for the saving and sanctifying action of Christ.

THE TIMES OF SACRAMENTAL CELEBRATION

Just as the events of human living can become carriers of sacramental meaning, so the structuring of time can disclose God's presence to the life of faith. After discussing the notion of liturgical time in general, the CCC discusses the weekly, yearly, and daily dimensions of liturgical worship.

Celebrating the *Lord's Day* once a week is foundational to the Christian structuring of time:

> 1193. Sunday, the "Lord's Day," is the principle day for the celebration of the eucharist because it is the day of the Resurrection. It is the day of liturgical assembly par excellence, the day of the Christian family, the day of joy and of rest from work. It is "the foundation and the core of the entire liturgical year" (SC 106).

It should be noted that in the Christian structuring of time, the celebration of the Lord's Day begins with Vespers on Saturday (traditionally associated with sunset), thus connecting the Christian and the Jewish keeping of time. Sunday, however, is *not* a "Christian Sabbath" but the "eighth day," the end-time signaled by the resurrection of Jesus, the first day of a new and endless week no longer grounded in the seven day creation narrative. The claims made for the Lord's Day frequently come into conflict with a late-twentieth-century structuring of time that divides "work week" from "weekend."

The *Liturgical Year* celebrates the mysteries of Christ both in paschal and incarnation cycles as well as in the annual commemoration of saints' feasts:

> 1194. The church "unfolds the entire mystery of Christ through the cycle of the year, from the Incarnation and the Nativity until the Ascension, the day of Pentecost, and the expectation of blessed hope and of the coming of the Lord" (SC 102).

1195. Making memory of the saints, in first place of the holy Mother of God, then of the apostles, the martyrs and the other saints, on fixed days of the liturgical year, the Church on earth manifests that it is united with the heavenly liturgy; it gives glory to Christ for having accomplished his salvation in his glorified members; their example stirs up the church on its path toward the Father.

These yearly cycles will be studied in more detail in another essay in this collection.

The *liturgical day* is marked by prayer at fixed hours, especially the "hinge" hours of Lauds and Vespers, in the Liturgy of the Hours:

1196. The faithful who celebrate the Liturgy of the Hours unite themselves to Christ, our Sovereign Priest, through the prayer of the psalms, meditation on the Word of God, canticles and blessings, so that they might be associated with his unceasing and universal prayer that gives glory to the Father and implores the gift of the Holy Spirit on the entire world.

While many Roman Catholics have little experience of the Liturgy of the Hours, associating it with the breviary obligation of bishops, priests, and deacons and the common choral prayer of monks and nuns, the Second Vatican Council encouraged all the faithful to join in this prayer as the circumstances of their life allowed, since "the divine office is the voice of the Church, that is, of the whole Mystical Body publicly praising God" (SC 99).

THE PLACES OF SACRAMENTAL CELEBRATION

In addition to human life and time, space itself can become a bearer of sacramental meaning. While the term "Church" most properly refers to the gathering of those who share the life of Jesus in baptism, it is also frequently applied to the architectural structure in which those followers gather. The "house of the church" can contain many places and objects by which sacramental worship is enacted: the altar or Lord's Table, the tabernacle, the place of reservation for the blessed oils (chrism, oil of catechumens, oil of the sick), the lectern or ambo for proclaiming God's word, the presidential chair (or the bishop's throne in the cathedral church), the baptismal font (and its surrounding baptistry), the confessional or reconciliation room. These places and objects tie the worshiping assembly to the celestial worship celebrated beyond time and space:

1197. Christ is the true Temple of God, "the place where his glory dwells"; by the grace of God, Christians themselves can become temples of the Holy Spirit, living stones from which the church is built.

1198. In its earthly condition, the church has need of places where the community can gather: our visible churches, holy places, images of the holy city, the heavenly Jerusalem toward which we journey in pilgrimage.

1199. It is in these church buildings that the church celebrates public worship to the glory of the Holy Trinity, that it attends the Word of God and sings its praises, that it lifts up its prayer and that if offers the sacrifice of Christ, sacramentally present in the midst of the assembly. These church buildings are also places of recollection and of personal prayer.

Conclusion

These few reflections on the sacramental life of Christians can be crowned with the inspiring words of a twentieth-century Orthodox theologian. Alexander Schmemann evokes the beauty and power of the sacramental life at the conclusion of his essay "And Ye Are Witnesses of These Things":

> The Church is the sacrament of the Kingdom—not because she possesses divinely instituted acts called "sacraments," but because first of all she is the possibility given to man to see in and through this world the "world to come," to see and to "live" it in Christ. It is only when in the darkness *of this world* we discern that Christ has already "filled all things with Himself" that these *things,* whatever they may be, are revealed and given to us full of meaning and beauty. A Christian is the one who, wherever he looks, finds Christ and rejoices in Him. And this joy *transforms* all his human plans and programs, decisions and actions, making all his mission the sacrament of the world's return to Him who is the life of the world.

At the Session

Review the Focal Points; view video "Sacramental Life" on Videocassette 4 (36 minutes).

After the Video

Choose one or two of the following questions for discussion:

1. If a sacrament is a "sign and instrument" of a divine reality, how is the humanity of Jesus a sacrament of God? How is the Church a sacrament of Christ? And how are baptism, confirmation, Eucharist, penance, anointing of the sick, matrimony, and holy orders sacraments of the Church?

2. What blessings can I identify in my own life, the life of my household, parish, civic community, nation, world? What are appropriate responses to these blessings?

3. How are the words and actions of Jesus salvific for human beings and how can the salvation accomplished by Christ be effective for human beings in the present and the future?

4. How does the Holy Spirit operate in my life, the life of my household, parish, civic community, nation, and the world?

5. What is the difference between a sign and a symbol? How are sacraments signs, symbols, and causes?

6. What does "sanctify" mean: to bring "profane" realities into the sphere of the "sacred" or to disclose the prior "sacredness" of all created reality?

7. How do the sacraments sanctify human life (rites of passage: birth, maturation, life-work, death)?

8. How do the sacraments sanctify time (cyclic rites: daily, weekly, monthly, yearly)?

9. How do the sacraments sanctify space (rites of position: posture, gesture, use of objects, arrangement of space)?

10. How does sacramental life recollect God's past saving events, manifest God's present grace, and give a fore-taste of God's consummation of history?

11. What obstacles to full sacramental life can I identify in myself or in my culture? What can overcome these obstacles?

BIBLIOGRAPHY

Catechism of the Catholic Church. English translations by Jan Michael Joncas from *Catéchisme de l'Eglise Catholique* (Paris: Mame/Plon, 1992).

McBrien, Richard. *Catholicism.* 2 vols. Minneapolis: Winston Press, 1980.

Schmemann, Alexander. *For the Life of the World: Sacraments and Orthodoxy.* New York: St. Vladimir's Seminary Press, 1973.

Structure of the Mass

JAN MICHAEL JONCAS

Before Arriving at the Session

Read Focal Points and the essay below.

Focal Points

This essay highlights the changes in forms of eucharistic celebration pre- and post-Vatican II and clarifies the components
and meanings of the texts and ceremonies occurring in the (1) Introductory Rites, (2) Liturgy of the Word, (3) Preparation and
Presentation of Gifts, (4) Eucharistic Prayer, (5) Communion Rites,
and (6) Dismissal Rites.

STRUCTURE OF THE MASS

If one were to ask Roman Catholics catechized prior to the Second
Vatican Council how many parts of the Mass there were, they would
normally respond "two," identifying them as "the Mass of the Catechumens" and "the Mass of the Faithful." They could also point to the
relative unimportance of the Mass of the Catechumens, since the three
events at which one had to be present in order to fulfill one's obligation to attend Sunday Mass were all part of the Mass of the Faithful:
the offertory, the consecration, and the priest's Communion.

Catechesis on the Mass after Vatican II involves significant changes
in terminology and the understanding of its structure. In articles
1328–32, the CCC describes the many terms now used to refer to the
sacrament: Eucharist, Lord's Supper, wedding feast of the Lamb,
breaking of bread, eucharistic assembly *(synaxis)*, memorial of the
Lord's passion and resurrection, holy sacrifice, divine liturgy, Communion, holy Mass. In articles 1348–55, the CCC presents the structure

of the Mass under five headings: (1) the gathering of the assembly, (2) the Liturgy of the Word, (3) the presentation of the offerings, (4) the Eucharistic Prayer *(anaphora)*, and (5) the Communion. The following article will supplement the CCC's teaching on the structure of the Mass with some further details on the ritual structure of the Order of Mass promulgated for the Roman Rite after the Second Vatican Council.

The Gathering of the Assembly

While it does not detail the various introductory rites, the CCC highlights the importance of Christ, the ordained presider, and the gathering of the assembly for Eucharist:

> 1348. All are gathered. Christians flock into the same place for the Eucharistic assembly. At their head is Christ himself, who is the principal agent of the Eucharist. He is the high priest of the New Covenant. It is he himself who presides invisibly over the entire Eucharistic celebration. It is in representing him that the bishop or priest (acting in the person of Christ the Head) presides over the assembly, breaks open the Word after the readings, receives the offerings and says the Eucharistic prayer. All have their active part in the celebration, each in their own way: the readers, those who present the offerings, those who give communion, and the entire people whose "Amen" demonstrates their participation.

The GIRM demonstrates how this differentiated gathering of the Church under Christ's presidency takes ritual shape:

> The parts preceding the liturgy of the word, namely, the entrance song, greeting, penitential rite, Kyrie, Gloria, and opening prayer or collect, have the character of beginning, introduction, and preparation.
> The purpose of these rites is to make the assembled people a unified community and to prepare them properly to listen to God's word and celebrate the eucharist (GIRM 24).

According to the GIRM, these introductory rites are of secondary ritual importance: they prepare the gathered Church for the elements of the ritual that are primary, namely the Liturgy of the Word and the Liturgy of the Lord's Table.

The entrance procession involving various ministers (incense-bearer, cross-bearer, candle-bearers, reader, and presiding ordained minister are the "normal" members of this procession; it may be augmented

with acolytes, choir members, deacon[s], and other ordained ministers) is not only a way of getting ritual actors into the sanctuary but
also a visual expression of the nature of the gathered Church with its
distinct offices and ministries.

An entrance song accompanies this procession. According to
GIRM (25) its further purposes are "to open the celebration, deepen
the unity of the people, [and] introduce them to the mystery of the
season or feast." Traditionally the Roman Rite resisted hymnody (a
"closed" musical form) at the entrance procession in favor of an anti-
phon refrain with variable psalm-verses (an "open" musical form).

The veneration of the altar by means of a kiss (and possibly by
incensation) concludes the entrance procession.

The dialogic character of Roman Catholic worship is established in
the sign of the cross and ministerial greeting. The sign of the cross as a
traditional form of self-blessing has strong baptismal overtones, since
a person is signed with the cross in the rites of Christian Initiation and
is baptized in the name of the Father, Son, and Holy Spirit. The ministerial greeting manifests the Lord's presence in and to the assembly.

The Sunday renewal of baptism ("Sprinkling Rite") is an adaptation of the rite known as the *Asperges/Vidi aquam,* which used to be
celebrated before the principal Sunday Mass. Sprinkling the assembly
with blessed water is a visual reminder of baptism and of the paschal
character of Sunday. It is celebrated as an alternative to the penitential
rite.

The penitential rite may take a variety of forms: a communal acknowledgment of sinfulness in the Confiteor, a dialogic set of acclamations addressed to Christ, or a "Lord have mercy" litany with special
invocations ("tropes") acclaiming Christ as the embodiment of God's
mercy.

A simple "Lord have mercy" dialogue follows the penitential rite if
the troped form has not been employed. This litany is sometimes sung
in Greek as *"Kyrie* [or *Christe*] *eleison."*

Emphasizing the festive character of certain Sundays and solemnities, the Glory to God *("Gloria in excelsis"),* an ancient hymn of praise,
marks Lord's Day worship outside of Advent and Lent. It may be sung
by the assembly in alternation with the choir or by the choir alone.

The opening prayer ("collect") brings the introductory rites to a
conclusion and makes a transition to the Liturgy of the Word.
Grounded in late antique Roman rhetorical patterns, the opening
prayer includes three elements: (1) an address to God (usually "God"
with some modifying adjectives such as "almighty and eternal," and
sometimes including a relative clause recalling the particular feast,
mystery, or motive for the petition), (2) a petition (usually quite gen-

eral since it serves to "collect" the unspoken prayers of all), and (3) a conclusion (usually underlining the mediatorship of Christ in the Holy Spirit).

It should be noted that the complexity of the introductory rites can be radically simplified in Masses with children and that a general simplification of the introductory rites currently is being proposed by the ICEL to the English-speaking bishops' conferences.

The Liturgy of the Word

Citing the outline of the Lord's Day Eucharist found in the First Apology of Justin Martyr (ca. 150 C.E.), the CCC sketches the structure and purpose of the Liturgy of the Word:

> 1349. The Liturgy of the Word comprises "the writings of the prophets," that is to say the Old Testament, and "the memoirs of the apostles," that is to say their epistles and the gospels; after the homily that exhorts the assembly to hear that Word as it truly is—the Word of God—and to put it into practice, come the intercessions for all humans, according to the word of the apostle: "Thus, I urge above all that one should make requests, prayers, supplications, and thanksgivings for all humans, for kings and for all those entrusted with authority" (1 Tim 2:1-2).

GIRM succinctly indicates the components of the Liturgy of the Word and their interrelationship:

> Readings from Scripture and the chants between the readings form the main part of the liturgy of the Word. The homily, profession of faith, and general intercessions or prayer of the faithful develop and complete it. In the readings, explained by the homily, God speaks to his people of redemption and salvation and nourishes their spirit; Christ is present among the faithful through his Word. Through the chants the people make God's word their own and express their adherence to it through the profession of faith. Finally, moved by this Word, they pray in the general intercessions for the needs of the Church and for the world's salvation (GIRM 33).

In Sunday and festival celebrations the first reading is usually taken from the Old Testament, manifesting the Church's strong belief that all Scripture is the word of God and that there is a continuity between Old and New Testaments centered in the person of Jesus.

The responsorial psalm, also generally taken from the Old Testament Psalter, is the only psalm sung in the Mass for its own sake and not to accompany a ritual action. It is neither a "meditation song" nor a "response to the first reading"; rather, it is proclamation in song of God's word, stimulating reflection on God's saving deeds and offering an opportunity for the assembly to mull over and digest this word.

The second reading in Sunday and festival celebrations is a passage from the New Testament outside of the Gospels. Although this reading is usually not chosen to harmonize thematically with the first reading and the Gospel, it allows the assembly to encounter the witness of the early Church in living its Christian faith.

The gospel acclamation (usually "Alleluia," although an acclamatory text not using the word is used during Lent) both accompanies the procession with the book of the Gospels ("evangelary") and expresses the community's joy at the word of God declared in the Gospel text.

The Gospel, proclaimed by a deacon or other ordained minister, is the high point of the Liturgy of the Word. Semi-continuous selections from Matthew during Sundays of Cycle A, Mark in Sundays of Cycle B, and Luke in Sundays of Cycle C structure the Gospel readings during Ordinary Time; the Gospel of John is read especially in Lent and Eastertide. Usually there is some thematic or symbolic connection between the first reading and the Gospel.

The homily continues God's saving message, eliciting faith and conversion by joyfully proclaiming God's saving deeds in Christ actualized in the liturgical assembly. The homily is not simply an exegesis of the Scriptures, catechetical instruction, moral exhortation, or an address on a religious topic (although it may involve any of these topics); rather, it is an authoritative proclamation of how what the Scriptures proclaim and promise is present in the worshiping assembly, leading to praise and thanksgiving.

By means of the profession of faith ("creed") the assembly responds, assents, and adheres to the word of God proclaimed in the Scriptures and preached in the homily. Although the Nicene-Constantinopolitan form of the creed is liturgically normative, other forms of the profession of faith may be used in particular celebrations; it is usually reserved for Sunday and festival celebrations.

The general intercessions or prayers of the faithful allow the assembly to exercise its baptismal priesthood by interceding for all humankind. Normally the intentions address the needs of the Church universal, public authorities, and the oppressed before turning to the concerns of the local community.

The Preparation and Presentation of the Gifts

The CCC emphasizes the significance of the presentation of bread and wine for the Eucharist with an accompanying collection of gifts for those in need:

> 1350. The presentation of the offerings (the "offertory"): Bread and wine are then carried, occasionally in procession, to the altar where they will be offered through the priest in the name of Christ in the Eucharistic sacrifice where they will become Christ's body and blood. This is the same gesture that Christ employed at the Last Supper, "taking some bread and a cup." "This unspotted oblation the church alone offers to the Creator, offering to him with thanksgiving that which has been provided from his creation" (Irenaeus, 4, 18, 4; cf. Malachi 1:11). The presentation of the offerings at the altar takes up the gesture of Melchizedech and confers the Creator's gifts into Christ's hands. It is he who, in his sacrifice, brought to perfection all the human attempts of offering sacrifices.

> 1351. From the beginning, Christians carried along with the bread and wine for the eucharist their gifts for sharing with those who were in need of them. This custom of the collection, always present, is inspired by Christ's example who made himself poor in order to enrich us (cf. 2 Corinthians 8:9):

> > "Those who have riches and who wish to do so, give them, each according to the measure that they impose on themselves; what is received is given to the one who presides and he uses it to assist orphans and widows, those that sickness or some other reason deprive of resources, prisoners, immigrants—in a word, he helps all those who are in need" (Justin Martyr, 1, 67, 6).

GIRM sketches in more detail the multiple elements involved in the preparation of the gifts:

> At the beginning of the liturgy of the Eucharist, the gifts, which will become the Lord's body and blood, are brought to the altar.

> First, the altar, the Lord's table, which is the center of the whole Eucharistic liturgy, is prepared: the corporal, purificator, missal, and chalice are placed upon it (unless the chalice is prepared at a side table).

> The gifts are then brought forward. It is desirable for the faithful to present the bread and wine, which are accepted by the priest or deacon at a convenient place. The gifts are placed on

the altar to the accompaniment of the prescribed texts. Even though the faithful no longer, as in the past, bring the bread and wine for the liturgy from their homes, the rite of carrying up the gifts retains the same spiritual value and meaning.

This is also the time to receive money or other gifts for the church or the poor brought by the faithful or collected at the Mass (49).

Once the gifts have been placed on the altar and the accompanying rites completed, the preparation of the gifts comes to an end through the invitation to pray with the priest and the prayer over the gifts, which are a preparation for the Eucharistic prayer (53).

It should be clear that although the preparation of the gifts opens the Liturgy of the Lord's Table, it has a secondary character since it prepares for and leads to the Eucharistic Prayer. (The preparation of the gifts leading to the Eucharistic Prayer and Communion rites parallels the introductory rites leading to the Liturgy of the Word.) The altar itself is prepared; the gifts of bread and wine are presented, prepared, and placed on the altar; the presiding minister is ritually empowered to speak in the name of the assembly; and the prayer over the gifts sums up the meaning of all that has taken place.

The Eucharistic Prayer

The amount of detail given to the Eucharistic Prayer in the CCC clearly indicates its central importance for an understanding of the Mass:

> 1352. The anaphora: with the Eucharistic prayer, a prayer of thanksgiving and consecration, we arrive at the heart and the high point of the celebration:
>
> In the preface the church gives thanks to God, through Christ, in the Holy Spirit, for all his works, for creation, for redemption and for sanctification. The entire community thus joins that unceasing prayer which the heavenly church, the angels and all the saints sing to God, the thrice-holy.
>
> 1353. In the epiclesis the church asks the Father to send his Holy Spirit (or the power of his blessing) upon the bread and wine, so that they would become, through his power, the body and the blood of Jesus Christ, and that those who take part in the Eucharist would become one body and one spirit (certain liturgical traditions place the epiclesis after the anamnesis).

In the institution narrative the strength of the words and action of Christ and the power of the Holy Spirit renders sacramentally present, under the species of bread and wine, Christ's body and blood—his sacrifice offered upon the cross once for all.

> 1354. In the anamnesis that follows, the church commemorates the passion, resurrection and glorious return of Christ Jesus; it presents to the Father the offering of his Son which reconciles us with him.
>
> In the intercessions, the church expresses that the Eucharist is celebrated with the entire church of heaven and of earth, with the living and the dead, in communion with the pastors of the church, the pope, the bishop of the diocese, its presbyterium and deacons, and all the bishops of the entire world with their churches.

GIRM likewise underscores the centrality of the Eucharistic Prayer:

> The Eucharistic prayer, a prayer of thanksgiving and sanctification, is the center and high point of the entire celebration. In an introductory dialogue the priest invites the people to lift their hearts to God in prayer and thanks; he unites them with himself in the prayer that he addresses in their name to the Father through Jesus Christ. The meaning of the prayer is that the whole congregation joins Christ in acknowledging the works of God and in offering the sacrifice (GIRM 54).

Currently there are ten officially approved Eucharistic Prayers for use in the dioceses of the United States; over one hundred different prefaces (taken both from the Sacramentary and from the Collection of Masses of the Blessed Virgin Mary) may be used with Eucharistic Prayers I, II, and III.

Eucharistic Prayer I is an adaptation of the ancient Roman Canon. Although the Roman Canon has been criticized for its length, repetitions, lack of structural cohesiveness and explicit invocation of the Holy Spirit, and its emphasis on petition to the virtual exclusion of elements of praise, the venerable character of the prayer makes it especially suitable for use on high feast days and characteristically Roman feasts.

Eucharistic Prayer II is based on a model given in the *Apostolic Tradition,* usually ascribed to Hippolytus of Rome and dated ca. 215. It is extremely brief and simple, quite suitable for daily Mass and for use with children. Although it has its own proper preface, variable prefaces could be employed.

Eucharistic Prayer III is a contemporary composition incorporating the themes of the Roman Canon with texts taken from other liturgical traditions. It would be appropriately used in Sunday and festival worship. Since it has no proper preface, an appropriate variable preface must be chosen for it if it is to be used.

Eucharistic Prayer IV is a reworking of the Anaphora of St. Basil, an Eastern Eucharistic Prayer of great antiquity. It would most appropriately be used with communities that have great familiarity with the Scriptures and salvation history. Variable prefaces may not be used with this text.

In 1974 three Eucharistic Prayers for Masses with Children were approved. All of these texts make extensive use of congregational interventions and acclamations, which should help children to experience the prayers as genuinely communal rather than simply presidential monologues.

In 1975 two Eucharistic Prayers for Masses for Reconciliation were also approved. While these texts are more poetic than Eucharistic Prayers I–IV, their thematic construction limits their use to situations when reconciliation is the special focus of the celebration.

It should be noted that ICEL has proposed new translations of all of these texts to the English-speaking bishops' conferences for adaptation and approval.

Communion Rites

Again citing Justin Martyr's account of the Eucharist at Rome ca. 150 C.E., the CCC outlines the structure and meaning of the Communion rite:

> 1355. In communion, preceded by the Lord's Prayer and the breaking of bread, the faithful receive "the bread of heaven" and "the cup of salvation," the body and blood of Christ who is given "for the life of the world" (John 6:51):
>
> Because this bread and this wine have been, according to the ancient expression, "eucharistized," "we call this nourishment 'Eucharist' and none can take part in it unless they believe the truth of what is taught among us, unless they have received the bath for remission of sins and new birth, and unless they do live according to the precepts of Christ" (Justin Martyr, 1, 66, 1–2).

MCW, a document issued in 1972 by the U.S. Bishops' Committee on the Liturgy, clearly outlines the individual elements of the Communion rite and their connections:

> The eating and drinking of the Body and Blood of the Lord in a
> paschal meal is the climax of our Eucharistic celebration. It is
> prepared for by several rites: the Lord's Prayer with embolism
> and doxology, the rite of peace, breaking of bread (and com-
> mingling) during the "Lamb of God," private preparation of
> the priest and showing of the Eucharistic bread. The eating and
> drinking is accompanied by a song expressing the unity of
> communicants and is followed by a time of prayer after com-
> munion. Those elements are primary which show forth signs
> that the first fruit of the Eucharist is the unity of the Body of
> Christ, Christians loving Christ through loving one another.
> The principal texts to accompany or express the sacred action
> are the Lord's Prayer, the song during the communion proces-
> sion and the prayer after communion (48).

The Lord's Prayer is an appropriate preparation for eucharistic
Communion because its petition for daily bread can be interpreted as
a request for eucharistic food, its petition for forgiveness of sins can be
seen as making holy those who are to receive the holy gifts, and its
doxology can be thematically linked with the eschatological banquet
when God's reign is fulfilled.

The rite of peace expresses faith in the risen Christ as the source of
all true *shalom*, a state of complete harmony with nature, self, and
God. At one and the same time it is a call to reconciliation before communion and a seal of the unity achieved in Christ. Ritual gesture appropriate to the depth of meaning of this rite has yet to be developed.

The fraction rite, accompanied by the Lamb of God chant, expresses the unity of Christians in their Lord. Just as the one bread has
become the body of Christ, so those who share in the one bread, whatever their ethnic, racial, gender, ideological, or socioeconomic differences, become one body in Christ.

The pre-Communion dialogue balances the right to eucharistic
Communion founded in baptism with the humility expressed toward
Jesus by the centurion. Some Eastern rites use the traditional form:
"Holy things for the holy!"

The Communion song accompanies the distribution and consumption of the consecrated elements. Communion under both species is
the preferred method of receiving the Eucharist as better fulfilling the
Lord's command and manifesting the fullness of sacramental symbolism.

The prayer after Communion is not so much a text of thanksgiving
(as is the Eucharistic Prayer) as a petition for the spiritual effects of the
Communion received.

The Blessing and Dismissal of the Assembly

Although the CCC does not comment on it, the dismissal of the assembly concludes the celebration of the Eucharist in the Roman Rite. As GIRM notes:

> The concluding rite consists of:
>
> a) the priest's greeting and blessing on certain days and occasions are expanded by the prayer over the people or other solemn form;
>
> b) the dismissal that sends each member of the congregation to do good works, praising and blessing the Lord.

Note that concluding music is optional. The concluding rite simply directs that those who have celebrated the Eucharist manifest its fruits by lives of service to one another and to the world.

At the Session

View video "Structure of the Mass" on Videocassette 4 (28 minutes), listing what you want to remember in each of the parts.

1. Introductory Rites
2. Liturgy of the Word
3. Preparation and Presentation of Gifts
4. Eucharistic Prayer
5. Communion Rites
6. Dismissal Rites

After the Video

Choose two of the following to discuss:

1. How can we prepare and encourage young people to celebrate the Mass?
2. What connections can we make between the introductory rites and the way other human groups gather for particular purposes?
3. What connections can we make between the Liturgy of the Word and storytelling (in family and recreational settings, personal reading, through drama, on television and radio)?
4. What connection can we make with others between the preparation of the gifts and the preparations needed for a special meal (deciding on the guest list, grocery shopping, spreading a tablecloth, setting the table, lighting candles, etc.)?

5. What connections can we make with others between the elements of the Eucharistic Prayer and their own personal prayer lives?

6. What connections can we make with others between the Communion rites and formal meals? (Celebrating the Passover Seder with Jewish friends might be a possibility.)

7. What connections can we make with others between the concluding rites and other forms of commissioning (graduating)?

8. How has eucharistic worship changed over the centuries?

9. How does the public prayer of the Eucharist feed off of, shape, and empower my personal prayer?

BIBLIOGRAPHY

Catechism of the Catholic Church. English translations by Jan Michael Joncas from *Catéchisme de l'Eglise Catholique* (Paris: Mame/Plon, 1992).

Hoffman, Elizabeth, ed. *The Liturgy Documents: A Parish Resource.* 3rd ed. "General Instruction of the Roman Missal," and "Music in Catholic Worship." Chicago: Liturgy Training Publications, 1991.

Irenaeus of Lyons. *Against the Heresies,* book 4, ch. 18, para. 4; cf. Mal 1:11.

Justin Martyr. *First Apology,* book 1, ch. 67, paras. 1–6.

Liturgical Year

JAN MICHAEL JONCAS

Before Arriving at the Session

Read Focal Points and the essay below.

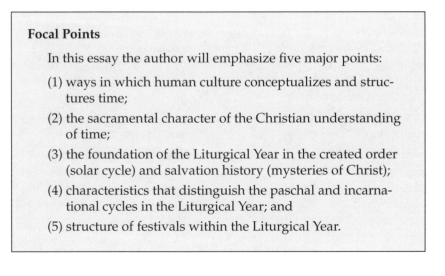

Focal Points

In this essay the author will emphasize five major points:

(1) ways in which human culture conceptualizes and structures time;

(2) the sacramental character of the Christian understanding of time;

(3) the foundation of the Liturgical Year in the created order (solar cycle) and salvation history (mysteries of Christ);

(4) characteristics that distinguish the paschal and incarnational cycles in the Liturgical Year; and

(5) structure of festivals within the Liturgical Year.

LITURGICAL YEAR

Christianity, faithful to its Jewish roots, is a religion that takes time seriously. For Christians and Jews time is a privileged locus for divine revelation: history is where God is made known. In contrast to religious world views where time is unimportant or illusory, Christianity does not proclaim "an atemporal salvation in general," but salvation accomplished in specific actions by God at particular times and places. It is in "the fullness of time" that God personally enters human history in the life and teaching, death and resurrection of Jesus of Nazareth. Christianity declares that time has a beginning, a direction, and a consummation, all focused on and disclosed in Christ.

It should not be surprising, then, that the centrality of time for Christianity is reflected in Christian worship. Regularly recurring rhythms of daily, weekly, and yearly events structure Christian prayer. This essay will concentrate on the annual cycle of the Christian keeping of time: the Liturgical Year.

Liturgical Time

Some earlier cultures have tended to view time as a circle: agricultural societies with their regular recurrence of "seed time and harvest" seem typical. Jewish society tends to image time as a line: historical events have definite consequences for the present and a genuinely new future is promised by God. The intelligentsia of some cultures divide time into various plateaus, speaking of "golden" or "silver ages" of literature, painting, drama, etc. The French paleontologist Pierre Teilhard de Chardin attempted to combine evolutionary theory with a Christian theology of time with his plateau-like concepts of biogenesis, neogenesis, and the "Omega Point." All of these conceptual schemes presumed that time (and its liturgical structuring) was meaningful and could disclose something about God, humanity, and the cosmos.

But these notions of liturgical time may be difficult for late-twentieth-century North Americans to grasp. We live, by and large, with a post-Einsteinian world view in which time is simply one variable factor in a random and relativistic universe. Time is less a medium of revelation and more a structuring of productivity: we "spend" time wisely or wastefully and our proverbs remind us that "time is money." The detaching of the "President's Day" festival from any concrete connection with a birth date in order to create a long weekend freed from work is typical of our technological manipulation of time. No wonder that the Christian insistence on the disclosive import of time becomes problematic!

In two dense paragraphs the CCC outlines a Catholic understanding of liturgical time:

> 1164. The People of God, from the time of the Mosaic Law, have known certain fixed festivals (beginning with the Passover) to commemorate the amazing actions of God the Savior, to give him thanks, to sustain the remembrance, and to teach the new generations how to shape their conduct. In the time of the church, situated between the passover of Christ, already accomplished once and for all, and its consummation in the Reign of God, the liturgy celebrated on fixed days is totally imprinted with the newness of the mystery of Christ.

> 1165. When the church celebrates the mystery of Christ, there is
> a word that marks its prayer: "Today!"—an echo of the prayer
> that its Lord has taught it (cf. Matt 6:11) and of the cry of the
> Holy Spirit (cf. Heb 3:7). This "today" of the living God into
> which humanity is called to enter is "the hour" of the Passover
> of Jesus that traverses and bears all of history.

What is central here is an implicit endorsement of the so-called
"Mystery Theology" of Odo Casel, an early-twentieth-century liturgical theologian. Casel held that in the liturgy the saving actions of
Christ were genuinely present to the participants, though "in
mystery": in the liturgy the temporal distance between the events of
salvation and the present were overcome in the "today" of the liturgy.
When we "recall" the originating events of salvation in liturgical
memorial (*anamnesis*), they come alive with all of their power to transform.

A contrast between the North American way of keeping a season
and the Roman Rite liturgical pattern should also be noted. Secular
culture tends to begin the preparation for a festival quite early (consider Christmas decorations and sales appearing in shopping malls
soon after Halloween), stir up a frenzy of anticipation (usually
through economic means), and collapse immediately after the central
event (consider the "letdown" after opening Christmas presents). This
style of keeping a season might be visualized as a lengthy ramp leading to a cliff. In contrast the Roman Rite liturgical pattern begins its
preparation relatively close to the feast (e.g., there are only four weeks
of Advent), reaches a high point in the designated festival (consider
the four Masses celebrating Christmas), and extends the festival celebration through a series of dependent feasts until one returns to "ordinary time" (consider Holy Family, the Octave of Christmas, Epiphany,
and Baptism of the Lord). This style of keeping a season might be visualized as a bell-shaped curve. Conflicts between secular and liturgical patterns of marking time should be expected.

The Liturgical Year

The CSL provides a helpful orientation for understanding the
Liturgical Year:

> The Church is conscious that it must celebrate the saving work
> of the divine Bridegroom by devoutly recalling it on certain
> days throughout the course of the year. . . . Within the cycle
> of a year . . . the Church unfolds the whole mystery of Christ,
> from his incarnation and birth until his ascension, the day of

Pentecost, and the expectation of blessed hope and of the Lord's return.

Recalling thus the mysteries of redemption, the Church opens to the faithful the riches of the Lord's powers and merits, so that these are in some way made present in every age in order that the faithful may lay hold on them and be filled with saving grace (102).

In celebrating this annual cycle of Christ's mysteries, the Church honors with special love Mary, the Mother of God, who is joined by an inseparable bond to the saving work of her Son (103). . . . The Church also has included in the annual cycle days devoted to the memory of the martyrs and the other saints (104). . . . Finally, in the various seasons of the year and according to its traditional discipline, the Church completes the formation of the faithful by means of devout practices for soul and body, by instruction, prayer, and works of penance and mercy (105).

Note that the Liturgical Year is centered on the commemoration of the mysteries of Christ: his enfleshment and nativity as well as the expectation of his return is celebrated in the incarnation cycle focused on Christmas, and his passion, death, resurrection, ascension, and sending of the Spirit are celebrated in the paschal cycle focused on Easter. Overlaying and intersecting with these fundamental cycles are the annual commemorations of various saints. Note that the keeping of a liturgical season is not just a matter of the texts and ceremonies used in public worship, but of individual and household practices as well.

The Paschal Cycle

Although popular piety dotes on the Christmas season with its gift-giving, carols, and creches, the heart of the Liturgical Year is the paschal cycle of Lent, Triduum, and Eastertide. In their linguistic roots, each of these elements of the paschal cycle simply refer to a fixed amount of time: *quadragesima* (Lent) = "the forty days"; *triduum* = "the three days"; *pentecostê* (Eastertide) = "the fifty days." In spite of the importance that Lent has assumed in popular piety, the Liturgical Year gives more weight to the fifty days of Easter festivity than to the forty days of lenten fast.

THE EASTER TRIDUUM

The GNLYC promulgated in 1969 outline the structure and character of the great paschal feast:

18. Christ redeemed us all and gave perfect glory to God principally through his paschal mystery: dying he destroyed our death and rising he restored our life. Therefore the Easter triduum of the passion and resurrection of Christ is the culmination of the entire liturgical year. Thus the solemnity of Easter has the same kind of preeminence in the liturgical year that Sunday has in the week.

19. The Easter Triduum begins with the evening Mass of the Lord's Supper, reaches its high point in the Easter Vigil, and closes with Evening Prayer on Easter Sunday.

20. On Good Friday and, if possible, also on Holy Saturday until the Easter Vigil, the Easter fast is observed everywhere.

21. The Easter Vigil, during the holy night when Christ rose from the dead, ranks as the "mother of all vigils." Keeping watch, the Church awaits Christ's resurrection and celebrates it in the sacraments. Accordingly, the entire celebration of this vigil should take place at night, that is, it should begin after nightfall and end before the dawn of Sunday.

First, it should be noted that the Triduum forms a single liturgical festival that lasts for three days. From the Mass of the Lord's Supper on Holy Thursday evening until Evening Prayer II of Easter (a celebration traditionally focused on the newly baptized), the Church marks time in a way unlike any other period of the year. The major liturgical services (evening Mass on Thursday, afternoon Passion service on Friday, Easter vigil from Saturday evening through Sunday morning, Easter Mass, Easter Vespers) may be supplemented by a wide variety of other liturgical forms and popular devotions (Compline to conclude the eucharistic vigil after the Holy Thursday evening Mass; the Liturgy of the Hours on Good Friday and Holy Saturday, Tenebrae, Stations of the Cross on Good Friday; blessing of Easter food on Holy Saturday). Yet all of these ceremonies form a single unitive celebration of Christ dying and rising.

Second, the liturgy of the Triduum is not so much historical commemoration as liturgical memorial. The Roman Rite liturgy of Good Friday, for example, does not dramatize the events of Jesus' crucifixion in a ritual context; rather, it proclaims the Johannine passion narrative in the context of other Scripture readings and psalmody, it intercedes for the needs of the Church and world in ten solemn intercessions, it venerates the cross in gesture and hymnody, and it celebrates communion from the presanctified gifts. The liturgy does not mourn a dead Jesus so much as acclaim a living Lord whose cross of suffering has become the throne of victory and the tree of life.

Third, the paschal Triduum is the premiere period for the celebration of Christian Initiation. A major component of the Easter Vigil is the baptism, confirmation, and first Eucharist of adults who have engaged the RCIA. In these initiation ceremonies the Church sees a powerful enactment of the victorious death and resurrection of Jesus. As the CCC poetically affirms:

> 1168. Beginning with the paschal Triduum, as from its source of light, the new time of the resurrection fills the entire liturgical year with its radiance. From place to place, on one side or the other from its source, the year is transfigured by the liturgy. It is really the "year of grace of the Lord" (cf. Luke 4:19). The economy of salvation is at work in the framework of time, but from its accomplishment in the Passover of Jesus and the outpouring of the Holy Spirit, the end of history is anticipated, "in a foretaste," and the Reign of God enters into our time.

> 1169. That is why Easter is not simply one feast among others: it is the "feast of feasts," the "Solemnity of solemnities," as the eucharist is the sacrament of sacraments (the great sacrament). Saint Athanasius calls it "the Great Sunday," as Holy Week is called in the East "the Great Week." The mystery of the Resurrection in which Christ has crushed death, fills our time with its powerful energy, until it has submitted everything to him.

EASTERTIDE

The GNLYC also highlight the character and structure of the Easter season as a fifty-day extension of the paschal festival:

> 22. The fifty days from Easter Sunday to Pentecost are celebrated in joyful exultation as one feast day, or better as one "great Sunday." These above all others are the days for singing the Alleluia.

> 24. The first eight days of the Easter season make up the octave of Easter and are celebrated as solemnities of the Lord.

> 25. On the 40th day after Easter the Ascension is celebrated, except in places where, not being a holy day of obligation, it has been transferred to the Seventh Sunday of Easter.

> 26. The weekdays after the Ascension until the Saturday before Pentecost are a preparation for the coming of the Holy Spirit.

The readings appointed for Sunday worship during the Easter season help to shape its liturgical commemoration. The first reading in all three Sunday cycles is taken from the Acts of the Apostles, which is a record of the life of the primitive Church, its witness, and its growth. The second reading in Year A is taken from 1 Peter (emphasizing initiation themes, since some exegetes believe this letter is a primitive baptismal homily), Year B is taken from 1 John (emphasizing the behavioral consequences of new life in Christ), and Year C is taken from the book of Revelation (emphasizing the consummation of history and the heavenly liturgy). The Gospels for the first three Sundays recount the appearances of Christ, the Fourth Sunday of Easter is always Good Shepherd Sunday (designated by the present Pope as "World Day of Prayer for Vocations"), and the last three Sundays of Easter recount Jesus' discourse and prayer at the Last Supper.

Crowning Eastertide, the importance of Pentecost is highlighted by its multiple texts for vigil and solemnity celebrations. On the vigil any one of four Old Testament readings may be chosen, each dealing with different aspects of the mystery of the Spirit; the second reading recounts the Spirit at work in the Church; and the Gospel reading recalls the promise of the Spirit made by Christ before his glorification. On the solemnity, the account of the events on Pentecost from Acts of the Apostles is taken as the first reading; the texts from Paul chosen for the second reading emphasize the Spirit's action in the Church; and the recommended gospel reading commemorates Easter evening when Jesus bestowed his Spirit upon the disciples in the Johannine account.

Eastertide is especially devoted to *mystagogia,* a systematic reflection upon the initiation sacraments received at the Easter Vigil. In fact, the first week of Eastertide is especially intended for the daily reunions of the newly baptized.

Lent

The GNLYC sketch the observance of Lent as a season of preparation for the great paschal festival:

> 27. Lent is a preparation for the celebration of Easter. For the Lenten liturgy disposes catechumens and the faithful to celebrate the paschal mystery; catechumens, through the several stages of Christian initiation; the faithful, through reminders of their own baptism and through penitential practices.

Traditionally three "orders" kept Lent in distinctive ways: those preparing for baptism entered a final forty-day retreat experience; those who were undergoing public penance for radically breaking with their Christian commitment through murder, adultery, or apostasy spent the forty days in penitential practice; and the faithful accompanied both of these orders with their prayer and witness. In the present reform, the presence of those preparing for Christian Initiation at the Easter Vigil strongly shapes the season.

On Ash Wednesday the Church calls catechumens, penitents, and faithful to begin the solemn keeping of Lent with personal commitments to three traditional disciplines: prayer, fasting, and almsgiving. Participants in the liturgy are marked with blessed ashes made from the burning of palms preserved since the last year's Palm/Passion Sunday liturgy.

The First Sunday of Lent features an account of Jesus' temptations in the desert. Catechumens undergo the "Rite of Election or Enrollment of Names," entering into their forty-day "period of purification and enlightenment."

The Second Sunday of Lent recounts Jesus' transfiguration.

The Third Sunday of Lent in Year A presents Jesus' interaction with the Samaritan woman at the well. When the elect are present, this Gospel may also be read in Years B and C, since the elect undergo the first scrutiny on this Sunday, a ritual whose texts are strongly connected to the theme of "living water" arising from the gospel. When the elect are not present, alternative texts from John (Year B) or Luke (Year C) are proclaimed.

The Fourth Sunday of Lent in Year A tells of Jesus healing of the man born blind. Like the preceding week when the elect are present, this Gospel may also be read in Years B and C since the elect undergo the second scrutiny whose texts connect to the theme of "illumination" on this Sunday. As on the Third Sunday, alternative texts from John and Luke are read in Years B and C when the elect are not present.

The Gospel on the Fifth Sunday of Lent in Year A narrates the raising of Lazarus. When the elect are present in Years B and C, this Gospel may still be used, since its theme of "new life" strongly connects with the Third Scrutiny celebrated with the elect on this Sunday. Alternative texts from John and Luke are provided for Years B and C when the elect are not present.

The Sixth Sunday of Lent, also known as "Palm/Passion" Sunday, both commemorates Jesus' triumphal entry into Jerusalem with a special procession and proclaims one of the Synoptic passions (Matthew in Year A, Mark in Year B, and Luke in Year C).

In each of these years the Old Testament readings for the Sundays of Lent have been chosen to outline salvation history from its beginning to the promise of the New Covenant. The readings from the apostolic letters have been selected to harmonize with the Gospels and Old Testament readings.

The Incarnation Cycle

While the paschal cycle remains foundational for the Christian keeping of time during the year, the Church also recognizes an incarnation cycle in its structuring of "strong seasons." As the GNLYC note: "32. Next to the yearly celebration of the paschal mystery, the Church holds most sacred the memorial of Christ's birth and early manifestations. This is the purpose of the Christmas season."

THE CHRISTMAS SEASON

Christmas admits four different sets of readings and liturgical texts to highlight its importance: a Vigil Mass, a Mass at midnight, a Mass at dawn, and a Mass during the day. All present different facets of the mystery of God entering human history in the life of Jesus.

The Sunday within the octave of Christmas is the feast of the Holy Family, a relatively new addition to the Liturgical Year. The Gospel reading is about Jesus' childhood and the other readings extol the virtues of family life.

On January 1 the Church celebrates the Solemnity of Mary, Mother of God. Although the secular calendar celebrates it as "New Year's Day," multiple themes intersect in the liturgical calendar on this day: the octave of Christmas, the circumcision of Jesus, the giving of the Holy Name, World Day of Prayer for Peace.

In the United States the celebration of Epiphany has been transferred from its traditional date of January 6 to the second Sunday after Christmas. Its readings commemorate the manifestation of Christ to the Gentile nations.

The Christmas season concludes with the celebration of the Baptism of the Lord.

ADVENT

The dual nature of Advent is well delineated by GNLYC:

> 39. Advent has a twofold character: as a season to prepare for Christmas when Christ's first coming to us is remembered; as a season when that remembrance directs the mind and heart to await Christ's Second Coming at the end of time. Advent is thus a period for devout and joyful expectation.

Each Gospel reading of the Sundays of Advent has a distinctive theme: the first Sunday focuses on Jesus' coming at the end of time, the second and third Sundays sketch the preaching and career of John the Baptist, and the fourth Sunday concentrates on Mary and the events that immediately prepared for Jesus' birth. The other Sunday readings comprise messianic prophecies (especially from Isaiah) and apostolic exhortations.

The period from December 17 to 24 is traditionally marked by the singing of the great "O Antiphons," a poetic version of which appears in the hymn "O Come, O Come, Emmanuel."

The Sanctoral Cycle

The "sanctoral cycle" refers to the annual commemoration of various saints in the liturgy. In every case the saint is venerated not so much for his or her own sake, but as a way of giving honor to Christ whose victory over sin and death has been actualized in the life of the saint.

The present reform of the Roman rite calendar distinguishes three levels of these commemorations. **Solemnities** are counted as principal days in the calendar, beginning their liturgical celebration with Vespers on the preceding evening (like the liturgical celebration of the Lord's Day). Examples of sanctoral solemnities include: Joseph, the Husband of Mary (March 19), the Annunciation (March 25), the Birth of John the Baptist (June 24), the Assumption (August 15), and All Saints (November 1). **Feasts** are usually celebrated without a vigil or vespers on the preceding day. Examples of sanctoral feasts include: the Conversion of Paul (January 25), the Chair of Peter (February 22), Mark (April 25), Philip and James (May 3), Matthias (May 14), the Visitation (May 31), Thomas (July 3), James (July 25), Lawrence (August 10), Bartholomew (August 24), Birth of Mary (September 8), Matthew (September 21), Michael, Gabriel, and Raphael (September 29), Luke (October 18), Simon and Jude (October 28), Andrew (November 30), Stephen (December 26), John (December 27), and the Holy Innocents (December 28). **Memorials** are either obligatory or optional, the former commemorating saints of universal importance to the Church, the latter saints particularly venerated by individual nations, cultures, or religious communities.

At the Session

Review Focal Points; view video "The Liturgical Year" on Videocassette 4 (21 minutes).

Discussion and Reflection

1. What models do I use for understanding time? Do I distinguish between *chronos* (the mechanical succession of instants) and *kairos*

(humanly significant time)? How can I communicate these concepts to others?

2. How can I keep time in a liturgical pattern rather than simply being overwhelmed by the secular structuring of the seasons?

3. How can I live the events of Triduum as liturgical memorials rather than simply historical dramas?

4. What marks of festivity can enrich one's experiences during Eastertide?

5. How can I take seriously the lenten disciplines of prayer, fasting, and almsgiving?

6. How can the sanctoral cycle with its complex structuring of solemnities, feasts, and memorials impact one's life?

BIBLIOGRAPHY

Catechism of the Catholic Church. English translations by Jan Michael Joncas from *Catéchisme de l'Eglise Catholique* (Paris: Mame/Plon, 1992).

Hoffman, Elizabeth, ed. *The Liturgy Documents: A Parish Resource.* 3rd ed. "General Instruction of the Roman Missal," and "Music in Catholic Worship." Chicago: Liturgy Training Publications, 1991.

Sacred Art

JAN MICHAEL JONCAS

Focal Points

  The author considers ten elements in the analysis of a visual artwork. The mystery of Jesus' crucifixion is pondered using three examples of visual theology.

At the Session

Engage in a brief discussion on "What is sacred art?" View video "Sacred Art" on Videocassette 4 (25 minutes).

After the Video

1. In what way did learning about the elements of art increase your appreciation of a piece of art?
2. In comparing three depictions of the crucifixion, which is your favorite and why?
   * Apse Mosaic of Sant' Appolinare in Classe (triumph)
   * Gruenwald's crucifixion from the Isenheim Altarpiece (agony)
   * Rouault's crucifixion from Miserere (challenge)

Further Reflection

1. How would this presentation help you to explore the theological dimension of other pieces of sacred art?
2. What art pieces in your church would you like to interpret theologically?

BIBLIOGRAPHY

Aimez-vous les uns les autres by George Rouault. From the collection of Richard L. Hillstrom. Minneapolis, Minn. Photographed by Roger Rich, University of St. Thomas.

Apse of Sant Appolinare in Classe. Ravenna, Italy. Photographer: Leonard Von Matt.

Isenheim Altarpiece by Matthias Grunewald. Musee Unterlinden, Colmar, France.

Sacred Pictures, Silent Talk

ADÉ BETHUNE

Adé Bethune presented a series of lectures on sacred art in the Focus on Theology sessions at the University of St. Thomas. The simple yet profound message Adé conveys through her extraordinary grasp of Christian symbolism articulated in the biblical tradition provides an added dimension to the video presentation. The Christian witness that she gives is as much from her personal life as from her art.

What the hymn is to the ear, the sacred image is to the eye. A conversation. A silent conversation.

What do we say when we sing a hymn of a psalm? We speak praise, praise to God—a cry of the heart from the lover to the beloved. "How great thou art!" We tell tales of divine justice and mercy. We give thanks to God—endless thanks for endless, exquisite gifts. We ask forgiveness for failure to love God, God's people, God's creation. And we also ask for additional favors. Often desperate asking, "Please, help me."

In some songs, the words are God's own words to us. We have to listen. In other hymns, the words are ours to God. We are asking God to listen. All of it is a conversation, a dialogue, moving back and forth between ourselves and the Lord our God. Awesome. A sacred conversation.

Can a conversation be wordless? Yes, between those who love each other, words are not always needed. Eyes look at eyes and heart speaks to heart. People can look at each other and communicate with the eyes. Eye contact. What the hymn is to the ear, the icon is to the eye. Unless there is dialogue, something is missing.

Conversation with a Picture?

How can we converse with a picture? When I was a child we prayed every day for Papa who was away at war. Set in a little frame, a small black and white photograph of an officer in his military uniform looked at us from the wall. Our prayers to God were for him. To Mama and the older children, the picture must have meant a great deal. Looking at it, I suppose they were able to recognize a loved person, to remember his presence.

Before we can recognize a person in a portrait, we need to know the real person. The portrait can only bring back to our hearts a remembrance of our love for the person depicted. In his wallet, a man keeps pictures of his wife and children. A young woman cannot keep her eyes from the portrait of her fiancé. It seems to talk to her. A mother will always cherish the picture of her baby as he then was, and now all grown. The portraits of grandparents become even more significant after they have gone. We question them. "What was it like? How did you feel?"

What of events? As we look at old snapshots, one event after another comes back to mind. "Remember the picnic at the old farm in Alton, when Uncle Joe jumped into the water and caught a fish?"

Our Family of Faith

If our loved ones can mean so much to us, even in portrait and anecdote, how much also can those of our brothers and sisters in the faiths—their portraits and the tales of their deeds. They greatly extend our family. But first we must know them, if not directly, at least through memory, through the community memory of the Church and through the tales of their lives and their actions.

To attempt making a picture of the invisible God would be impossible. It goes counter to human reason. The first commandment wisely rules it out. We have no way of understanding the unseen divine being except by metaphor. Thus, fabricating idols to worship them— as though pieces of wood, stone, or bronze, even when cleverly carved, could have divine power—is nonsense.

However, we can indeed represent our visible human brothers and sisters, even those who lived in the past, provided we know something about them, their lives, and their personalities. For us, obviously, the chief among our brothers and sisters are Jesus and his mother, Mary. But we have many, many others in addition.

Representation as Presence

Something about a portrait suggests the person's presence and continuing dialogue with us. The portrait of Rabbi Lewis in our local Jewish Community Center always reminds me of the years he spent there as teacher to his congregation. I am comfortable looking at the painting and recalling the interesting and sometimes amusing things he used to say.

Some years ago, I was commissioned to paint a set of icons for a Melkite church. When they were almost finished, an old Monsignor, a friend of the client, came to see the icons before they were to be shipped away. In front of the image of Saint Nicholas, Monsignor Najmy stopped short. "But, that is St. Nicholas," he exclaimed. "It is he! It looks just like him." Tears welled in his eyes. Despite a distance of so many centuries, Nicholas must have been a dear friend to him. He must have felt close to him. He recognized Nicholas. I was deeply touched at his love for Nicholas, and also thankful that I had managed to produce a recognizable likeness that could speak (silently) to a faithful friend.

The Human Face

How can you make a portrait that "talks" to people? Simple. Show the subject front face, both eyes open, looking straight at the viewer. A first grader can do it.

A picture of Jesus looking at you straight in the eyes tells you that he is interested in YOU. In contrast, one that shows him from the side or the back—even if it is an interesting painting with delicate colors and skilled brush strokes—can only give you the unhappy impression that he does not really care who you are and even whether or not you are there. It is as if you do not count; he has other things to do. Why, instead, did the San Damiano crucifix "talk" to Saint Francis, telling him to rebuild his church? Look at those beautiful eyes. They looked at Francis and reached deep into his heart. They still look at us and talk to us, if we will look at them and listen.

The face is the most individual, recognizable part of the human being. And the eyes are the window to the soul. That is why portrait icons usually show only the person's face and shoulders, though, in some cases, the hands might be significant as well. Some situations call for a full figure, perhaps standing head to toe. That too is fitting, provided that it still looks at you as would a close-up portrait.

In a large church building that holds many people, the eyes in a wall mosaic or a fresco painting may seem to range right and left. That is because the conversation is not with only one person (me), on a one-to-one exclusive basis, but it encompasses the whole congregation of which I too am a part.

Lectors who proclaim the word of the Lord in church also need to look at the congregation no less than at the page. As they read, they might move their heads ever so slightly to include the people on the

right, on the left, those who are near, those who are far. In communicating God's word, hearing is critical but eye contact also plays an essential role. Even a person who is visually impaired can feel, in the
sound and direction of the voice, whether the reader is addressing the
people convincingly with eye to eye—soul to soul—contact.

Narrative Pictures

How do we depict events, tales from the Bible, scenes from the
lives of holy people, Church heroes? Easy. As a child does. Facing the
viewer, in a sort of silhouette, yet with a partially three-quarter, even
semi-profile view of the body when trying to express movement, action.

For example, to show a person walking or running the face and
shoulders would be presented almost in front view, but not the legs.
Attempting to suggest speed of running in a front-view figure, rush-
ing toward the viewer, is seldom convincing. While one leg touches
the ground, the other leg, raised in the air, seems to be amputated,
giving an uneasy sense of frozen impermanence.

Some scenes show two figures talking to each other. A favorite
example illustrates Luke 1:26, in which the angel Gabriel brings a message to a virgin named Mary who replies and a conversation ensues.
How does one depict this beautiful event? In earlier examples, Gabriel
stands on the right. Actually he seems to be walking in or alighting
from the right, one foot behind the other sideways. On the left, Mary
is seated, spinning yarn. While they face each other, they are also facing us, the viewers. Gabriel's right hand is stretched out in speech. In
his left he usually holds a staff. It is really quite simple, yet very deep.

To some extent, the position of figures in a sacred image is much as
it would be in a play, where the actors face the public so that their
voices may be heard clearly, while by gesture they also appear to be
talking to each other. Players' speech would not carry if they stood
with their back to the audience when delivering their lines. The same
is true in the icon of an event.

Biblical narrations such as Exodus 14 (Moses leading his people
across the Red Sea) can involve a great many figures. This can present
as many difficulties for composing an illustration as in gathering and
training young performers for a pageant or a mystery play. Usually
the scene is reduced to its chief characters while the crowd is suggested
by just a few figures representing "thousands." That is an acceptable
solution.

Unidentified people in a crowd might even be shown with their
faces in profile. Why? Because they are not really talking to us; they

are in the picture only because they are taking a lesser part in the event depicted. Sometimes they are also shown in a smaller size because of their lesser role.

A Perspective of Size

As a sign of their importance, main characters are often drawn in a larger size. Appropriate to a sacred icon, that view is not quite the way a camera would catch the picture. In a photograph or in a picture drawn in correct linear perspective, the things and people nearer the eye are large, regardless of their significance, while those farther away appear smaller and smaller with the receding space. An eminent person who was farther from the camera would appear tiny and might even be partly hidden by insignificant figures who happened to be in the foreground. That is the way things look in real life. But the timeless view of the spirit is not absolutely bound to earthly perspective or even virtual reality.

A sacred image can be more universal, ageless. Earthly perspective is not essential to it. The icon may take poetic license as it leads from the visible to the invisible, from time to the timeless.

For example, the Epiphany in Matt 2:11 is basically depicted in a quite sober manner that closely reflects the gospel verses. The child Jesus is not presented as a newborn in swaddling clothes, as he is to the shepherds in Luke 2:12, but as a young child (echoing the words, "king of the Jews") he talks to the wise men with his hand. The words "on entering the house" might be suggested by an arch or a doorway, perhaps barely large enough to surround the enthroned figures. Realism is not important here; the Gospel mystery is. Sometimes "Bethlehem of Judea" is suggested by a few small roof tops forming a "city" in a quasi "perspective of importance." Often the wise men are a little smaller than the two chief figures. If space is tight on the page, they might be grouped almost as a unit, but the words "they prostrated themselves" and "presented him with gifts" are clearly delineated by their gesture.

The Bible Made Visible

A true sacred image, painted on a panel or on a wall, stays as close as possible to the words of Scripture and rehearses the ageless mystery. While it describes a historic event which actually happened (or will happen) in time, the icon also shows a significance beyond time, a mystery yet to be unveiled to the soul. When our eyes follow the icon's lines and savor its colors, the Bible words almost form themselves on our lips, much as they do when our ears perceive the familiar melody of a great and timeless hymn.

BIBLIOGRAPHY

Catechism of the Catholic Church. Part Three: §2, ch. 2, art. 8. Washington, D.C.: United States Catholic Conference, 1994.

Sacred Music

JAN MICHAEL JONCAS

Focal Points

This presentation explores sacred music as a form of theology. The presenter discusses the elements in analyzing a musical work and then distinguishes the four textures of music. Three musical settings of the "Sanctus-Benedictus" are considered and compared.

At the Session

View video "Sacred Music" on Videocassette 4 (23 minutes).

After the Video

In listening to the "Sanctus-Benedictus," we experienced three musical settings. Which of these settings created the greatest appreciation of sacred music for you?

- Gregorian Chant, "Mass of the Angels"
- Mozart, "Sanctus in C" K 258, from *Missa Brevis*
- Arvo Pärt, "Sanctus" from *Berliner Messe*

Further Reflection

The great Lutheran composer, Johann Sebastian Bach, would write a motto at the beginning of his handwritten scores—"to God alone be the glory." Is all music sacred?

BIBLIOGRAPHY

Mozart, Wolfgang Amadeus. "Sanctus and Benedictus in C Major," K 258. *Music of Mozart's Missa Brevis.* BMG Music.

_____. "Sanctus and Benedictus in C Major," K 258. *Score of Six Masses in Full Score.*

Pärt, Arvo. "Sanctus." *Berliner Messe* and *Berliner Messe* score. ECM Records, Munich, Germany.

"Sanctus" from the *Mass of the Angels,* the Cathedral Singers with Richard Proulx, conductor.

CHAPTER SEVEN

MORAL LIFE

Christian Moral Life

CHRISTOPHER THOMPSON

Before Arriving at the Session

Read Focal Points and essay below.

Focal Points

At one point in the history of the world, Jesus' offer of a divine friendship was "good news." Given our contemporary culture's emphases, it is likely to be "good news" once again. Catholics have tended to see the moral life as a set of external rules to be followed rather than a form of life centered around gratitude for what God has done for us in Jesus.

This essay situates the Christian moral life within the context of our faith. Christian moral life is our response to what we believe God has done for us through Jesus Christ. When moral life is seen as a response to divine love, it becomes a form of life rooted in gratitude and celebration and not one of control or mere "rules" to be followed. Moral actions become situated within the broader context of a life centered on prayer, the Church, and the sacraments.

CHRISTIAN MORAL LIFE

To live the Christian moral life is to live life as a response, a response to what we believe God has done for us in sending God's Son, Jesus the Christ. For the early followers of Jesus, discovering what it meant for God to send his Son as a sign of love involved a long process of discerning and responding. They wondered what it meant for God to be so interested in God's people. They wondered what it could mean to have the Scriptures fulfilled in their midst, what good could come from Nazareth, and who this is that speaks with such authority.

Jesus presents the possibility of another account of ourselves, another story of what it is that our lives are all about. Through the accounts of Jesus in the Gospels we are met with the challenge of re-configuring our lives in accordance with the Good News. That challenge often entails resistance and struggle as all of us are confronted with the prospect of setting aside our individualistic, often distorted accounts of ourselves for the truer story of God. Students especially can be invited to encounter the Gospels as a means whereby their own "cover stories" can be challenged.

Slowly over time, through signs and wonders, and especially through his death and resurrection, the disciples came to discover the significance of Jesus the Christ for their lives. Today in our community, the Christian discovers what it means to become a new creation in Christ. Death is no longer the ultimate cover story; in the new community of Jesus the Christ, our love for one another in imitation of what God has done for us is to be the new narrative.

But to grasp the depth of what was disclosed in the event of Jesus involves a process, a continuing conversion over time, as one dwells in wonder about what God has done for us and struggles to respond adequately. The New Testament tells of this process of growth, as the early disciples engage the reality of Jesus at ever deepening levels. Peter, for example, took a bold, unreflective step to confess Jesus as the Messiah, only later to abandon him at that crucial time in which Jesus' messianic mission was to be played out. Yet the story of Peter does not end in failure. Later we read of his devotion to the Cross and resurrection of Jesus, a reality for which he would soon give his life. From affirmation to rejection, from rejection to devotion, St. Peter marks the story of one being taken in by the Good News. St. Paul is the paradigm of Christian discipleship, but was once an enemy of Christ, "breathing threats and murder against the disciples of the Lord" (Acts 9:1). And Thomas declared, "My Lord and my God!" (John 20:28), but only after demanding more than the rest of the disciples. For so many of the followers of Jesus in the New Testament, the expectations were thwarted in the person of Jesus who, "by taking the form of a slave" (Phil 2:7), inaugurated the new kingdom of God, a new form of life for all men and women.

In grasping the gospel of Christ one grasps the persistence of the covenantal presence of God's love for us, and so the metaphors of "return" and "response" dominate the moral narrative of the Christian. For many students, however, it is perhaps a matter of hearing this story for the first time. Or like the prodigal son, the story of the Church is a matter of an inheritance to be taken for granted and squandered. Coming to their senses, though, students can begin to discern the genuine possibility of being taken up in a divine friend-ship, of accounting for their lives from the perspective of God's story of ourselves. Through the process of re-configuring the significance of their lives they can come to recognize the Father who, "while still a long way off, caught sight of him and was filled with compassion" (Luke 15:20).

That embrace in divine friendship, or what the Christian tradition has called charity, expresses one of the deepest insights of Jesus' choice for our fellowship. No longer slaves of sin, the new life in Christ signals a new life in friendship with God. What this divine friendship offers to the world is a new form of life, a new way of understanding what our human struggles are all about.

Throughout its history, Christianity had to confront a variety of competing cover stories, rival accounts about the nature of human happiness. Against the portrait of the Stoic sage, the Christian could not imitate a studied indifference to one's neighbor, nor could "self-control" be the dominant form of life. Under the cover story of Stoi-cism, like so many other visions of the ancient world, an individual was not caught up in the drama of salvation history. He or she was not pursued in divine love. The Stoic, with an attending theology of indif-ference, could only stand confused, challenged, and shocked before the story of Christ, of one who offered himself for us on the cross for the sole purpose of divine friendship. For the Stoic the divine prin-ciple stands before the world as impersonal *logos*—never as the Father who was filled with compassion at the sight of his son, who was still a long way off (Luke 15:20). The Father, from the perspective of Stoi-cism, made a grave mistake. He allowed himself to be unsettled by the wayward son.

Few students would overtly identify themselves with Stoic phi-losophy, yet many are tantalized with the essential features of that cover story. The impersonal nature of the created order, the allure of "self-control" and the appeal of "keeping one's cool" amidst the tur-moil of society, provides an appealing account of their lives. The invi-tation of the Gospels, on the other hand, is an invitation to consider one's self as caught up in the narrative of divine love. It is an invita-tion to set aside the need for dominance and control and to adopt the dispositions of gratitude and humility.

With the in-break of the revelation of Christ the previously ordered world is now overturned only to be reordered in divine love. Charity, not indifference, becomes the new form of one's life as Christians are called to a newer kind of "self-control." One's self is ordered no longer through repression, but invitation—an invitation to respond to the divine friendship established by Christ himself.

"See what love the Father has given us," the author of 1 John proclaims, "that we should be called children of God; and that is what we are" (3:1). To be invited to a divine friendship in Christ is incomprehensible to so many of us who understand God and creation to be anything but a world ordered toward love. The author of 1 John is sensitive to the challenges of competing accounts of ourselves and continues, "The reason the world does not know us is that it did not know him" (3:1). As if to say that those who do not know God, who do not know the one who offers a divine friendship to us through his Son, cannot understand that community who is caught up in a passionate pursuit of that friendship. Christianity remains a puzzle before those who do not comprehend the nature of divine love.

More specifically, the Christian moral life remains a puzzle before those who do not see it primarily as a form of dwelling in divine love. Justice becomes a nexus of extrinsic rules to be followed, instead of an order of mutual relations in love. Fortitude appears as an unbridled will to power instead of an enduring commitment to the truth of God's ways. Temperance means repression rather than an invitation to delight in God's truth. And prudence becomes a mere cunning in the absence of a commitment to the wisdom of Christ and the saints. Charity, as the form of the happiest life we may hope for, orders the activities of the Christian around that divine love in Christ. Charity transforms the form of the happy life itself—what was once perhaps a life ordered around power and control is now ordered toward sacrifice and joy.

Students who hear of such a form of life are often in the same position of that ancient Stoic sage. For so many it has not been a real possibility that they may be the object of a divine love. Though they do not know or follow Epictetus, the form of self-control and a studied indifference is dominant in their culture. Convinced that to risk oneself on the truth of divine love is too great, they opt instead for something less—far less. The teacher of Christian moral theology can witness to an alternative form of life. Yet even in failing to live up to that form— we do, after all, hold a treasure in earthen vessels—the teacher can encourage them to seek the resources that sustain us in that quest: the saints, the sacraments, and personal prayer.

No portrait of a Catholic moral life can be complete without some appeal to the saints, the sacraments, and, above all, prayer. Prayer is perhaps one of the most striking contrasts to the dominant cover story of our age, as the action of prayer affirms the primacy of God, our inability to maintain control, and the need for a sustaining relationship of reconciliation and worship. In prayer the student learns the discipline of attentiveness to the Holy Spirit, the habit of gratitude, and the form of charity. The discipline of attentiveness is demanded of those who seek to live, in the vortex of modern culture, a life present to the love of God. The habit of gratitude captures the moral life of the Christian. For what else can one live but sheer gratitude before the gift of eternal love? Grateful prayer is the curative of a spiteful heart and the foundation of service for one another. Finally, prayer is the expression of charity, the form of the happiest life, for deep down in our heart of hearts, St. Augustine reminds us, "humanity wishes to praise Him who has made us for Himself." Without some habitual commitment to prayer, both with the community through the sacraments and privately through meditation, the demands of the Christian moral life are hollow and incoherent. One can speak with the tongues of men and angels, St. Paul reminds us, but without charity it is mere noise (1 Cor 13:1).

And so Christian moral life, as a life lived in response to what God has done for us in Jesus, is a process—like the growth of a mustard seed, the swelling of leavened bread, or the sprouting of seed on good soil. It is a process of living in the mystery of divine love and allowing oneself to be ordered by that love which has been "poured out into our hearts by the Holy Spirit that has been given to us" (Rom 5:5). In the New Testament that process is often a portrait in human failure. Yet it is always a failure transformed into hope through love—a wayward son is welcomed back, a dying seed springs to new life, a lost coin is found, a treasure is recovered (Luke 8:5-8; 15:8-10; Matt 13:44).

And so the New Testament offers a model for us today as we struggle to respond to what is difficult to fathom. In teaching about the Christian moral life one speaks of a divine mystery of love that is a broader reality than any person can fully comprehend. It is to recognize oneself as very often an inadequate messenger of the Good News; yet still, in the confidence of the presence of God's grace, one takes up the challenge of introducing students into the life-giving reality of God's Church.

For so many of us, though, it is an introduction by way of humble pointing. Pointing toward the reality of a friendship with Christ becomes the challenge for ourselves as well. As members of the body of Christ, we recognize—even as we teach—our utter dependence upon the head. We recognize what St. Paul means in bearing a treasure in an earthen vessel (2 Cor 4:7). What we have to offer is beyond what we on our own can give. And so the invitation to the Christian moral life is to see things beyond the ordinary. The love of God in Christ surpasses human understanding, and to call one another to live in that love is to call one another to a life that is beyond us.

It is in this tension of holding on to a treasure, of seeking to grow in divine friendship, that the commands of the Christian moral life take shape. To love one's neighbor as oneself, to take up the cross, to deny oneself for the sake of the gospel, to be poor in spirit—for so many of us such commands seem beyond what we are capable of doing. And yet as members of the body of Christ, such commands are invitations into a deeper love beyond our ordinary knowing.

The Christian moral life is lived in hopeful humility. The moral life is marked by humility in that as "doers of the word" we recognize our need for the grace and forgiveness of Jesus in the Church. It is marked by hope in that an invitation to true happiness becomes a real possibility—the blind see, fathers welcome sons, a precious coin is found, and dying seeds spring to new life (Luke 7:21; 8:5; 15:8-10, 11-32).

At the Session

Review Focal Points; view video "Christian Moral Life" on Videocassette 5 (26 minutes).

After the Video

1. What would life be like if God, our first principle of reality

- were indifferent to us?
- pursued us in divine love?

2. How would you apply this to your lives?

Further Discussion and Reflection

1. To what extent have I taken the invitation of divine friendship for granted?
2. How do I display gratitude to God in my own life?
3. In what ways have I inadvertently led others to believe that life is essentially about control, power, prestige, or prominence?
4. How might a person behave if she believed that she were truly a friend of God? How would she respond to the world and others?

BIBLIOGRAPHY

Catechism of the Catholic Church. Part Three: §1, ch. 1, arts. 1, 2, 7. Washington, D.C.: United States Catholic Conference, 1994.

Catholic Social Thought and Catholic Education

MICHAEL NAUGHTON

Before Arriving at the Session

Read Focal Points and the essay below; use the lists at the end of the session for preparation and for review.

Focal Points

The Catholic Social Tradition has a long and rich history in the Church. It addresses social ills and principles that act as a guide. These issues are found in the teachings of the Church.

CATHOLIC SOCIAL THOUGHT AND CATHOLIC EDUCATION

It is often stated that the Catholic social tradition is the Church's best kept secret. While Catholics may know what the Church teaches regarding abortion, divorce, homosexuality, birth control, and other sexual and personal matters (although not always why), they are unaware of the Church's teaching on various economic and sociopolitical matters such as work, property, environment, state, social communications, economic participation, and so forth. Dorothy Day, the co-founder of the Catholic Worker movement, observed that too often "when it came to private morality the Catholics shone but when it came to social and political morality, they were often conscienceless" (Day, 71). Walter Burghardt, S.J., puts the matter in more specific terms:

> Our post immigrant Catholicism has rarely heard Pope Leo
> XIII in the context of greed and exploitation affirm private
> property and the common purpose of property, distinguish just

ownership from just use, declare the obligation of employers to pay a living wage, proclaim workers' right to organize for group protection, insist on collaboration rather than class struggle as the fundamental means for social change (Burghardt, 36).

There are various reasons why Catholics are unaware of the social teachings of the Church. Since we live in a highly individualistic culture, we tend to see the moral life only in personal, not social, terms. We restrict moral questions to a small quarantine of issues such as lying, cheating, infidelity, impurity, and so forth, and have a difficult time seeing moral issues in economic systems, political structures, or business practices.

But the most important and immediate reason for Catholics not aware of their social tradition is us, Catholic educators. In 1995, Archbishop John Roach commissioned a task force on Catholic social thought and Catholic education. The report states that while great strides have been made in many Catholic parishes and schools, too often the social mission of the Church has not become an integral part of a student's education. Too often Catholics have not been introduced to the substance of the Church's social teaching and cannot draw on these principles to help inform their actions (*Sharing Catholic Social Thought,* facing 1).

In this essay I will sketch an outline on what the Catholic social tradition means, explain the virtue of justice and its different meanings in the United States, and conclude with the important contribution Catholic social thought can effect in making Catholic education more Catholic.

What Is the Catholic Social Tradition?

The beginning of modern Catholic social thought is often associated with the encyclical *Rerum novarum* (On the Condition of Labor) by Pope Leo XIII in 1891. This encyclical was the first official response to the Industrial Revolution and the modern economy. Yet, it would be a mistake to think that the Church first started thinking about social issues in 1891. Leo XIII himself would never have written the encyclical unless a social tradition preceded him. The Hebrew prophets, the teachings of Jesus, the early Church Fathers, Thomas Aquinas, and many others represent a tradition on social issues such as labor, the state, property, poverty, finance, etc., that have been an integral part of the Church's moral teachings.

That tradition continues today. On May 1, 1991, Pope John Paul II promulgated a very important social encyclical *Centesimus annus* (One

Hundred Years) in honor of the one-hundredth anniversary of *Rerum novarum*. Within those one hundred years, there were several other papal encyclicals along with bishops' pastoral letters and council documents from Vatican II (see Appendix I). In CA John Paul provides a rereading of *Rerum novarum*, along with the social tradition as a whole, by looking at the text itself, not simply for nostalgia's sake, but to examine and reinterpret the fundamental principles of the document in light of today's situation. For John Paul II, this process of looking back and reinterpreting manifests "the true meaning of the Church's Tradition which, being ever living and vital . . . builds upon the foundation laid by our fathers in the faith" (CA 3). The Church's social tradition contains the gospel treasure of what is old and new by passing on what has been received in Scripture and tradition and by interpreting new events "in the midst of which the life of the Church and the world unfolds" (CA 3).

By looking at what is both old and new, the Church's social tradition engages the world and its specific issues and problems. By formulating moral teachings on the social problems of society, the Church's social teaching helps people to make judgments about them and to indicate directions toward just and peaceful solutions. (See Appendixes II and III for motivating principles and virtues.) Rather than merely reacting to modern situations and attempting to reinvent the wheel when it comes to ethical problems of today, the Church sees the new and the old "always closely interwove[n]. The 'new' grows out of the 'old,' and the 'old' finds a fuller expression in the 'new'" (*Tertio millennio adveniente* 18). The social tradition of the Church is precisely so important because it helps us to mediate the profound meaning of our faith and see the world as it is—created and redeemed by God.

The Church's social tradition is not only the words of popes and bishops, but also the actions of women and men who live out the deepest aspirations of their vocation and who promote the dignity of others, especially those who are most vulnerable. One without the other weakens the Church's mission to the world. The teacher, the student, the parent, the faith formation director, the parishioner are all a part of the Catholic social tradition, either contributing to its vitality and growth or letting it lie dormant in apathy and self-interest.

Two Conflicting Traditions of Justice:
Individual Rights versus Right Relationships

Central to the Church's social tradition is the virtue of justice. Yet, justice has different meanings in our culture. When the Catechism was first published in 1992, Daniel Seligman in *Fortune* magazine (2/22/93) published an article criticizing the Church's social teaching as being too "communitarian," too idealistic, and ultimately too naive. Seligman accuses the Church of being "gripped by a communitarian ethic . . . [that] continues to focus on the motives of economic players rather than the outcomes of economic behavior and remains oblivious of Adam Smith's great insight: that individuals pursuing their own self-interest end up enriching the whole community." For Seligman, economic activity has little to do with being a particular person (motives), and everything to do with having more material goods (outcomes).

What drives Seligman's critique of the Church's social teaching is not that he does not believe in justice, but that he has redefined it within an individualistic tradition. For Seligman, justice has nothing to do with a movement outward toward others, nor is it related to the social nature of our humanity. Rather, justice for Seligman is a series of individual claims or rights that allow people to pursue their own self-interests without others getting in the way. Justice is attained when individuals are given the maximum amount of liberty so they can pursue their own projects without infringing upon the rights of others.

When it comes to deciding how we should live or what project should be taken up, Seligman pleads a certain agnosticism toward any idea of a common good. His refrain is "Let people decide on their own good." He is asserting that people are right or developed when they are autonomous, not by the nature of their choice. As the common rhetorical question for modern culture goes "Who is to decide what is good for others?"

For the Catholic social tradition, justice is much more than autonomy. Justice comes from the Latin word *ius*, which means "right," that is, the just person is in right relationship with others. In the words of Thomas Aquinas, the just person is "well disposed towards another" (*ST* II–II, q. 58, a. 12). It is precisely this "right" relationship that serves as the basis for one's own development. Autonomy, while necessary, is insufficient to an integral development of the human person. Justice is the constant pursuit to give each person his or her due. Without this fundamental solidarity of right relationships with other people, without being wholly possessed by justice, we tend to shrivel into small-minded maximizers. It matters very much what our motives are! As T. S. Eliot puts it: "To do the right deed for the wrong reason is the greatest treason" (Eliot, 44).

What we have here are two different understandings of justice. For Seligman, the American Individualist, the focus of justice is on "individual rights" that lead to greater autonomy; whereas for the Church it is "right relationships" based on the Trinity that lead to greater community (see the cover of this book). In the Catholic social tradition, we become right, that is, developed, not only in human freedom and autonomy, but when we are freely in right relation with others and we live in a community that fosters conditions for others to develop (common good). We are right when our choices reflect the good of others. To understand what my good is, I must understand the good of the other, since the two are woven by the social nature of our humanity.

For example, in their pastoral letter on economic justice the United States Catholic bishops define rights not as claims on autonomy, but rather as the "minimal conditions for communal living." In commenting on this definition, David Hollenbach recalls the Exodus story where the people are liberated from bondage into community, "a community of persons who are both free and co-responsible for one another's fates" (Hollenbach, 70–94). It is not a liberation to autonomy and independence that sets the conditions for human development, but liberation to community and interdependence. We are most free when we are most responsible—when our ability to respond to God's call is fully grasped. Autonomy and freedom are not ends to strive for, but rather means to be in right relationship in a community that promotes the common good.

Why Is Catholic Social Thought So Important to Catholic Education and Faith Formation?

In their reflections on Catholic social thought and Catholic education, the United States bishops write that "If Catholic education and formation fail to communicate our social tradition, they are not fully Catholic" (*Sharing Catholic Social Thought*, 2).

God is the source of all we know and can learn. For this reason true Catholic education emphasizes the importance and interrelationship of all learning. Often there is a danger of restricting the incarnational dimension of our faith. The Catholic social tradition can be an integrative power in the curriculum especially in social studies and history. The Catholic social tradition teaches and integrates the social implications of faith in how people vote, how they make political decisions, how they understand poverty and the environment, how they view their property and work, and how they organize a business. These issues cannot be answered merely in a secular fashion, nor can they, when dealing with spiritual and moral dimensions, be relegated to religion class as though that is the only place we talk about God.

Catholic social thought helps students to see how important the human person is in God's plan. It engages students, appropriate to their ages, with their vocations in society. What does God want from them? How can they be their brother's keeper? What sacrifices are they to make? The social tradition of the Church invites all of us into a broader perspective, a perspective that is always expanding our horizons to explore the moral and spiritual dimensions of social issues and problems. It also helps us to understand that solutions to our problems in society cannot be solved unless they are rooted in the deepest understanding of the Gospel, which enables us to participate in the truth about the person. The social problems of our day are not merely the matter of getting the right techniques in place (although certainly this is part of the solution), but they are always moral and spiritual at their core. That is, our social problems always have at their core the meaning of the human person. As John Paul II explains:

> In order better to incarnate the one truth about man in different and constantly changing social, economic and political contexts, [Catholic social thought] . . . enters into dialogue with the various disciplines concerned with man. It assimilates what these disciplines have to contribute, and helps them to open themselves to a broader horizon, aimed at serving the individual person who is acknowledged and loved in the fullness of his or her vocation (CA 59).

Our deepest aspirations about life, about others and ourselves, and about God must penetrate our understanding of the world. This is why we gravitate to people like Dorothy Day, Mother Teresa, Archbishop Romero, as well as parents who witness to their children, business people who practice justice, politicians who work for the poor and marginalized. We find in them an integrity of life where they bring together their deepest aspirations of moral and spiritual conviction to their day-to-day living. There are no shadows about them, but a vibrant light of integrity that witnesses, in both their actions and words, to God's grace and goodness.

The Catholic social tradition is an extremely exciting part of Catholic education and religious formation precisely because it can get integrated through the whole curriculum, especially social studies. The Institute for Catholic Social Thought at the University of St. Thomas' Center for Catholic Studies has developed a national project to develop curriculum materials for Catholic education and faith formation to better integrate Catholic social thought (see bibliography).

At the Session

Briefly discuss Focal Points, view video "Catholic Social Thought and Catholic Education" on Videocassette 5 (28 minutes).

After the Video

What topic in the Catholic Social Tradition is most known and acted on in the lives of Catholics? Which topic is the least known and acted on? Give reasons.

Further Reflection (with Emphasis on Curriculum)

Read and discuss the following list of ideas for integrating Catholic social thought throughout the curriculum. Make an additional list of programs, ideas, lesson plans, and so forth that promote the theme of justice in the world. Three areas where teachers can help students integrate the Catholic social tradition are social studies, literature, and history. In your discussions be sure to bring out the spiritual and moral underpinnings of these issues. The following topics are venues for bringing in the Catholic social tradition:

1. **Peace and War:** Many of the peace movements had religious inspirations such as Pax Christi. These movements supported conscientious objectors (see Jagerstatter, a Catholic conscientious objector to Nazism; a video called *The Refusal* tells his story). Also the just war theory has its origins in St. Augustine, who lived in the fourth century.

2. **International Human Rights:** Pope John XXIII's encyclical *Pacem in Terris* would work well with the United Nations' *Declaration on Human Rights*.

3. **Catholic and Christian Professional Associations:** Study people who are trying to make their work an expression of prayer and their workplaces more just (e.g., Christians in Commerce, Thomas More Society—Catholic Lawyers).

4. **Poverty:** Often our students are unaware of their position of privilege in society. Most do not have to deal with high levels of crime, violence, drugs, broken homes, and inadequate housing, education, and health care. While we are all equal in the sight of God, we are not all born with equal opportunity. The Scriptures and the Church's tradition, especially the patristic period (the first four centuries), have some powerful ideas concerning poverty and our responsibility to the poor.

5. **The Industrial Revolution and the Meaning of Labor:** What is the condition and treatment of the worker? Examine the condition of labor today in Mexico, Latin America, and Asia, as well as in the United States, especially for immigrant workers.

6. **The Religious Inspiration of Various Movements in the United States:** Dorothy Day and the Catholic Worker movement, Martin Luther King Jr. and Civil Rights Movement, the hippie movement, the founding fathers, and so forth all have some form of religious inspiration that often gets submerged in history books.

7. **Key Catholic Figures Who Worked for Justice:** Bartolomé de las Casas was a Dominican priest who defended the Indians when the Spanish and Portuguese came to America. The Paulist Press has a video on Archbishop Romero (though it may not be appropriate for all ages). Other saints such as Nicholas, Patrick, Francis, and Clare can bring out justice themes.

8. **The Universality of the Church:** Establish a sister school with one in a developing country. This could be part of a Spanish program in Latin America or an inner city school or both.

9. **Examine Our Consumptive Habits in Light of Justice:** Examine faith and the consumer economy, particularly consumption habits and the virtue of simplicity. How do we spend our money? What do we spend it on?

APPENDIX I: CATHOLIC SOCIAL PRINCIPLES

I. **Human Dignity:** Everything in the economic and organizational realm must be judged in light of whether it protects or undermines human dignity. This dignity is grounded in the transcendent dimension: the person is created in the image of God. Each individual's life is intrinsically valuable and sacred, and hence ought never be treated as a means.

II. **Common Good:** The Catholic understanding of the common good is not "the greatest good for the greatest number." Rather, as John XXIII stated in *Mater et Magistra,* the common good is "the sum total of those conditions of social living, whereby men are enabled more fully and more readily to achieve their own perfection" (65). The person is social by nature and hence must be seen in relationship to the community.

III. **Subsidiarity:** The common good is the task of both the public and the private sector; some matters belong to one or the other, but many matters belong to both (such as distribution of goods). However, social and economic control should be kept at the lowest possible level, thus giving primacy to individual initiative. Intermediate associations (families, local communities, unions, societies, etc.) should be free to perform operations proper to themselves without interference from the state. The state, though, in its vigilance over the common good, is to encourage, assist, and, when necessary, supplement this private initiative.

IV. **Universal Destination of Material Goods/Private Property:** God's creation is intended for everyone. To deny access to the fruits of the earth is to disobey God's command of dominion. God's divine command has a harmonious relationship with the moral structure of creation, that is, God's divine command forms the moral structures of human relationships. Hence, part of the Creator's ordering is a just distribution guided by the principle of common use. In general, the best way to attain the universal destination of material goods is through the exercise of private property. Yet "the Church teaches that the possession of material goods is not an absolute right, and that its limits are inscribed in its very nature as a human right. . . . Of its nature private property also has a social function which is based on the law of the common purpose of goods" (CA 30). Hence, the right to private ownership is not absolute; property has a social mortgage.

V. **Preferential Option of the Poor:** All have an obligation to those most vulnerable. Not everyone has an equal start in economic life and hence blame for poverty does not lie exclusively with the individual. Regardless of the cause of poverty, those in poverty have equal dignity with all others.

Appendix II: Catholic Social Virtues

I. **Solidarity:** In *Sollicitudo Rei Socialis,* John Paul II explains that all economic activities, including work, have an interdependent nature. He maintains that this interdependence should be formed by the virtue of solidarity, which is "a firm and preserving determination to commit oneself to the common good; that is to say, to the good of all and each individual, because we are all really responsible for all" (38). Solidarity does not represent a struggle as found in the divisiveness and hostility between labor and management, which has until recently characterized the labor/management relations in North America. Rather, solidarity reflects unity in struggle "for" justice, not "against" a particular group.

II. **Moderation:** In light of growing awareness of environmental degradation, depleting resources, and the plain obesity of the West, moderation is a necessary virtue for today. In *Centesimus annus,* John Paul II criticizes market economies for the increasing phenomenon of consumerism, which sees moderation as more of a vice than a virtue. If the production and consumption of goods and services are "the centre of social life and society's only value, not subject to any other value" (CA 39), then that particular society reveals a materialistic philosophy. This emphasis of consumer sovereignty abstracts people from their other social and economic roles by exaggerating the pleasure of consumption. If consumption is ordered without the good of society as well as the good of the person, consumption becomes indulgence. Such a vice becomes destructive of the physical and spiritual health of people.

III. **Entrepreneurial Virtues:** John Paul provides a list of what can be called entrepreneurial virtues: "diligence, industriousness, prudence in undertaking reasonable risks, reliability and fidelity in interpersonal relationships, as well as courage in carrying out decisions which are difficult and painful but necessary, both for the overall working of a business and in meeting possible set-backs" (CA 32).

IV. **Courage (Magnificence):** While witnessing massive world-wide unemployment at the time of writing *Quadragesimo anno,* Pius XI stresses the creation of employment opportunities that create products and services which contribute to the social good. He defines this as the virtue of magnificence or, more generally, courage. Products should not be produced solely for the purpose of fulfilling the wants of the market; rather, investments and products have a moral and even a spiritual character that provide people an opportunity for virtue.

V. **Charity:** Charity is what enables us to respond to God's universal call to holiness, which directs the human person to friendship with God. Charity is the form of all virtues, in that it directs our acts to the final end of human life. Charity is what unites the virtues. It is the virtue that enables us (doctors, factory workers, managers, farmers, etc.) to respond to God's call to work to build the kingdom, to be stewards of the earth, to collaborate, and have dominion over the land because we are made into God's image. Through the virtue of charity we become God's hands and God's co-workers.

Appendix II: Catholic Social Tradition
The Major Documents

Leo XIII (1878–1903)

Rerum novarum (The Condition of Labor) 1891

The encyclical came about as a reaction to the inhumane condition of the worker and the growing option of socialism. With the rise of the Industrial Revolution came a flight to cities where the factories were. With the market flooded with human resources, workers were paid poorly and treated poorly. The encyclical came as a response to the abuses of capitalism and also to the proposed solution of socialism.

Pius XI (1922–39)

Quadragesimo anno (On Reconstructing the Social Order) 1931

As Leo responded to the abuses of the industrial revolution, Pius responded to its apparent demise in the Great Depression. Similar to Leo, Pius was still very concerned about the conditions of the worker. However, Pius went further to challenge the structures of the economic order.

Pius XII (1939–58)

Summi pontificatus
(Function of the State in the Modern World) 1939

This document examines the moral foundation as the world prepares to enter its second war. He states that when "the divine is denied . . . an autonomy is claimed which rests only upon a utilitarian morality, there human law itself justly forfeits in its more weighty application the moral force which is the essential condition for its acknowledgement and also for its demand of sacrifices" (55).

John XXIII (1959–63)

Mater et Magistra (Mother and Teacher) 1961

John XXIII responded to the increasing complex and interdependent nature of social relations and social institutions. In the 1950s and 60s, this was brought about by progress in technology, the increasing role of government, and the furthering education of the worker. He responded to these historical circumstances by expanding the concept of human dignity into a wage principle of justice and equity and a production process principle of participation.

PACEM IN TERRIS (PEACE ON EARTH) 1963

Often considered the "rights" encyclical, John XXIII examines the problems of war, the arms race, state authority, political refugees, and international relationships.

The Vatican Council II (1962–65)

DIGNITATIS HUMANAE (ON RELIGIOUS LIBERTY) 1965

The bishops developed the teaching of recent popes on the inviolable rights of the human person and on the constitutional order of society.

GAUDIUM ET SPES (CHURCH IN THE MODERN WORLD) 1965

This was the only document that was addressed to the whole world and not just the Church. It took three years of dialogue, debate, and controversy to produce the document, which was published by the world bishops and their theologians. The social issues of the document are divided into three major sections: (1) family, (2) economics, and (3) politics. It is probably the most comprehensive document the Church has in the social realm. If one wanted to get a good idea of what the Church teaches on the social issues, this would be a good place to start.

Paul VI (1963–78)

POPULORUM PROGRESSIO (THE PROGRESS OF THE PEOPLES) 1967

Focused on the inequalities exiting in developing countries, this encyclical examines the importance of an integral human development and of a development in solidarity with all of humanity.

OCTOGESIMO ADVENIENS (APOSTOLIC LETTER ON THE EIGHTIETH ANNIVERSARY OF *RERUM NOVARUM*) 1971

This document, like *Populorum progressio,* is more international in scope. Paul spent much of his time on the macro dimensions of economics.

JUSTITIA IN MUNDO (JUSTICE IN THE WORLD) SYNOD OF BISHOPS (1971)

John Paul II (1978–present)

LABOREM EXERCENS (ON HUMAN WORK) 1981

Certainly the most systematic exposition on the nature of work by any pope. According to John Paul II, to understand work one must have a sound anthropology that originates from Genesis, that is, the person is the image of God, who is called to subdue, dominate, and till the earth. This doctrine from Genesis provides the meaning of work, namely that in work people remain true agents and that both the means of production and the fruit of labor are at the service of those who work (the person has a transcendent value). Because people are made in the image of God, every aspect of work is subject to each person's dignity.

SOLLICITUDO REI SOCIALIS (ON SOCIAL CONCERN) 1987

Celebrates the twentieth anniversary of *Populorum progressio* by revisiting the question of development. He argued that one major reason for lack of development in many countries was the Eastern (former Soviet Union) and Western (U.S.) blocs' manipulation of such countries.

CENTESIMUS ANNUS (ONE HUNDRED YEARS) 1991

Whereas *Laborem exercens* is systematic, *Centesimus annus* is historical. John Paul II discusses the fall of the Eastern bloc, explains the increasing importance of information regarding skills and technology, and encourages the entrepreneurial virtues necessary for a healthy economy. His evaluation of the market economy is positive overall; however, he is concerned over the increasing phenomenon of consumerism, which he believes is a partial cause to the various social problems, in particular environmental degradation.

U.S. Catholic Bishops Statements

THE CHALLENGE OF PEACE (1983)

The bishops examine the role of nuclear and conventional weaponry as part of the U.S. defense policy.

PROGRAM OF SOCIAL RECONSTRUCTION (1919) AND ECONOMIC JUSTICE FOR ALL (1986)

The U.S. bishops have attempted to apply the papal and conciliar teaching to the specific situation in the United States. They have also attempted to develop the tradition. Issues such as unemployment, poverty, plant closings, worker ownership, and participation are examined in both documents. When the bishops wrote their recent pastoral letters, controversy ensued as to the role of the bishops in the public discourse on these social issues.

Sharing Catholic Social Teaching: Challenges and Direction

This publication contains two documents—the bishops' reflection on the title and the *Summary Report of the Task Force on Catholic Social Teaching and Catholic Education.*

Bibliography

Burghardt, Walter. *Preaching the Just Word.* New Haven, Conn.: Yale University Press, 1996.

Calvez, Jean-Yves, and Jacques Perrin. *The Church and Social Justice: The Social Teachings of the Popes from Leo XIII to Pius XII.* Chicago: Henry Regnery Co., 1961.

Catechism of the Catholic Church. Washington, D.C.: United States Catholic Conference, 1994.

Charles, Rodger. *The Social Teachings of Vatican II: Its Origin and Development.* San Francisco: Ignatius Press, 1982.

Day, Dorothy. *The Long Loneliness: The Autobiography of Dorothy Day.* New York: Harper and Row, 1981.

Dorr, Donal. *Option for the Poor: A Hundred Years of Vatican Social Teaching.* Maryknoll, N.Y.: Orbis Books, 1983.

Dwyer, Judith, ed. *The New Dictionary of Catholic Social Thought.* Collegeville: The Liturgical Press, 1994.

Eliot, T. S. *Murder in the Cathedral.* San Diego: Hartcourt Brace Jovanovich, Inc., 1935.

Habiger, Matthew. *Papal Teaching on Private Property 1891–1991.* Lanham, Md.: University Press of America, 1990.

Hollenbach, David. *Claims In Conflict: Retrieving and Renewing the Catholic Human Rights Tradition.* New York: Paulist Press, 1979.

———. "The Common Good Revisited." *Theological Studies* 50 (1989).

John Paul II. "Encyclicals and Documents of John Paul II." December 14, 1996. <http://www.cin.org/jp2doc.html> (February 1, 1999).

Kammer, Fred. *Doing Faith Justice: An Introduction to Catholic Social Thought.* New York: Paulist Press, 1991.

McGinnis, Kathleen, and James McGinnis. *Parenting for Peace and Justice: 10 Year Later.* Maryknoll, N.Y.: Orbis Books, 1990.

Naughton, Michael. *The Good Stewards.* Lanham, Md.: University Press of America, 1992.

Nell-Breuning, Oswald von. *Reorganization of Social Economy.* Milwaukee: The Bruce Publishing Co., 1936.

O'Brien, David, and Thomas A. Shannon, eds. *Catholic Social Thought: The Documentary Heritage.* Maryknoll, N.Y.: Orbis Books, 1992.

Pius XII. *"Summi pontificatus."* October 20, 1939. <http://www. catholic.net/rcc/documents/> (February 1, 1999).

Ryan, John A. *Distributive Justice.* 3rd ed. New York: The Macmillan Company, 1942.

_____. *A Living Wage.* New York: The Macmillan Company, 1906.

Schuck, Michael. *That They Be One.* Washington, D.C.: Georgetown University Press, 1990.

Sharing Catholic Social Teaching: Challenges and Directions. Washington, D.C.: United States Catholic Conference, 1998.

For ideas on incorporating Catholic social thought within the curriculum see the following Website: www.stthomas.edu/cathstudies/cst.

Theological Virtues

CHRISTOPHER THOMPSON

Before Arriving at the Session

Read Focal Points and essay below.

Focal Points

Many Catholics have lost the language of virtues, especially the language of theological virtues. This tradition is an important one, for it helps us understand the progressive character of Christian growth and maturity. It is not an all-or-nothing affair. The language of virtues also helps us situate our lives within the broader context of the life of the Church and its sacraments—the principle means of growing in Christ.

This essay has three objectives: (1) to introduce the reader to the notion of the theological virtues, or qualities of character that are rooted specifically in our relationship with God; (2) to emphasize the importance of openness and reliance upon God as the mark of Christian maturity; and (3) to recognize that, in contrast to the contemporary notions of "adulthood," the Christian adult is one who comes to affirm his or her dependence on God's grace.

THEOLOGICAL VIRTUES

Have you ever heard yourself saying to your child or student, "It's time you start acting like an adult" or "It's time you learn to be responsible"? Usually, the remark is made in some moment of frustration and so does not necessarily reflect what we really wish to convey, but the episode can nonetheless tell what we think maturity involves. Take a moment to think about what you might mean when asking someone to act like an adult. Having done that, I encourage you to reflect on another question: What is happiness? In answer to this question, we might get still another range of responses, this time quite distinct from the first. Being happy involves "kicking back," "taking it easy," "being free from responsibility."

But notice the contrasting responses. If by "acting like an adult" we mean "acting responsibly," and by "happiness" we mean "being free," aren't we setting up a strange dichotomy between happiness and adulthood? Still worse, aren't we telling our children and students that to be an adult means that you cannot be happy? It's no wonder, then, that with these messages our students are reluctant to grow up, are reluctant to become mature Christian adults.

It is in this context that the tradition of the virtues, especially the theological virtues, can help us sort through the conflicting tension within our everyday remarks. In other words, the tradition of the theological virtues challenges the "cover stories" of maturity and happiness.

The cover stories tell us that to be an adult means to stand alone, to think alone, to be independent, to need no one—at least not in any essential sense, maybe for companionship but not for wholeness. Maturity consists in creating a citadel of the self, an edifice of qualities that suggests no need for further growth or completion. To admit one's neediness is to admit immaturity.

However, the theological virtues, especially the virtue of charity, tell us quite the opposite. Charity tells us to recognize our absolute dependence on the redeeming love of Christ, to set aside the self for the sake of God, to learn to lean on Christ as a companion and guide, to need God not simply for an interesting companion, but for our very livelihood. To dwell in charity, the tradition tells us, is to dwell in a relationship of eternal significance and depth. It is to rest in the sustaining love of God. Unless you become like a child, the gospel says, you cannot enter into the reality of God's kingdom.

It is for this reason that St. Thomas Aquinas calls charity the most important of the virtues. Without charity, without a living sense of our absolute dependence on the friendship of Christ to sustain us in every aspect of our lives, the rest of our virtues—our character—develop like a neglected child. In popular psychology and in the media we have heard much of "dysfunctional" homes and their effects on our character. We might apply that to the virtue of charity, then, and see that our failure to develop a companionship with Christ is to deny the place of charity as the "mother" of our happiness. Unlike human parents, though, the love of God never abandons the child, and it is in this context, too, that one understands the deeper significance of calling faith, hope, and charity "theological" virtues.

They are theological virtues because they have their origin in the initiative of God. Unlike the "cardinal" or natural virtues in which personal temperaments play such important roles—your challenge to be courageous is probably not identical to mine—the theological virtues come to all of us through God's initiative. It is not my "personality" that makes charity a sign of myself, but God's love in action for me. Recall that for Christians, human fulfillment does not consist only in us pursuing goodness; rather, Christians struggle to attain a "good" who is also seeking us. How God embraces us in our lives is what the theological virtues are all about. Charity, as the mother of the virtues, is that divine companionship Christ wishes to enjoy with all of his disciples. Hope is our sustained trust in the reality of that friendship someday coming to a completion and faith is our recognition of the truth of Christ, his Church, and his sacraments. It is true that as virtues they are qualities of myself, my character; but as theological virtues they are sustained by Christ himself.

The entire life of virtue, Aquinas says, is fueled by the dynamism of love. For Aquinas love is a passion, that is, it is something that begins from the agency or action of another. To be passive is to allow another to affect us in important ways. For Aquinas, the passion of love means that we allow the good of the other to move us. Our love for God, our charity, is principally our ability to allow the reality of God's presence to move us profoundly, to affect us at the center of ourselves. In this sense, the passion of love allows the good to penetrate our lives. To grow in the virtue of charity, then, means that we grow in ways that allow Christ to become more and more the principal agent in our lives. We grow to the point where we say with St. Paul, "It is no longer I who live, but it is Christ who lives in me" (Gal 2:20).

Christian maturity, then, does not consist in building an impenetrable ego. It does not consist in making one's own will the still point at the center of one's universe. Christian maturity consists in growing in faith, hope, and charity. It consists in allowing Christ to become one's raison d'être. It is not to "think for one's self," but to "let the same mind be in you that was in Christ Jesus" (Phil 2:5). Finally, it does not mean that one perfects a kind of sustained frown, a look of constant concern and worry; rather, to grow in God is to fall in love with the person of Jesus Christ. And to fall in love with the person of Jesus means we bear the sign of the Christian saint: joy.

But here too the cover story can distort the truth of authentic happiness. Many think that happiness consists in doing only what I want, when I want. Christian joy is deeper, however, and is rooted not in the citadel of the self, but in the kingdom of God. Authentic happiness is the effect of a life lived in virtue, of a life lived in conformity to our true and authentic good, in the truth of God. Here the cover story's portrait of maturity cuts to the quick of Christian growth. The cover story says that to work toward a deeper sense of dependence is to work toward weakness, that maturity consists in needing no one. And so instead of relying on the grace of God, we rely on our own fallen schemes, we rely on our capacities to "go it alone," to be independent.

Moreover, genuine virtue takes effort since we are not always inclined—due to sin—to think along virtuous lines. To fall in love with the person of Christ is our supreme beatitude to be sure, but it is not always our initial inclination. Sin, in other words, means that the path to joy involves work, effort, patience, and suffering. And it is in this long journey to happiness that the process of authentic maturity takes place. We grow along the way, sometimes painfully and with halting steps, toward further reliance on the reality of our friendship in Christ.

The portrait of discipleship often affirms this painful process of our fulfillment in God. When the cock crowed, St. Peter recognized the essential relationship between his happiness and the cross. At that moment he saw what Christ had seen earlier, that to be a companion of Jesus means more than feelings of satisfaction and contentment; rather, to be a friend of Jesus in triumph means to be a friend of Jesus on the cross. St. Paul was thrown to the ground and blinded when he came to see that the God whom he fiercely loved and Jesus crucified are one and the same (Acts 9:4-8). For Augustine, it came to the point of a nervous breakdown in a little garden in Milan before he saw wherein his happiness lay. Because of the reality of sin, in other words, suffering has always been the forge in which Christian joy is tested and purified (Augustine, book 8).

We might allow the tradition of the theological virtues to recast our conceptions of happiness and maturity. Through the tradition of the virtues one learns of the conditions of our authentic happiness and at the same time jettisons the self-centered bifurcation with Christian growth and maturity. To become an adult in Christ is not to become independent, but to become confirmed in one's faith, hope, and friendship with God. In this context then we can encourage our children to act like adults, that is, to act like children of God.

At the Session

Review Focal Points; view video "Theological and Cardinal Virtues" on Videocassette 5 (26 minutes).

After the Video

1. "As we grow in Christian virtue, we learn to be moved by God, to become dependent on God, to allow God to be the principle agent in our lives." To what extent have I allowed the culture to determine what being an adult means?
2. What does it mean to be a mature person? When I expect others to "grow up," do I expect them to grow in faith, hope, and charity?

Further Discussion and Reflection

1. In my own life, to what extent do I exhibit a life of dependence and need? How do I, in my daily life, show others that I am one who needs the friendship of Jesus?
2. To what extent do I characterize myself as having to carry many burdens alone? To what extent do I tell others, directly or otherwise, that I alone am in charge?

BIBLIOGRAPHY

Augustine. *The Confessions of St. Augustine.* Trans. John K. Ryan. New York: Doubleday, 1960.

Catechism of the Catholic Church. Part Three: §1, ch. 1, art. 7; §2, ch. 1, art. 1. Washington, D.C.: United States Catholic Conference, 1994.

Cessario, Romanus. *The Moral Virtues and Theological Ethics.* Notre Dame, Ind.: University of Notre Dame Press, 1991.

Wadell, Paul. *The Primacy of Love: An Introduction to the Ethics of Thomas Aquinas.* New York: Paulist Press, 1992.

Integrating Work and Leisure

MICHAEL NAUGHTON

Before Arriving at the Session

Read Focal Points and the essay below.

Focal Points

Participants will reflect on the importance of a unified life. Work and leisure are "not two periods of time in human life, but moments in a person's self-realization which exist only in relation with another and are the primary constituents of human existence itself" (Rahner, 379).

We will examine the secular notions of work and leisure and the cover stories they propose, along with the Church's rich social tradition on the meaning of work and leisure.

INTEGRATING WORK AND LEISURE

A traveler asked three bricklayers what they were doing. The first said simply, "I am laying bricks." The second responded, "I am feeding my family by laying bricks." The third responded, "Through my work of laying bricks I am constructing a cathedral, and thereby giving honor and praise to the Lord." Implied in the traveler's question "What are you doing?" is not only "What act are you doing?" but also "What are you working for?" What is the purpose or end to your work?

But to answer this question "What are you working for?" we must also ask the question "What do you rest or leisure in?" Initially, these two questions may seem unrelated, since we may think that work and leisure represent two periods of time unrelated in human life. Yet, if we see our leisure or rest as St. Augustine does (who states "because you have made us for yourself, our hearts are restless until they rest in you, O God"), then our leisure and rest is that moment where we begin to see our work in a new light. Within the Catholic tradition, work and leisure are "moments in a person's self-realization which exist only in their relation with one another and are the primary constituents of human existence itself" (Rahner, 379). The notion that work and leisure have little to do with each other for certain people may be true, but it is true in a life that represents conflict and disunity (the Catholic in the Mafia or the pacifist in the defense industry). Within the Catholic social tradition, self-realization is a unified life of work and leisure, of activity and contemplation.

At the Second Vatican Council, the bishops were very concerned about a disunity among the laity between what they rested in and what they worked for:

> The split between the faith which many profess and their daily lives deserves to be counted among the more serious errors of our age. . . . Let there be no false opposition between professional and social activities on the one hand, and religious life on the other. The Christian who neglects his temporal duties, neglects his duties toward his neighbor and even God, and jeopardizes his eternal salvation (GS 43).

This essay is about two words: work and leisure. As Christian educators, we are constantly tempted by both internal and external pressures, "to cover up" the profound theological meanings of these words by restricting them to material or psychological interpretations. Yet, within the Catholic social tradition, we have a rich vision that can help us as well as our students to achieve self-realization based on Christian principles. In this essay I contrast a careerist and Catholic view of work and leisure, and explore how we as Catholic educators can better practice our Christian vocation.

Career

When I ask my students what they want most out of their work they usually say personal satisfaction. They see work as a psychological value to enhance their self-esteem. With the higher levels of education and skills among people, work is increasingly becoming valued in psychological terms such as creativity, autonomy, and fulfillment. People who perceive work as a career expect more out of their work than those who perceive work just in terms of money. Their career becomes an important means to their personal identity.

The careerist's primary emphasis on personal preference and satisfaction, however, suffers from an individualism that lacks any sense of social responsibility. What resounds for the careerist is Cain's rhetorical question, "Am I my brother's keeper?" (Gen 4:9). This can be seen in the very word "career" which has the same root as "car." They both refer to movement, and increasingly a private way of movement. Our "auto-mobile" or self-driven car lets us travel alone. Even though the car drives us out into society, it does so with a "glass-enwrapped privacy" (May, 31) that shields us from traveling with others. In similar terms, careerists calculate their travels not in public but in private terms. Like the privacy of a car, the careerist is interested in what means, in terms of education, contacts, money, skill, power, etc., are necessary to get from here to there. While such means are within the law, they have little connection to the common good. William F. May explains that "questions of public obligation and responsibility seem marginal and episodic at best, distracting and suicidal at worst. The careerist travels by public thoroughfares and largely obeys the rules of the road, but toward his or her own private destination" (May, 31).

The careerist tends to see work as the main source of personal meaning and self-esteem. When this happens, leisure often becomes understood as a "regenerative function." This can be seen for two reasons.

The first reason is internal intentions. For those who see work as the fundamental locus of meaning and self-esteem, leisure is not only a break from work. Leisure time is also used for rest so one can be more productive when returning to work. Leisure serves as a tension release; however, it is not done for its own sake. Whether a coffee break, Sunday worship, or time with the family, leisure is viewed as a means of renewal to be more efficient at work, not as an end in and of itself. Leisure is a means to make better workers for a more productive, efficient, and profitable enterprise. It is merely another productive function. For careerists, the dictum is not "we work to live," rather, "we live to work."

The second reason leisure becomes understood as a regenerative function is external pressures. Careerism has also been foisted upon people. For people to succeed in organizations there is great pressure to work long hours at an intense pace. Leisure is either literally squeezed out or people are so tired that all they can or wish to do is to rest up for the next day through extra sleep or television watching. The only nation that works more than the United States, Japan, is the only nation to watch more TV than the United States.

The presence of careerism and its regenerative notion of leisure have had a significant effect on education in the United States. Joseph Pieper points out that the Greek word for leisure is *skole*, the English word for school. For the ancient Greeks, leisure was a time not to flee reality, but rather to penetrate its meaning. By looking at art, science, math, history, philosophy, literature, theology, etc., one could glimpse the mystery of creation. For the careerist, however, school is relegated to the technique of so-called successful living. Rather than a form of leisure in which the mind rests in the contemplation of creation, school takes the form of techniques where knowledge is power to provide personal satisfaction, success, markets, and income. Careerist students come to see themselves as masters and owners of creation. Their education has instilled a view of the world as raw material on which to act simply for their own personal purposes. Careerists have difficulty in seeing the goodness of creation, in seeing the world as a created order that one participates in and has reverence for. They are so busy that they cannot stop to receive anything beyond their own initial preferences.

This is rather a harsh indictment of the careerist; yet, it is not meant to deny the place of professional assistance to students seeking work opportunities, nor is it to deny the importance of psychological growth in the workplace. Rather, the point, as John Paul II states, is that once self-actualization becomes detached from God's created order, the person is more likely to enter into a "self-love which leads to an unbridled affirmation of self-interest and which refuses to be limited by any demand of justice" (CA 17). Work and leisure should not be understood primarily in terms of personal preference and inter-pretation, but primarily in terms of a created and redeemed reality.

Vocation

In contrast to a career, the question for a vocation is not simply "Who am I?" but "Whose am I?" A vocation is a friendship with God for other people. God calls all workers—retired workers, those who work in the home, teachers, doctors, factory workers, managers, lawyers, farmers, etc.—to work to build the kingdom, to be stewards of the earth, to collaborate, and to have dominion over the land. The reason we are called to such nobility is because we are made in God's image. One way we image God is in God's activity: God creates and God rests. It is precisely in creating and resting like God that we live our Christian vocation.

God creates and we are asked to collaborate in this creation. We are asked to collaborate because creation is not finished; creation is not a one-time event. It is a continuing process, sustained through God's power and love, in cooperation with people. John Paul II explains that work can actually place the person in a relation with his/her ultimate destiny, "becoming an ally with the living God" (LE 5). We can image God's creative activity not by becoming our own creators, but by participating and collaborating with God. In our work we should see ourselves as partners with God. Just as we collaborate with God and continue God's creation through the procreation of children, our work should be seen as a collaboration with God to build organizations in which all employees can develop their human potential and develop goods and services that serve human society. At the end of the day, we should be able to reflect as God did: "God looked at everything he had made, and he found it very good" (Gen 1:31)—good not just in a technically correct sense, as stressed in the quality movement, but morally good.

A vocation calls attention to our contribution to serve the needs of the larger community. Our work is not only a private or psychological affair (career). Our work must be directed toward the common good in which the fulfillment of our work is intrinsically connected to the fulfillment of the community. In relationship to work, the Catholic social tradition defines the common good as creating those organizational conditions that foster human development. All organizations, whether educational, medical, government, business, and so forth, have an important part in creating those conditions that favor human development. Organizations share the moral call to serve others and contribute to the good of society. They are an indispensable factor in placing people at the service of the natural law, that is, in the development of the human personality, supporting the family, and achieving the common good through what it produces. It is in this community of work where virtue is practiced and the common good is attained. Consequently, our vocation is not only an individual vocation, but an organizational one as well.

However, our collaboration with God runs the danger of becoming a form of idolatry, if work becomes our only activity with God. We lose perspective when work is performed in a life without rest or leisure, even when it is supposedly done for God. Work must pattern God's activity. This pattern is an alternative one between work and leisure. The pattern itself is learned and given in leisure (the creation story in Genesis). Leisure, in part, provides reflection and grace on the question "What we are working for?" And work provides a manifestation of what is given in leisure.

God not only creates, but God rests. At the end of each day God looks back on God's work and sees that it is good. This form of rest expresses a celebration that what has been made has order and is fundamentally good. This goodness and order is a precondition to celebration and consequently a precondition to rest. For who would celebrate and find rest in a world that is disordered, chaotic, and meaningless? Pieper explains that "those who do not consider reality as fundamentally 'good' and 'in the right order' are not able to truly celebrate, any more than they are able to 'achieve leisure'" (Pieper, 141, 142). That is why the deepest form of leisure is the celebration and worship of God, the Creator of all that is good. It is the deepest form of leisure because it is the deepest form of affirming the goodness of creation.

Precisely in affirming God's creation as good, the person is able to participate in God's ongoing work of creation. The goodness of work is affirmed on the basis of God's created order, not on the basis of one's individual preference. For example, the careerist has nothing in his or her vocabulary to call work good. It may be productive, efficient, profitable, and even personally satisfying, but the criteria of work is either a calculation or at best provides a sense of personal satisfaction. For the careerist, entering the vocabulary of goodness becomes a form of oppression of imposing one's good upon another. In a vocation, goodness is based on the created order revealed by a personal God. Leisure in its Christian meaning places work in a created context that uncovers the moral and spiritual meaning to work. Work within the Christian tradition does not have an independent meaning, but is incarnated with meaning that is received from "divine rest."

In the Judeo-Christian tradition, to leisure is to rest, to rest is to worship, and to worship is to affirm that which is most worthy. The Hebrew word for "sabbath" comes from the verb "to rest," and "worship" and "worth" have the same etymological root. In order to have leisure, one must rest in that which the person believes is of most worth. Rest is not simply idleness from work, but rest in God, who gives rest. It is a rest to hear God's word, to receive God's sacrament, and to be informed by God's grace. Work is not enough in the realization of a person's vocation. Within the very system of a Judeo-Christian notion of work there resounds the statement:

> Thus the heavens and the earth were finished, and all their multitude. And on the seventh day God finished the work that he had done, and he rested on the seventh day from all the work that he had done. So God blessed the seventh day and hallowed it, because on it God rested from all the work that he had done in creation (Gen 2:1-3).

Conclusion: The Vocation of Catholic Educators

What are the implications of the Christian vocation for the Catholic educator? I would like to raise four possible areas that we can think about: yourself, students, faculty and administration, and Catholic identity. I conclude here with some brief comments and questions on each of these four areas.

YOURSELF

How do you perceive your work as an educator (career, vocation, other)? Are there beliefs and/or practices that are preventing you from fulfilling a vocation?

STUDENTS

Do we practice the virtue of hope? Do we show that we have hope for them, a hope that is divinely inspired? Are we on guard from the vices of apathy and despair? Do we see our teaching in terms of virtue? Are the virtues of diligence (being prepared, professionally updated, reading in your area, etc.), prudence (learning how to educate and deal with diverse students; knowing when to discipline and to knowing when to listen), and courage (to confront problems and attitudes when they will be unpopular) present in our relationship with our students?

COLLEAGUES AND ADMINISTRATORS

Do you share among all the employees at your school or parish a "community of work"? Do you share a vision of your work that promotes the common good? What can we do to make our school and parish a true community of work? What is your teachers' lounge like? Is decision making at your school or parish organized on the principle of subsidiarity? Is faculty participation valued?

CATHOLIC IDENTITY AND MISSION

The mission of a Catholic educational institution is religious at its core, and its core must pervade the whole institution. Do we help our students in their moral formation based on the Christian Scriptures and tradition? One colleague told me that her students were afraid to take a stand since they were unable to determine right and wrong. This moral indetermination, she felt, came from an educational training in elementary and secondary schools which stressed that life was somehow neutral and non-committal—no one is wrong and no one is right. The students, she felt, became distrustful of themselves since they became paralyzed by a belief that they are unable to take a position besides the one which takes no position. A valedictorian from Harvard expressed this point in her graduation speech:

> Among my classmates, I believe there is one idea, one senti-
> ment, which we have all acquired at some point in our Harvard
> careers; and that, ladies and gentlemen, is, in a word, confu-
> sion. . . . They tell us it is a heresy to suggest the superiority
> of some value, fantasy to believe in moral argument, slavery to
> submit to a judgment sounder than your own. The freedom of
> our day is the freedom to devote ourselves to any values we
> please, on the mere condition that we do not believe them to be
> true.

Although difficult, we must provide a vision, proclaim truth, issue challenges, make judgments, and not let freedom be defined in terms of personal preference. Fortunately, we are not asked to do these things by ourselves. We cannot do it alone. God's grace is fundamental, which is why the basis of our work must be the leisure expressed in our worship of God.

> Come to me, all you that are weary and are carrying heavy
> burdens, and I will give you rest. Take my yoke upon you, and
> learn from me; for I am gentle and humble in heart, and you
> will find rest for your souls. For my yoke is easy, and my
> burden is light (Matt 11:28-30).

At the Session

Review Focal Points; view video "Work and Leisure" on Videocassette 5 (26 minutes).

Discussion

A Story to Ponder:

A traveler asked three bricklayers what they were doing. The first said simply, "I am laying bricks." The second responded, "I am feeding my family by laying bricks." The third responded, "Through my work of laying bricks I am constructing a cathedral, and thereby giving honor and praise to the Lord."

1. Do you see your work primarily as a job, career, vocation, or other?

2. What obstacles do you face at work that prevent you from seeing your work as a vocation?

3. What forms of leisure do you practice? What forms of leisure take most of your time?

4. Does your leisure help or hinder your work as a vocation?

Further Discussion and Reflection

1. While some people work to rest, and others rest to work, why is it so critical in the Christian tradition to ask the questions, "What do we work for?" and "What do we rest in?"

2. How is it that "recreation" needs to indicate a re-creation of ourselves and not a de-creation or distraction of ourselves?

3. How can Christians make moral decisions in the realm of their work that are congruent with their belief system and that nurture their spiritual lives?

BIBLIOGRAPHY

Bellah, Robert, et al. *Habits of the Heart.* New York: Harper and Row, 1985.

Catechism of the Catholic Church. Part Three: §2, ch. 1, art. 3; §2, ch. 2, art. 7. Washington, D.C.: United States Catholic Conference, 1994.

Haughey, John C. *Converting 9 to 5: A Spirituality of Daily Work.* New York: Crossroad Publishing Company, 1989.

_____. *The Holy Use of Money.* Garden City, N.Y.: Doubleday & Company, 1986.

John Paul II. *Laborem Exercens* (1981). *Proclaiming Justice and Peace: Papal Documents from* Rerum novarum *through* Centesimus annus. Ed. Michael Walsh and Brian Davies, 271–311. Mystic, Conn.: Twenty-Third Publications, 1984.

Kammer, Fred. *Doing Faithjustice: An Introduction to Catholic Social Thought.* Mahwah, N.J.: Paulist Press, 1991.

May, William F. "The Beleaguered Rulers." *The Public Obligation of the Professional.* Kennedy Institute of Ethics Journal 2 (1992) 25–41.

McGinnis, Kathleen, and James McGinnis. *Parenting for Peace and Justice: 10 Years Later.* Maryknoll, N.Y.: Orbis Books, 1990.

Michel, Virgil. *Christian Social Reconstruction.* Milwaukee: Bruce Publishing, 1937.

National Conference of Catholic Bishops. *Economic Justice For All: Pastoral Letter on Catholic Social Teaching and the U.S. Economy.* Washington, D.C.: United States Catholic Conference, 1986.

Naughton, Michael. *The Good Stewards: Practical Applications of the Papal Social Vision of Work.* Lanham, Md.: University Press of America, 1992.

Pieper, Josef. *An Anthology.* San Francisco: Ignatius Press, 1989.

_____. *Leisure: The Basis of Culture.* New York: A Mentor Book, 1952.

Ratzinger, Joseph Cardinal. "Market Economy and Ethics." Ordo Socialis: *Making Christianity Work in Business and Economy.* Ed. Association for the

Advancement of Christian Social Sciences, 62–7. Philippines: Divine Word Publications, 1992.

Schor, Juliet B. *The Overworked American.* New York: Basic Books, 1992.

Schumacher, E. F. *Good Work.* New York: Harper and Row, 1979.

Wuthnow, Robert. *God and Mammon in America.* New York: The Free Press, 1994.

For information about Catholic social teaching and Catholic education on the Internet see: http://www.stthomas.edu/cathstudies/cst/educ/

CHAPTER EIGHT

FULFILLING THE KINGDOM

Mary

ARTHUR KENNEDY

Before Arriving at the Session

Read Focal Points and the essay below.

Focal Points

In Mary the Christian sees a life of mystery. The reader is invited to reflect on Mary's specific role in the mystery of redemption. We are invited to play a part in this mystery.

I Acclaim the Greatness of the Lord

In the Catholic tradition and many other Christian churches, Mary has an essential place in the mystery of our redemption revealed and effected through the birth, death, and resurrection of Jesus Christ. Mary has a unique place in each of these central actions that affect both our personal lives and the whole Church. Christians have constantly honored Mary for the unique graces that informed her life. Through these graces she was open to God's complete will to manifest in human flesh and human nature the mystery of the divine love as the response to our suffering and our nature wounded by the fall of Adam and Eve.

We honor Mary as one who united the fullness of God's grace and the perfect reception of that grace. Because of God's grace and Mary's fidelity, she enjoys a primary place among all the saints. She is the one in whom the unity of grace, the action of human liberty, and physical life are so proper that she is given the mysterious vocation of being the Virgin Mother of Jesus Christ.

The four Gospels focus on her life as the unique person through whom the Word, Jesus Christ, the second person of the Holy Trinity, has taken human flesh and heals our fallen human nature. It is Mary who receives and accepts the grace of God to begin the opening of our nature to this divine healing.

The Gospels speak about the unique place of Mary in the life of Christ. It is particularly in Matthew and Luke that Mary is identified as one in whom the action of God is extraordinary. Matthew places Mary in the genealogy of the birth of the Messiah; Luke focuses on the annunciation, with Mary's hymn of praise, the Magnificat (1:46-55), and Zechariah's response with his Benedictus, blessing, and his interpretation of the relationship between John the Baptist and Christ, who is a mighty Savior.

Thus in different ways the Gospels speak of Mary's life as connected with the life and ministry of her son. Of primary importance is the testimony of Matthew and Luke that speaks of Mary as both mother and virgin. The same testimony is also indirectly present in Mark, who refers to Jesus as "Son of God" (Mark 1:1) and "son of Mary" (Mark 6:3). In no place in Scripture is Christ called "son of Joseph."

The Gospel of John focuses primarily on the divine origin of Christ as the Word *(logos)* spoken by the Father before all creation. In this Gospel, Mary has a special place among all those who believe that her son is the Messiah; both her unique stature and her complete sharing in human nature are seen in the account of the wedding feast at Cana. Again these same dimensions are affirmed at the crucifixion where Jesus places her in the care of "the beloved disciple" (John 19:26).

The epistles of Paul do not speak of the person, Mary, but of her grace-filled role in the mystery of God's taking on human flesh, nature, and life. In the epistle to the Galatians (4:4-5) Paul speaks of how in time, "God sent his Son, born of a woman, born under the law, in order to redeem those who were under the law, so that we might receive adoption as children."

Most important in the Scripture, and in the whole of the tradition, are the affirmations of Mary's unique life of grace and faith. It is for these actions of God in her life and of her graced response and cooperation in the divine plan that love, grace, and liberty are available to those who follow her son. We honor her as first among the saints. Because we acknowledge her as a recipient of God's unique gift of her vocation and her role in history, we seek to learn from her remarkable faith. We learn from her humility as she points away from herself to focus on God acting in and through her.

We learn from her suffering as she allows it to be transformed by her faith, trust, and love. We learn from Mary about the mystery and holiness of the Jewish people. She, the flower of the Jewish people, is ever a reminder to Christians of God's action in the people of Israel. Both men and women learn respect for flesh and grace as they imitate Mary's cooperation with God's action in her life.

Mary's place in salvation is celebrated throughout the year in a variety of liturgical feasts and devotions. These feasts are ancient in their origins and they have had a central role in the formulation of the Church's doctrines about Mary, especially the feasts of the Immaculate Conception and the Assumption.

The Rosary, as prayed by Roman Catholics, is addressed to Christ through the intercession of Our Lady. The Hail Mary originated in the Church in the middle of the sixth century; then in the Middle Ages it was repeated 150 times by many who could not or did not have time to read every day the 150 psalms. The entire rosary was prayed with a focus on how God's historical action and grace unfolded in Mary's life. This prayer is especially connected to the teaching and preaching of both the Dominicans and the Franciscans.

The importance of Mary in Christian imagination can be found in the litanies that were created to honor her. The earliest were written in the seventh century; the most well known is the Litany of Loreto, which was first published by Peter Canisius in 1587. The litany has had many additions over the centuries and now contains forty-nine metaphors for Mary. There is also the artistic tradition of the images of the Madonna in every age and culture, painted and sculpted in materials of all types.

The significance of Mary's place in the Church was an important part of the theological discussion at Vatican II. In the constitution, chapter 8 of *Lumen gentium* is titled "On the Blessed Virgin Mary in the Mystery of Christ and the Church." It recalls the ancient teachings about Mary and her place in the Church.

The place of Mary in the Church has been a source of division between the Catholic and Protestant communities. Unfortunately, during the Reformation, the Marian feasts and prayers were removed from the Protestant communities because of a particular focus on grace and the Bible. In the reformed catechisms she is mentioned only rarely; the Anglican tradition is an exception. At the present time ecumenical dialogues have affirmed the unique place of Mary in Christian faith and the Church.

At the Session

Review Focal Points; view video "Mary" on Videocassette 6 (9 minutes).

After the Video

1. What is Mary's role in the mystery of redemption?
2. How can each person share in the mystery of redemption?

Further Reflection

1. How does Mary's life present the Christian dynamism of grace and freedom?
2. How does Mary's life teach us about virtue and ministry?

BIBLIOGRAPHY

See "Mary" in the index of the *Catechism of the Catholic Church.* Washington, D.C.: United States Catholic Conference, 1994.

Ecumenism

ARTHUR KENNEDY

Before Arriving at the Session

Read Focal Points and essay below.

Focal Points

Ecumenism is seen as a mission of the Church. We see particular facets of Christian unity and division. The unity of the Church is a gift of the Holy Spirit. Christian unity is an essential aspect of the mystery of the Church.

ECUMENISM

It is important today to consider, both practically and systematically, the situation of our ecumenical age. The Church's ecumenical mission has as its goal the unity of all Christians, and so of the Church itself. This unity is understood in Scripture and the developing tradition as the manifestation of the Church as the body of Christ as intended by Christ's own teaching about the Church in his prayer: "Holy Father, protect them in your name that you have given me, so that they may be one, as we are one" (John 17:11).

On May 30, 1995, Pope John Paul II signed an encyclical entitled *Ut unum sint* (That They May Be One), in which he reminds us that the quest for God's gift of unity is "an organic part of her [the Church's] life and work, and consequently must pervade all that she is and does" (para. 20). The letter reminds us of the practical dimensions of ecumenism, in that "believers in Christ . . . if they wish truly and effectively to oppose the world's tendency to reduce to powerlessness the mystery of redemption, they must profess together the same truth of the cross" (para. 1).

At the very beginning of his letter, Pope John Paul makes reference to modern ecumenical witness to the Christian reality. He states:

> The courageous witness of so many martyrs of our century, including members of churches and ecclesial communities not in full communion with the Catholic Church, gives new vigor to the [Vatican II] council's call [to unity] and reminds us of our duty to listen to it and put into practice its exhortation. These brothers and sisters of ours, united in the selfless offering of their lives for the kingdom of God, are the most powerful proof that every factor of division can be transcended and overcome in the total gift of self for the sake of the Gospel.

Practically then, ecumenism means that Catholics have a special bond with each other and have a responsibility to develop spiritual bonds with other Christians and churches. On one hand, ecumenism is an officially and institutionally developed conversation with all Christian church communities who share a common faith in God who, in the New Testament, reveals that the divine life is both a Unity and a Trinity of Persons. All Christians affirm that Jesus Christ is the second person of the Trinity, the Word made flesh, and the Savior of all. We commonly affirm that the Bible is the revelation of God, that it unveils the power of the Holy Spirit through whom "God's love has been poured into our hearts" (Rom 5:5), and that it affirms the fact that we are all incorporated into the Church through baptism. On the other hand, ecumenism is experienced by different members of the Church in different settings with different graces and with different responsibilities.

Some persons are engaged in detailed study of the theological documents, the histories, the debates, and conclusions with which the different divisions within the Church began. In some measure, these persons are concerned with examining how and why different claims about the Church were made and how further developments have been made within different churches over the past few centuries. Other persons are engaged in studying the Scriptures together, in praying together, and in commonly addressing the evils of our age through living their lives in common witness to the teachings of Christ and the Church. But, as the encyclical notes, in all situations "the commitment to ecumenism must be based upon the conversion of hearts and upon prayer, which will lead to the necessary purification of past memories" (para. 2).

A concern that needs to be addressed is how we act and interact with people from other Christian traditions. The sensitivity which this requires is paralleled with the need to be very clear about what Catholic teachings are so that we will be able to acquire an understanding of the common Christian teaching, as well as those differences which most likely are a part of daily experiences. In many large dioceses, policies have been established so that parents know ahead of time that the teachers will be instructing the children in Catholic faith, beliefs, and virtues, and where possible relating them to other Christians' traditions. Parents and teachers together need to address this issue.

Marks of the Church

First, then, it can be helpful for us to realize that the ecumenical dimension of the Church is related to what we call "the four marks or notes" of the Church, "one, holy, catholic, and apostolic." These notes, named in the ancient creeds, identify certain characteristics of the mystery of the Church's existence as it is constituted by God and by men and women in time. While ecumenism seeks primarily to address certain aspects of the mark of unity, it is also concerned about the full expression of the whole Church in living out the call to holiness in manifesting its catholic, or universal, promise of redemption, and in its clear apostolic testimony, or teaching all that Christ has taught us. The Church in its members is called to show the mystery of Christ to the world! The Church is provided with the graces to live out this calling, which opens God's presence in human history and offers the divine response to sin, evil, and death.

Having an Ecumenical Sense

It should be clear at the start that no one can be expected to know all the different Christian beliefs, or the expressions of those beliefs, which are at the heart of each Christian community. One of the hopes related to ecumenism is that a shared Christian faith will continue to unfold, through the help of the Holy Spirit and the traditions of the churches, in a common understanding of central beliefs.

One of the central roles of religion teachers is to communicate the beliefs of that tradition. It is important not to confuse children about what those beliefs are, because the beliefs are passing on a reality about the divine mystery, which includes these children in an eternal redemption. It is only through Catholic teachings that one can help students understand the other Christian traditions. Teachers can also aid students in learning to pray together and to recognize what is truly common among Christians.

Fundamentalist Tradition

In order to develop one's own ecumenical awareness and to recognize some practical differences among students from different traditions, it is helpful to understand some of the theological and historical differences between Catholic, Orthodox, and Reformed Christians. These differences may often manifest themselves more deeply if students of the different traditions have also been trained, at home, in faith that is more in the fundamentalist tradition. In such a situation, they are being trained at home to read and listen to the Bible differently than the Catholic tradition does, and they may bring that to the attention of their teacher and the other students. Teachers should be prepared to help their students understand the differences in understanding the Bible and, for Catholics, how the Church is the guiding interpreter.

The Protestant Tradition

One of the differences among Christian traditions is that between faith and human knowledge. Such a difference will have considerable implications in a Christian school that is concerned with providing full intelligent explanations of human experience and history—as is any public school—but which also is concerned with helping students relate that secular knowledge to the knowledge they learn about God and the Church. There is a difference then in how Catholic Christians and some Reformed Christians understand the relationship of faith and knowledge. In a practical sense this can mean that faith and biblical teachings may not be as fully related to the study of secular knowledge in some of the reformed traditions.

This difference arises as a result of the efforts of the Protestant reformations to heighten the role and importance of faith in Christian life, to give different weight to the effects which follow from the Fall, and to focus on the absolutely unique redemption of Christ as one's personal savior. Correlative to this, there can be different understandings of the books of the Bible, of the place of the Bible in the Church, different understandings of the number and meaning of the sacraments, and a different vision of the relationship of human effort, or works, and divine grace.

While there are different expressions of these elements in different reformed communities, it is most often understood, named, and identified as in the Lutheran tradition: "The Protestant Principle: Faith, Grace and Scripture Alone."

The Catholic Tradition

In the Catholic tradition, there is affirmed a fuller integration of faith with knowledge, grace with works, and Scripture with unfolding traditions. In relationship to the Protestant principle, Catholic life is underpinned by sacraments. The sacraments are institutional mediations of God's grace through the Church. Thus there is the important role of the Church, in all of its aspects, as vessel of the mystery of divine redemption. Each of the sacraments effects God's grace in us and prepares children to recognize their vocations for carrying God's mystery in their tasks in the world.

Faith and Formation in Our Catholic Institutions

It is important for Catholic students to know the faith and piety of other children and to respect that faith. It is important for them to be able to understand and to explain Catholic belief to their friends from other Christian traditions and from other religions.

Because teachers also participate in planning prayer and sacramental practice, there should be sensitivity to ecumenism in school prayer. As Pope John Paul II notes in his encyclical:

> "Ecumenical" prayer, as the prayer of brothers and sisters, who because they are separated from one another . . . meet in Christ, with all the more hope, entrusting to him the future of their unity and their communion. . . . The change of heart which is the essential condition for every authentic search for unity flows from prayer and its realization is guided by prayer. In the deep personal dialogue which each of us must carry on with the Lord in prayer, concern for unity cannot be absent (*Ut Unum Sint*, 26, 27).

Children of other Christian traditions should be invited to participate in the prayer of the school as much as is possible and as they feel comfortable. Such prayer should include hope for the day when all Christians will be able to share a common eucharistic union.

So it is that teachers of religion have a very important role in promoting the ecumenical mission of the Church.

They will not only have a place in education and prayer but also in practical cooperation, witnessing by Christian responses to the needs of the local communities and to the development of solidarity in addressing the important issues of "freedom, justice, peace and the future of the world" (para. 43).

At the Session

Review Focal Points; view video "Ecumenism" on Videocassette 6 (7 minutes).

After the Video

1. Why is Christian unity important for the full mission of the Church?
2. In what way does it require a spiritual conversion?

Further Reflection

1. How is ecumenism much more than a toleration of other Christians?
2. Why is it important that ecumenism does not merely cover up our differences as Christians?

Information, Formation, Transformation

MARY DANIEL HARTNETT, C.S.J.

Before Arriving at the Session

Read Focal Points and the essay below.

Focal Points

In this essay we will explore ways in which we can assist young people in developing a closer relationship with God. Through the gift of faith and through a process called information, formation, and transformation, we will attempt to focus on the importance of presenting religious truths in a way that will enable those we teach to accept the beliefs and eventually inculcate them into their daily lives.

INFORMATION, FORMATION, TRANSFORMATION

"For many young people, a critical look at the world they are living in leads to crucial questions on the religious plane. They ask whether religion can provide any answers to the pressing problems afflicting humanity. Large numbers of them sincerely want to know how to deepen their faith and live a meaningful life" (*Religious Dimension,* 10).

We must know before we can believe and then our knowledge and belief can lead us to deeper understandings. We need to build on what our young people know, expand that knowledge on the appropriate level, and help them translate it into their lives. When this building is accomplished in a meaningful way, using stories and examples to which students can relate, we are accompanying them on their faith journey as they struggle to understand and appreciate the power of Jesus and the need for him in their lives. This process involves three steps.

First, information provides us with the basic knowledge and facts on which to build and develop deeper insights. It also provides us with the necessary skills and the ability to translate that knowledge into one's capacity to understand, always realizing that understandings grow gradually. Reinforcing the concept of always teaching from the known to the unknown, we strive to present a new idea or concept by seeing it in relation to something we already know and understand.

Second, formation is an inner development. It is the ability and willingness to share religious concepts with those we encounter in our teaching. Our goal is that the religious concepts we are discussing in our classroom will begin to take root in the students' behavior. This often happens because we have shared with them our own values such as the importance of Sunday liturgy, the Eucharist, and a commitment to personal prayer and meditation on the stories of Jesus found in sacred Scripture. In doing this, we make an effort to open students to new religious knowledge and experiences in which the incidents in the life of Jesus grow in their own importance. As students open their minds and hearts to Christ, they begin to desire to live as he did. "Let each of you look not to your own interests, but to the interests of others. Let the same mind be in you that was in Christ Jesus" (Phil 2:4-5). The life-long process of formation has begun.

Third and finally, transformation is the personal response to the gifts we have received through information and formation. This step occurs when the person chooses to make the gospel message of Jesus his or her own. Transformation happens when God and the individual enter into a deep spiritual relationship; it is our own personal encounter with Christ.

As educators, we try to impart the information we teach in a careful and relational way. We may often see slight movements of formation within students. We may sometimes even see that they accept and integrate into their lives the religious truths and the gospel message we have shared. The transformation process is a deeply personal commitment between God and the student and is seldom ever known to us. But it does happen.

At the Session

Review focal points; view video "Information, Formation, Transformation" on Videocassette 6 (29 minutes).

Discussion

1. How are information, formation, and transformation related?

2. In our personal lives, can we name instances when we have been transformed?

Further Discussion and Reflection

1. Which part of information, formation, and transformation do I accent the most?

2. Which part do I neglect the most?

3. How do I, or can I, make God present in the world?

BIBLIOGRAPHY

Catechism of the Catholic Church. Part Four: §1, ch. 2, art. 3. Washington, D.C.: United States Catholic Conference, 1994.

The Religious Dimension of Education in a Catholic School. The Congregation for Catholic Education: Rome, 1988.

Eyes of Faith

MARY DANIEL HARTNETT, C.S.J.

Before Arriving at the Session

Read Focal Points and the essay below.

Focal Points

We will be introduced to new terms which will help us understand the relationship between spiritual and intellectual learning, and the learning that leads us to a further deepening of our understanding of God and to a stronger spiritual commitment.

We will discover a new way of looking at "blindness" and "seeing."

EYES OF FAITH

St. Bonaventure gives us a model for the way in which a person gains knowledge. He tells us that we have three sets of eyes: the eye of the flesh, the eye of the mind, and the eye of contemplation. St. Augustine names the eye of contemplation the eye of the soul, and John Shea, a noted author, often refers to the eye of the soul in his writings. The first two enable us to see and learn more about life, humanly and intellectually. The eye of the soul goes beyond this; it enables us to see transcendental realities and it helps us to see as Jesus sees. It facilitates the ability to recognize our gifts by refocusing attention and by refocusing our level of consciousness in a way that will help us see things differently. The eye of the soul offers us an opportunity to remember that we belong to a long tradition of men and women who already know what is within them and who have an insatiable desire to transmit that to us so that we, too, may acknowledge the great gift of sharing in the life of Jesus. "I am the resurrection and the life. Those who believe in me, even though they die, will live" (John 11:25). To give life is Jesus' gift to each of us, and that life is found first of all in the reception of the sacraments. It is often discovered through our interaction with others who invite us to be attentive to that which is within us.

We are invited to share in this gift in a three-fold pattern. First, through injunction we are invited to share things others have experienced that have been a means of spiritual growth for them—perhaps reading a spiritual book or exploring some insights into contemplative prayer. Second, through illumination we are invited to accept the invitation to consider some of these ideas, witness their value, and discuss them in the light of our own spiritual journey. Third, confirmation allows us to make these experiences part of our lives, and results in a more personal relationship with God. Through the example of others we have met on the way, and through our own cooperation with the gift of God's grace, we become a very vital part of the rich tradition of the Church. These three steps, which are very similar to information, formation, and transformation, lead us to a knowledge of God on a much deeper level.

We learn to appreciate the importance of going beyond the capacity to see only with the eye of the flesh and the mind. Jesus, through what he said and what he did, taught us how to live, how to transform our lives, and how to overcome the struggles that occur in the life of a Christian. He taught us through his daily encounters with people. For example, some Pharisees considered rules and regulations to be the criteria by which to live. In the story of the blind man who received his sight from Jesus on the Sabbath, some of the Pharisees immediately instructed the blind man to beware: "This man is not from God, for he does not observe the sabbath" (John 9:16). When the man born blind attempted to confirm what Jesus did to him in restoring his sight, they called him a liar and doubted that he had ever been blind. They saw things with the eye of the flesh only, and so they missed the importance of the event: the healing that took place, the restored humanity, and the cure of the blind man. They did not rejoice over the person restored to life; they were only concerned about the day on which it happened and who it was who performed these acts. They saw only with the eye of the flesh, rather than with the eye of the soul. As we read sacred Scripture, it is important for us to reflect on our own interpretation of these stories so that we, too, may begin to see with the eye of the soul.

To open the eye of the soul is to see things from the divine point of view because now we are in touch with God at our deepest level.

Because we are transcendental, incarnational people, we find God within and contemplate God's presence there; we then move out into the world and put flesh on all we have experienced in prayer. This Christian tradition to which we belong begins with Jesus and continues on to the present day. When we begin to see with the eye of the soul, we begin to see in the way Jesus sees. Each of us, in our daily struggle to overcome our own "blindness," is given the grace to join with the blind man in saying after occasions of doubt and uncertainty, "One thing I do know, that though I was blind, now I see" (John 9:25).

As we read sacred Scripture, it is important for us to reflect on these stories in the light of our own lives so that we, too, may begin to see with the eye of the soul.

This is a great and glorious invitation and challenge.

At the Session

Discuss the terms eye of the flesh and eye of the soul; view video "Eyes of Faith" on Videocassette 6 (25 minutes).

Discussion

1. How are blindness and "seeing" symbolic?
2. Name some ways in which we might begin to see with the eye of the soul.

BIBLIOGRAPHY

Catechism of the Catholic Church. Part Four: §1, chs. 2, 3. Washington, D.C.: United States Catholic Conference, 1994.

Shea, John. *Gospel Light.* New York: Crossroads Publishing Company, 1998.

PART THREE

PRAYERS

Invitation to Prayer

PEGGY O'LEARY, C.S.J.

Because prayer is an integral part of the *Focus on Theology* program, information about the forms and expressions of prayer are included. The variety of prayers which follow integrate many of the forms and expressions.

Following the rich tradition of the Church, emphasis is placed on prayer as the means by which we learn to know God and, in gratitude, to believe in the divine presence in our lives. It is through faithfulness to daily prayer that we acknowledge our dependence on God, and through which our faith is strengthened and enlivened as we encounter God's presence in sacraments and sacramentals.

We are invited to use various forms and expressions in our prayer life.

Forms of Prayer

Blessing: God first blesses all men and women and they, in turn, bless God.

Petition: We pray for all our spiritual and temporal needs.

Intercession: We intercede for others: those who love us, those who do not love us, and for strangers.

Thanksgiving: We thank God for all gifts: our lives, our joys, and our sufferings that allow us to share in redemption.

Praise: We give glory to God for being God; we put aside our own selfish reasons to pray.

Expressions of Prayer

The three expressions of prayer are vocal prayer, meditation, and contemplative prayer.

One form of prayer may employ one, two, or all three expressions of prayer. For example, our prayer of praise may be the oral reading of a psalm followed by a meditation on the glory of God.

226

The following prayer models give examples of the forms and expressions of prayer that you may find helpful.

BIBLIOGRAPHY

Catechism of the Catholic Church. Part Four: §1, ch. 2, arts. 1, 2, 3; §1, ch. 3, art. 1. Washington, D.C.: United States Catholic Conference, 1994.

Advent

Opening Song	"As the Watchman"
Leader	God of love, you have raised Jesus from death to life, resplendent in glory as King of creation. Open our hearts, free all the world to rejoice in his peace, to glory in his justice, and to live in his love. Bring all humankind together as we praise and acclaim your glory.
Psalm 113	(Alternate sides)
Leader	Praise the LORD!

Side One	Praise, O servants of the LORD;
	    praise the name of the LORD.
	Blessed be the name of the LORD
	    from this time on and forevermore.
	From the rising of the sun to it setting
	    the name of the LORD is to be praised.
	The LORD is high above all nations,
	    and his glory above the heavens.

Side Two	Who is like the LORD our God,
	    who is seated on high,
	who looks far down
	    on the heavens and the earth?
	He raises the poor from the dust,
	    and lifts the needy from the ash heap,
	to make them sit with princes,
	    with the princes of his people.
	He gives the barren woman a home,
	    making her the joyous mother of children.

All	Praise the LORD!
Reader	Rev 4:11; 5:9; 12:10-11
Response	God's kingdom will endure forever, and all the kings of the earth will serve God.

Leader	Advent Reflection:
	My friends, now is the acceptable time spoken of by the Spirit, the day of salvation, peace, and reconciliation: the great season of Advent. This is the time eagerly awaited by the patriarchs and prophets, the time that holy Simeon rejoiced to see. This is the season that the Church has always celebrated with special solemnity. We too should always observe it with faith and love, offering praise and thanksgiving to our Creator for the mercy and love he has shown us in this mystery.
Closing Song	"O Come, O Come, Emmanuel"

BIBLIOGRAPHY

Joncas, Jan Michael. "As the Watchman." *Every Stone Shall Cry.* Washington, D.C.: Cooperative Ministries, 1986.

Neale, John M. Trans. from Latin. "O Come, O Come, Emmanel." *Worship: A Hymnal and Service Book for Roman Catholics.* Chicago: G.I.A. Publications, 1986.

Blindness and Vision

Silent Reflection

Mark, in his Gospel, spends a great deal of time on the subject of blindness both in the physical sense and in the spiritual sense. In the first story, he speaks of Jesus curing a blind man who then saw people who looked like trees walking. However, when the blind man cooperated and "looked intently," his sight was restored (Mark 8:22-26).

Further on in his Gospel, Mark also tells us about another interaction, this time between Jesus and the disciples. After Jesus tells about his coming suffering and death, the disciples ask for positions of power. Jesus said to them, "Whoever wishes to become great among you must be your servant." It took the disciples much longer to overcome their blindness and understand what Jesus was talking about (Mark 10:37-43).

A little later in this Gospel, blind Bartimaeus asks that he might see again. His restored sight allowed him to see in two ways, physically and in faith, as he regained his sight and followed Jesus on the way (Mark 10:46-52).

As we pray together, let us ask God for the gift to see others in faith and in trust.

BLIND MAN STORY

Narrator	Jesus took the blind man by the hand and led him out of the village; and when he had put saliva on his eyes and laid his hands on him, he asked him:
Jesus	Can you see anything?
Narrator	And the man looked up and said,
All	I can see people, but they look like trees walking.
Narrator	Then Jesus laid his hands on his eyes again; the blind man looked intently and his sight was restored and he saw everything clearly.
Song	"God of Day and God of Darkness," verse 1

JESUS AND THE DISCIPLES

Jesus	The Son of Man will be handed over to the Gentiles; they will mock him, and spit upon him, and flog him, and kill him; and after three days he will rise again.
Narrator	James and John, the sons of Zebedee, came forward to him and said:
All	Teacher, we want you to do for us whatever we ask of you.
Jesus	What is it you want me to do for you?
Narrator	And they said to him,
All	Grant us to sit one at your right hand and one at your left in your glory.
Narrator	Jesus said to them:
Jesus	Whoever wishes to become great among you must be your servant.
Refrain	"God of Day and God of Darkness," verse 3

BARTIMAEUS

Narrator	A blind beggar was sitting by the roadside. When he heard that it was Jesus of Nazareth, he began to shout out and say:
All	Jesus, Son of David, have mercy on me!
Narrator	Many sternly ordered him to be quiet, but he cried out even more loudly:
All	Jesus, Son of David, have mercy on me!
Narrator	Jesus stood still and said:
Jesus	Call him here.
Narrator	And they called the blind man, saying to him, "Take heart; get up, he is calling you." So throwing off his cloak, he sprang up and came to Jesus. Then Jesus said to him:
Jesus	What do you want me to do for you?

Narrator	The blind man said to him:
All	My teacher, let me see again.
Narrator	Jesus said to him:
Jesus	Go; your faith has made you well.
Narrator	Immediately he regained his sight and followed him on the way.
Refrain	"God of Day and God of Darkness," verse 4

BIBLIOGRAPHY

Haugen, Marty. "God of Day and God of Darkness." *Gather.* Chicago: G.I.A. Publications, 1985.

Christmas Season

Read Silently   Christian, remember your dignity. In the fullness of time, chosen in the unfathomable depths of God's wisdom, the Son of God took for himself our common humanity in order to reconcile it with its creator. He came to overthrow the devil, the origin of death, in that very nature by which he had overthrown humankind. And so at the birth of our Lord the angels sing in joy: Glory to God in the highest, and they proclaim peace to his people on earth as they see the heavenly Jerusalem being built from all the nations of the world. Let us give thanks to God, through his Son, in the Holy Spirit, because in his great love for us, he took pity on us, and when we were dead in our sins he brought us to life with Christ, so that in him we might be a new creation (St. Leo the Great).

Song   Any appropriate song of the season

Reader   Judg 13:2-9

Response   In the mystery of Jesus' birth, we receive the gift of your loving Son. May the love and gentleness of his being permeate our lives in a way that the world will know Jesus because of us. The Son is our light and our salvation!

Intercessions

Leader   With faith, we join in prayer with all those who believe and hope in the salvation that Jesus Christ has bestowed on us:

All   Jesus, may your coming as one of us be a source of faith; may we, the Church, make known your presence to the world, we pray.

Leader	You accepted human frailty for our sakes; help us to recognize our weaknesses and look to you for strength, we pray.
All	Through your birth, you brought hope to the world; may we grow in trust, we pray.
Leader	Comfort the sick and dying; give them the grace to accept their sufferings, we pray.
All	You came to share your love and your life; lead us to your kingdom, we pray.
Silent Reflection	
All	God our Creator, our Redeemer, our Comforter: through your coming may we recognize the power of your love, and be witnesses of that love to all those with whom we share life. Amen.
Song	Psalm 98: "All the Ends of the Earth"

BIBLIOGRAPHY

Haas, David, and Marty Haugen. "All the Ends of the Earth." *Gather*. Chicago: G.I.A. Publications, 1994.

St. Leo the Great. Nativitate Domini, Sermo 1:1-3; *Patrologia latina* 54, 190–3. *Liturgy of the Hours*. Christmas Office of Readings, Second Reading.

Church

Reader 1   "Christ loves us individually but not separately, saying to each of us, as he said to Moses, 'I know you by name'; he loves us in his Church, for which he shed his blood. Our personal destiny can work itself out only in the common salvation of the Church, who is the 'Mother of Unity'" (De Lubac, 44).

Reader 2   "Existing as she does by the will of God, the Church is necessary to us—necessary as a means. And more than this. The mystery of the Church is all mystery; it is our own mystery, *par excellence*. It lays hold on the whole of us and surrounds us; for it is in his Church that God looks upon us and loves us, in her that he desires us and we encounter him, and in her that we cleave to him and are made blessed. She is the rallying-point for all, "inviting those who as yet have no faith, and assuring her own children that the faith which they profess has the firmest of foundations" (De Lubac, 45).

Reader 3   To a person "who lives her mystery, she is always the city of precious stones, the Heavenly Jerusalem" (De Lubac, 46); the city that we build up in this world to the city which is in heaven. "It will always be the City of Yahweh, the Sion of Holy Israel. We ought, indeed, to love that very element of the Church which is transitory—but we ought to love it as the one and only means, the indispensable organ, the providential instrument, and at the same time as "the pledge, the passing image, the promise of the communion to come" (De Lubac, 81, 83).

Silent Reflection

Petitions

Leader	O God, you send your Spirit to renew the Church, the people of God, and call them to holiness in the world. We give you thanks and pray:
	We pray for Pope John XXIII whom you inspired to open the windows to the breath of the Spirit. Keep our hearts and attitudes open to you in the sign of our times:
All	Lord, hear our prayer.
Leader	We pray for the Church of Christ: that it may be seen more clearly as the place of reconciliation and generous service to the needs of the entire human family:
All	Lord, hear our prayer.
Leader	We pray for the Church throughout the world: that by word and action it may proclaim the mystery of the Cross, the power of sacrificial love, and the path to human joy:
All	Lord, hear our prayer.
Leader	We pray for our young people: that they will be enriched by the Word of God and come to a genuine love of the Church and a deep love of the Catholic tradition:
All	Lord, hear our prayer.
Leader	O God, you graced your Church to be a witness to the world. Bless all who are in positions of Church leadership. Make them holy and true witnesses of the gospel. May all come to know their calling to be a priestly people, so that the Church will be seen by the world as God's holy people. We ask this in the name of Jesus who founded the Church on Peter. Amen.
Closing Song	"We Have Been Told"

BIBLIOGRAPHY

De Lubac, Henri. *Splendor of the Church.* San Francisco: Ignatius Press, 1986. Quotations used with permission.

Haas, David. "We Have Been Told." *Gather.* Chicago: G.I.A. Publications, 1994.

Creation

All	We acknowledge your presence, Creator of the universe.
Leader	Help us, God, to respect and protect all of your creation, remembering that you created it and gave it to us for our use.
Reader	God saw everything that he had made, and indeed, it was very good (Gen 1:31).
Response	Help us to recall your command to take care of your handiwork.
Reader	The God of all creation settled humankind on the earth. In the Scriptures, God tells us to "till it and keep it" (Gen 2:15).
Response	Help us to recall your command to take care of your handiwork.
Reader	We celebrate our unique creation, our individual gifts. St. Paul says, "For as in one body we have many members, and not all the members have the same function, so we, who are many, are one body in Christ, and individually we are members one of another" (Rom 12:4-5).
Song for Reflection	"We Are Many Parts"
Leader	St. Paul reminds us of how wonderful we have been made by our Creator.
All	We are temples of God with the Spirit of God living in us. God's temple is holy and we are that temple.

Silent reflective reading by each person

> "O God, I must confess to myself as well as to you that which has come to me again and again.

It is with great difficulty that I behold your creation as wondrous, although indeed it is. The Scriptures deem your creation glorious; the poets sing praises to it; St. Francis, too in his "Canticle to the Sun" of which the final verse about death still moves me deeply (Rahner, 40, 42).

"Should I be patient with myself or rather force myself into joining that chorus of poets who extol the power, the sublimity, the infinite mercy and the awful splendor of your creation, and therefore have an inkling of who you truly are?" (Rahner, 41).

Song   "Canticle of the Sun"

BIBLIOGRAPHY

Rahner, Karl. *Prayers for a Lifetime.* New York: Crossroad, 1984.

Haugen, Marty. "Canticle of the Sun." *Gather.* Chicago: G.I.A. Publications, 1950.

_____. "We Are Many Parts." *Gather.* Chicago: G.I.A. Publications, 1994.

Easter

Song	"Easter Alleluia"
Leader	Alleluia, Alleluia! Blessed are you, Lord our God, who raised up Jesus from the tomb and has gathered us together to rejoice because we have been saved.
All	As the light of God overcame the darkness of death, may this candle we now light be for us a sign of the flame of life that burns within our hearts.
Leader	As we come to pray together, we continue our celebration of the ever-newness of the resurrection of our Lord Jesus Christ. May we, in this Easter season, share with each other the great joy of life.
Reader	St. Luke tells of the appearance of Christ on the evening of his resurrection. This time it was to his apostles that he came and offered his peace. He helped them understand all the things that had been said concerning his death and resurrection (Luke 24:36-40).
Response	Help us to profess the Easter faith with joy and live always in the light of Christ.
Leader	By baptism we share in this paschal mystery. We die with Christ and we rise with him. We become adopted sons and daughters of God. We renew our commitment to live and grow in the love of Christ. We reject sin so as to live in the freedom of God's children.
All	Like a green olive tree in the house of God, I trust in the kindness of God.

Leader	And the dove came back to him in the evening, and there in its beak was a freshly plucked olive leaf; so Noah knew that the waters had subsided from the earth (Gen 8:11).
	Mary sings, "Suddenly sorrow has been changed to joy and all has become joyous and a cause for rejoicing. I do not hesitate to say, 'I have been glorified as Moses for I have seen, I have seen—not on the mountain but in the tomb, not concealed by a cloud, but by flesh, the Lord of the Immortals and of the clouds, Lord of old, now and forever. And he said,
	"'Mary, hasten and tell those who love me that I have risen. Take me on your tongue like a branch of olive.
	"'To the descendants of Noah, announce the good news, pointing out to them that death is destroyed and that he has risen, He who offers resurrection to the fallen'" (*Romanos*, sixth century).
All	O God, our rainbow, our dove, our promised land: in the resurrection of your Son you have brought us to your ark. Protect us from storm, and ferry us to your welcoming shore. This is the day the Lord has made, alleluia; let us rejoice and be glad in it, alleluia.
Song	"Easter Alleluia"

BIBLIOGRAPHY

Haugen, Marty. "Easter Alleluia." *Gather.* Chicago: G.I.A. Publications, 1994.

Kontakia of Romanos. Byzantine Melodist. 1: *On the Person of Christ,* trans. Marjorie Carpenter, 1970.

Justice and Peace

Leader	Divine source of all wisdom and truth, we come before you asking your help as we prepare to teach, to listen, and to learn. We are aware that we have been called by you.
All	Nourish our spirit, remove our doubts, and help all of us who are in need of your love and who search for your truth. Strengthen us and be with us. Amen.
Reader	Eph 3:14-19
All	To know the Lord is to act justly.
Right side	Come, Spirit of Wisdom, teach us to value the dignity of every person.
Left side	Come, Spirit of Understanding, show us the need for community to protect the common good.
Right side	Come, Spirit of Counsel, guide us toward enabling all to participate in the social and economic life of this country.
Left side	Come, Spirit of Courage, strengthen us to opt for the poor, to speak with the voiceless, to defend the defenseless.
Right side	Come, Spirit of Godliness, stir our minds and hearts to work for human dignity and the protection of human rights.
Left side	Come, Spirit of Fear of the Lord, make us into your image—loving sons and daughters who serve our God all our days.
All	To know the Lord is to act justly.

Leader	God of compassion we beg you to help and defend us:
Reader 1	Deliver the oppressed and be present to all people.
Reader 2	Raise the fallen and show yourself to the needy.
Reader 3	Heal the sick and give peace to the dying.
Reader 4	Bring back those who have gone astray.
Reader 5	Enlighten us so that we may be receptive to the Gospel message.
All	May every nation come to know that you alone are God, that Jesus is your Son, and that we are your people.
Reader 6	We pray for peace in the world that a spirit of respect and forbearance may grow among nations.
Song	"Wood Hath Hope" by John Foley

BIBLIOGRAPHY

Foley, John. "Wood Hath Hope." *Wood Hath Hope*. Phoenix: North American Liturgy Resources, 1978.

Lent

Psalm 51

All   In your love make Zion lovely.

Leader   Have mercy on me, O God, according to your steadfast love; according to your abundant mercy blot out my transgressions. Wash me thoroughly from my iniquity and cleanse me from my sin. For I know my transgressions, and my sin is ever before me.

All   Indeed, I was born guilty, a sinner when my mother conceived me. You desire truth in the inward being; therefore, teach me wisdom in my secret heart. Purge me with hyssop, and I shall be clean; wash me, and I shall be whiter than snow.

Leader   Let me hear joy and gladness; let the bones that you have crushed rejoice. Hide your face from my sins, and blot out all my iniquities. Create in me a clean heart, O God, and put a new and right spirit within me. Do not cast me away from your presence, and do not take your Holy Spirit from me.

All   Restore to me the joy of your salvation, and sustain in me a willing spirit. Then I will teach transgressors your ways, and sinners will return to you. Deliver me from bloodshed, O God, O God of my salvation, and my tongue will sing aloud of your deliverance. O Lord, open my lips, and my mouth will declare your praise.

Leader   For you have no delight in sacrifice; if I were to give a burnt offering, you would not be pleased. The sacrifice acceptable to God is a broken spirit;

a broken and contrite heart, O God, you will not despise. Do good to Zion in your good pleasure; rebuild the walls of Jerusalem, then you will delight in right sacrifices, in burnt offerings and whole burnt offerings; then bulls will be offered on your altar.

All	In your love, make Zion lovely.
Song	"Like Burning Incense" (optional)
Reader	Isa 55:10-11
Intercessions	
Leader	Compassionate Savior, you watch over us, you raise the weak: **We trust in your mercy.**
	Compassionate Savior, you protect the poor, you overcome adversaries: **We trust in your mercy.**
	Compassionate Savior, you sustain our efforts, you bring blessings upon your people. **We trust in your mercy.**
All	O God who guards and protects, you watch over your holy people with care and compassion: be with us today as a shield that surrounds us, and help us to trust in your mercy now and always. Amen.

BIBLIOGRAPHY

Joncas, Jan Michael. "Like Burning Incense." *Gather.* Chicago: G.I.A. Publications, 1963.

Mary

Song	"Mary's Song" (or some other appropriate song)
Prayer	God, you have given us the mother of your Son to be our queen and mother. With the support of her prayers, may we come to share the glory of your children in the kingdom of heaven.
Response	Blessed are you for your firm believing that the promises of the Lord would be fulfilled.
All	O Mary, bright dawn of the new world, mother of the living, to you do we entrust the cause of life.
Right side	Look down, O Mother, upon the vast numbers of babies not allowed to be born, of the poor whose lives are made difficult, of men and women who are victims of brutal violence, of the elderly and the sick killed by indifference or out of misguided mercy.
All	Grant that all who believe in your Son may proclaim the Gospel of life with honesty and love for the people of our time.
Left side	Obtain for them the grace to accept the Gospel as a gift ever new, the joy of celebrating it with gratitude throughout their lives, and the courage to bear witness to it resolutely, in order to build, together with all people of good will, the civilization of truth and love, to the praise and glory of God, the Creator and lover of life (John Paul II).
All	Lord, in celebrating the gift of your mother, Mary, we offer our gifts and prayers. May you

who offered yourself as a perfect sacrifice bring
humankind the peace and love of your kingdom,
where you live forever.

Song   "I Found the Treasure"

BIBLIOGRAPHY

John Paul II. "On the Value and Inviolability of Human Life: *Evangelium
      Vitae.*" <http://listserv.american.edu/catholic/church/papal/jp.ii/
      jp2evanv.html> (February 1, 1999).

Joncas, Jan Michael. "Mary's Song." *On Eagle's Wings.* Phoenix: North Ameri-
      can Liturgy Resources, 1979.

Schutte, Dan. "I Found the Treasure." *The Steadfast Love.* Phoenix: North
      American Liturgy Resources, 1985.

Spirit

All	The God who knows and understands all things is with us. Come, Holy Spirit, and send your light upon us. As we gather here, inform our reason and enlighten our reflection. With you our work will come to good and our efforts will lead to fruition. Let us not be moved by hasty judgments, but grant us your wisdom and understanding. In complete trust in your providence, we pray to you, ever-faithful God.
Leader	Send your Spirit into the Church to strengthen the hearts of all who believe.
All	Send your Spirit into the world to fulfill the work of the gospel.
Leader	Come, Holy Spirit, fill the hearts of your faithful and enkindle in them the fire of your love.
All	Send forth your Spirit and they shall be created and you shall renew the face of the earth.
Leader	Let us pray:
All	O God, who taught the hearts of your faithful by sending them the light of your Holy Spirit, grant us by the same Spirit, to have a right judgment in all things and ever more to rejoice in your holy comfort. Amen.
Song	"Dwelling Place"

BIBLIOGRAPHY

Foley, John. "Dwelling Place." *Gather*. Chicago: G.I.A. Publications, 1976.

Trinity Icon Meditation

(See the cover of the book)

Reader 1 Though three figures are pictured, the three figures are profoundly one. Each is robed in blue
and winged, symbols that they abide in heavenly realms. Each has the same face, symbol that
they share an identity, that to know one of them
is to know all. Each sits on an identical throne
and holds an identical scepter, symbolizing the
equality of their power. They sit around a common table, symbol of their hospitality and the
openness of their dialogue with one another as
they share their common life together. And they
are gathered around a single cup of wine, symbol of the blood of the covenant and the new
wine of festivity and joy to which we are all
invited.

Reader 2 Set your eyes on the face of the figure at the left
and let them follow naturally. They will move to
his feet, then to the feet of the others and up to
the shoulders of the figure on the right. Continue
across the top again back to the face of the figure
on the left. The three figures form a single circle,
symbol that they are absolutely one.

Reader 3 Yet, within this profound unity, the three figures
are distinct from each other, each possessing a
unique identity.

Reader 4 The Creator, on your left,
is clothed in luminous gold
the creator of light, the beautiful one
ever ancient, ever new, the origin of all
that is.

The Word, seated in the center,
  wears an undergarment of earthen color,
    symbol of a basic humanity though clothed
    with divinity,
      symbol of oneness with earth
        as the gift of the Creator offered within
        creation.

The Spirit, to your right,
  is robed in green,
    symbol of life, generativity,
    hope, and vitality.

Reader 5	Each has a slightly different posture. The Word, the redeemer and healer of humankind, gazes upon the Creator. The Creator, the fountain of mercy, gazes upon the Spirit, the giver of life. The Spirit, the Consoler, the Advocate who proceeds from the Creator and the Word, gazes toward the open space at the center of the icon.
Reader 6	The open space on which the Spirit gazes is the place at table left for us. The Spirit looks to this open space in invitation. Each of us is invited to join them at table. The Trinity invites us to share their equality, to share their power, to share their hospitality, to share their openness and dialogue, to share their festivity and joy as they celebrate their distinctiveness within their absolute unity. For the Trinity is the source for all of us. The Spirit's gaze invites us to share that freedom, that security, that fulfillment. Their relationship with each other is a ministry we are invited to share and to extend.
Reader 7	For whenever we extend freedom, security, and fulfillment to others, we extend to them the life of the Trinity. Whenever we extend exclusivism instead of freedom, coercion instead of security, or selfishness instead of fulfillment, we withdraw from our place at this table and we live outside the life of God. The life of the Trinity can only be found in the freedom, security, and fulfillment of the life they know together, the life

that we are invited to share with them—and to extend on their behalf.

Reader 8   Our God is absolutely one, yet our God is a community of three. The goal of the spiritual life is Trinity. And the mystery of Trinity is this: we are invited into a relationship with our Creator, Redeemer, and Spirit, all three. We are invited to share in the immense freedom, security, and fulfillment that is the life of the Trinity.

Reader 9   The fourth place at the table is for you (Author Unknown).

On the next page please find a prayer to the Trinity for your use.

When I ponder the gospel of my life,

my God reveals a Trinity.

As to action, I discern this in myself:

Initiative from the Father, sparing me the dead weight of inertia.

Responsiveness from the Son saving me from deadening insensitivity.

Animation from the Spirit dispelling the death of boredom.

As to the fruit of the Trinitarian action, I celebrate:

Equality with others that erases the oppression of
superiority or inferiority.

Distinctiveness of gifts free of conceit or competition or intimidation.

Oneness in love encircling the equality and distinctiveness of each,
non-possessive, yet all-inclusive.

Mission that bursts with purpose delivering me from the mire of
meaninglessness.

—Gerald Keefe

To paraphrase Paul:

I am an icon of Christ, painted by the Spirit of the living God on
canvas of flesh, transformed from glory to glory, tinted with mystery
divine, a gospel teeming with Trinity.

Virtue:
Living a Life of Faith, Hope, and Love

Song	"Ubi Caritas"
Leader	Let us pray for faith.
Response	As a believing people, we gather in prayer before our faithful God.
	We know that material things can be a hindrance to love of God and love of our neighbor. Help us to be willing to make sacrifices and to give of ourselves in order to be faithful to all that God asks of us.
Leader	For just as the body without the spirit is dead, so faith without works is also dead (Jas 2:26).
	Silent Reflection on Faith
	"Lord Jesus Christ, You Yourself have shown me a way to a faith that is real and determines my life. It is the way of the ordinary and actively generous love of neighbor. I meet you on this road as unknown and known. Guide me on this path, light of life" (Rahner, 80).
Response	As people seeking to grow in faith, we offer this prayer in Jesus' name.
Leader	Let us pray for hope.
Response	We place ourselves in the presence of God, who is the source of all hope. God of justice, hear our prayers for conversion. May we place your love and the love for our neighbor before the accumulation of material wealth or worldly ambition. Help us to walk with the poor as friends, and to seek the justice that the prophets acclaim

as the surest sign of your presence. We place our hope and trust in you.

Leader

I consider that the sufferings of this present time are not worth comparing with the glory about to be revealed to us (Rom 8:18).

Silent Reflection on Hope

"We ask you, God of grace and eternal life, to increase and strengthen hope in us. Give us this virtue of the strong, this power of the confident, and this courage of the unshakable. Make us always have a longing for You, the infinite plenitude of being. Do not let me be embittered by suffering, but mature, patient, selfless, gentle, and filled with longing for that land where there is no pain and for that day when You will wipe away all tears from the eyes of those who have loved You and in sorrow have believed in Your love, and in darkness have believed in Your light" (Rahner, 98, 100, 101).

Response

We offer this prayer, firm in the hope that Jesus offers us. Amen.

Leader

Let us pray for love.

Response

Let us call to mind that You, God of love, are present and we ask for your guidance and grace. Help us to acquire clarity of purpose and purity of heart so that we might truly love you and our sisters and brothers.

Leader

Owe no one anything, except to love one another; for the one who loves another has fulfilled the law (Rom 13:8).

Silent Reflection on Love

"You meet me, Jesus, in my neighbor towards whom I have ventured without guarantee; in all love and joy which is still only promise, and asks me for the courage to believe in eternal love and joy" (Rahner, 82).

Response

God of love, we ask you to continue to hear our prayer.

Leader   Divine source of all wisdom and truth, we have
                  been called by you. This challenge reminds us
                  that we must, by prayer and service, transform
                  our lives into a revelation of you. Deepen our
                  reverence and nourish our spirit. Remove our
                  doubts and help all of us because we are in need
                  of your love, and because we search for your
                  light and your strength. Gracious God be with
                  us.

Response   Let us put our faith into action that we may
                  work in love and persevere in hope.

Song   "We Are Called"

BIBLIOGRAPHY

Berthier, Jacques. "Ubi Caritas." *Gather.* Chicago: G.I.A. Publications, 1994.

Haas, David. "We Are Called." *Gather.* Chicago: G.I.A. Publications, 1994.

Rahner, Karl. *Prayers for a Lifetime.* New York: Crossroad, 1984.

Vocation

Isaiah's Call

Leader	The pivots on the thresholds shook at the voices of those who called, and the house filled with smoke (Isa 6:4).
Reader	And I said: "Woe is me! I am lost, for I am a man of unclean lips, and I live among a people of unclean lips; yet my eyes have seen the King, the LORD of hosts!" Then one of the seraphs flew to me holding a live coal that had been taken from the altar with a pair of tongs. The seraph touched my mouth with it and said: "Now that this has touched your lips, your guilt has departed and your sin is blotted out." Then I heard the voice of the Lord saying, "Whom shall I send, and who will go for us?" (Isa 6:5-8).
Song	"Here I Am, Lord"
Leader	When he [Jesus] saw the crowds, he had compassion for them, because they were harassed and helpless, like sheep without a shepherd. Then Jesus said to his disciples, "The harvest is plentiful, but the laborers are few; therefore ask the Lord of the harvest to send out laborers into his harvest" (Matt 9:36-38).
All	You did not choose me but I chose you. And I appointed you to go and bear fruit, fruit that will last, so that the Father will give you whatever you ask him in my name (John 15:16).

Peter's Call

Leader	"Very truly, I tell you, when you were younger, you used to fasten your own belt and to go

wherever you wished. But when you grow old, you will stretch out your hands, and someone else will fasten a belt around you and take you where you do not wish to go." (He said this to indicate the kind of death by which he would glorify God.) After this he said to him, "Follow me" (John 21:18-19).

Leader   When he [Jesus] saw the crowds, he had compassion for them, because they were harassed and helpless, like sheep without a shepherd. Then he said to his disciples, "The harvest is plentiful, but the laborers are few; therefore ask the Lord of the harvest to send out laborers into his harvest" (Matt 9:36-38).

All   You did not choose me but I chose you. And I appointed you to go and bear fruit, fruit that will last, so that the Father will give you whatever you ask him in my name (John 15:16).

Song   "Come with Me Into the Fields"

Jeremiah's Call

Leader   Now the Word of the LORD came to me saying,
            "Before I formed you in the womb I knew you,
            and before you were born I consecrated you;
            I appointed you a prophet to the nations."
            Then I said, "Ah, Lord GOD! Truly I do not know how to speak, for I am only a boy." But the LORD said to me,
            "Do not say, 'I am only a boy';
            for you shall go to all to whom I send you,
            and you shall speak whatever I command
                you" (Jer 1:4-8).

All   Then the LORD put out his hand and touched my mouth; and the LORD said to me,
            "Now I have put my words in your mouth.
            See, today I appoint you over nations and over
                kingdoms,
            to pluck up and to pull down,
            to destroy and to overthrow,
            to build and to plant" (Jer 1:9-10).

Song   "A Song of Hope"

Refrain:

I know the plans I have for you, says the Lord;
Plans of fullness, not of harm;
    To give you a future and a hope.
    After a time has gone by, then I will visit you,
    fulfill my promise to you, and bring you back.

Refrain

    Then you will call upon me and you will pray
        to me;
    and I will listen to you, and bring you back.

Refrain

    You will seek me, and find me.
    When you seek me with all of your heart,
    I will be found by you.

Refrain

BIBLIOGRAPHY

Schutte, Dan. "Come With Me into the Fields." *Glory and Praise.* Phoenix: North American Liturgy Resources, 1977.

_____. "Here I Am, Lord." *Gather.* Chicago: G.I.A. Publications, 1994.

Foley, John. "A Song of Hope." *The Steadfast Love.* Phoenix: North American Liturgy Resources, 1985.

PART FOUR

REFERENCE

Glossary

The terms in this glossary originated from discussions among participants.

allegory:
> A literary composition in which the various terms and details are to be interpreted. It is a comparison in which the general sense of the whole story is directed toward illustrating a truth.

anagogy:
> Interpretation of a word, passage, or text (as of Scripture) that finds the sense beyond the literal, allegorical, and moral senses, going to a fourth spiritual or mystical sense.

apperceptive mass:
> The body of knowledge, attitudes, and behaviors stored within one and on which future knowledge, attitudes, and behaviors are built.

catechesis:
> To teach through oral instruction. Instruction given to Christians preparing for baptism.

cosmogonic story:
> A story about the origin of the universe in which everything comes from "evil gods" who have ordered human life toward evil; it reduces reality to natural repetitive cycles—truncating human intelligence and liberty.

cover story:
> The cover story covers up and tries to replace the true story; it confuses the distinction, introduced by the Scriptures, between natural and supernatural, and so confuses the relationship between the creature and the Creator, etc.

divinity:
> The quality or state of being divine—God.

doctrine:
> A principle of law established through past decisions that form a tradition.

dogma:

A doctrine or body of doctrines concerning faith or morals formally stated and authoritatively proclaimed by a church.

ecumenism:

A collective name for all efforts to reunite Christians of various persuasions; the recovery of the unity of all believers in Christ.

eschatology:

Pertaining to the "last things"—end of the world; belief about or in the end of the world; belief in the second coming of Christ; resurrection, judgment.

ethical:

Entire form of right and proper behavior.

evangelization:

Pertaining to the Gospels. The act of announcing the Good News. It suggests a ministry of preaching the Gospel. Teachings based preeminently on the Gospel.

evolution:

Process of change in a certain direction. Process of continuous change from a lower, simpler form to a higher, more complex, or fuller state.

gift:

A meaning or reality freely offered by one person to another intended to provide a substantive benefit for the well-being of the whole person. It has its source in the freedom and good will of another.

grace:

God's self-disclosure to human beings. It is God's personal condescension and absolute gratuitous clemency to us. In Christian theology the supernatural assistance of God bestowed upon rational beings with a view to their sanctification.

heresy:

An error in matters of faith; can only occur in baptized persons who wish to remain Christians. Heresy is the formal denial or doubt of any defined doctrine of the Catholic faith.

humility:

A moral virtue which consists in keeping oneself within bounds; not reaching out to things above one (St. Thomas Aquinas).

Catholic theology regards it as part of the cardinal virtue of temperance in that it represses inordinate ambition and self-esteem without allowing one to fall into the opposite error of exaggerated or hypocritical self-abjection. Humility is considered the foundation of the spiritual life because it subjects reason and will to God.

mission:

(of the Church) The duty and right of the Church to preach the Gospel without hindrance among all peoples and in all historical situations in order to help all grow in faith.

mystery:

Truths that we cannot fully understand because they are a reality beyond a complete comprehension for the human mind.

myth:

Religious interpretations of nature, her power, and her phenomena that are seen as the manifestations of a sacred reality.

parable:

A short story that illustrates a moral attitude or a religious principle. The kind of stories in which we can find an opening or a glimpse of meaning revealed by God that continues to be a mystery. Similitudes drawn from nature or from human affairs (short narratives) that Christ used to convey a spiritual meaning.

passive diminishment:

The continuous action in which this world's goods (positive gifts and negative realities) are utilized to the fullest (Pere Teilhard de Chardin quoted by Flannery O'Connor in "A Memoir of Mary Ann"). How Christ can use even the evil of unmerited suffering as a vehicle of grace. Acceptance of suffering; acceptance of the Cross; handing over one's suffering to Christ; overcoming the cover story that says we are all victims; experiences of the creature as expressing the wound in the creative order. It is the offering or acceptance of life in relationship to hope. It becomes the material on which the Redemption of Christ operates.

providence:

The plan that God has for the created world.

redemption:

To be saved. The condition of humans is overcome by Jesus' act of obedience. It is a deliverance from sin and a restoration of humans and the world to communion with God. Our desire to be delivered from sin, suffering, and death.

revelation:

The act of revealing or communicating divine truth. The truth God discloses to us about God and the process by which the communication of it takes place.

salvation history:

The fact that God has graciously embraced the whole human history and in it has offered all persons salvation. It is the history of all experiences of salvation throughout the human race and reveals history as "saving history."

tradition:

In order to keep the Gospel forever whole and alive within the Church, the apostles left bishops as their successors, handing over to them the authority to teach in their own place. This sacred tradition and sacred Scripture are like a mirror in which the Church on earth looks at God until she can see him face to face. It is not something that is "handed down" but rather "handed over," for there is growth in the understanding of the realities and the words which have been handed down (DV 7–8).

transcendence:

Technical term often used to explain the mystery of the divine life itself. Designates that God is not immediately present to our senses and is often used as the opposite of immanence; beyond ordinary human knowing.

Trinity:

The name of the fundamental mystery of Christianity, that of the one nature and the three persons—Father, Son, and Holy Spirit. One God exists in three persons and one substance. A mystery in that it can neither be known by unaided human reason apart from revelation nor cogently (convincingly) demonstrated by reason after it has been revealed. It is maintained that though the mystery is above reason, it is not incompatible with the principles of rational thought.

virtue:

Habit of doing good. Theological virtues relate directly to God. These virtues are faith, hope, and charity, which are the basis of the Christian life. Moral virtues dispose us to live good lives. Cardinal virtues are prudence, temperance, fortitude, and justice.

These moral virtues are called "cardinal" because they act as hinges on which is linked our whole moral life.

vocation:

The recognition by an individual that a particular career or way of life corresponds to God's permissive will for that person, and that this "call" will gain him or her eternal salvation.

Bibliography

Anderson, Bernhard. "Creation in the Bible" and "Creation in the Noachic Covenant." *Cry of the Environment: Rebuilding the Christian Creation Tradition.* Ed. Philip Joranson and Ken Butigan. Santa Fe: Bear and Co., 1984. These pieces are more difficult theologically than Boadt and Vawter.

Apse of Sánt Appolinare in Classe. Ravenna, Italy. Photographer: Leonard Von Matt.

Association for the Advancement of Christian Social Sciences. "Market Economy and Ethics." *Ordo Socialis: Making Christianity Work in Business and Economy.* Ed. Joseph Cardinal Ratzinger, 62–7. Philippines: Divine Word Publications, 1992.

Augustine. *The Confessions of St. Augustine.* Trans. John K. Ryan. New York: Doubleday, 1960.

Bellah, Robert, and others. *Habits of the Heart: Individualism and Commitment in American Life.* New York: Harper and Row, 1985.

Berthier, Jacques. "Ubi Caritas." *Gather.* Chicago: G.I.A. Publications, 1994.

Boadt, Lawrence. *Reading the Old Testament.* Ch. 6. New York: Paulist Press, 1984.

Brown, Raymond, and others, eds. *Jerome Biblical Commentary.* Englewood Cliffs, N.J.: Prentice-Hall, 1968. See especially Richard F. Smith's entry, "Inspiration and Inerrancy."

Burghardt, Walter. *Preaching the Just Word.* New Haven, Conn.: Yale University Press, 1996.

Calvez, Jean-Yves, and Jacques Perrin. *The Church and Social Justice: The Social Teachings of the Popes from Leo XIII to Pius XII.* Chicago: Henry Regnery Co., 1961.

Catechism of the Catholic Church. Washington, D.C.: United States Catholic Conference, 1994.

The Catholic Spirit. St. Paul, Minn.: Archdiocese of St. Paul and Minneapolis, 1997.

Cessario, Romanus. *The Moral Virtues and Theological Ethics.* Notre Dame, Ind.: University of Notre Dame Press, 1991.

Charles, Rodger. *The Social Teachings of Vatican Two.* San Francisco: Ignatius Press, 1982.

Coles, Robert. *The Call of Stories.* Boston: Houghton Mifflin, 1989.

_____. *Harvard Diary.* New York: Crossroad, 1988.

_____. *Spiritual Life of Children.* Boston: Houghton Mifflin, 1990.

Congregation for Catholic Education. *The Religious Dimension of Education in a Catholic School: Guidelines for Reflection and Renewal.* Washington, D.C.: United States Catholic Conference,1988.

Cooke, Bernard. *Sacraments and Sacramentality.* Mystic, Conn.: Twenty-Third Publications, 1994.

Council of Chalcedon. Confession of Chalcedon.

Council of Nicea. Creed of Nicea.

Dawson, Christopher. *The Dynamics of World History.* Ed. John J. Mulloy. New York: Sheed and Ward, 1956.

Day, Dorothy. *The Long Loneliness: The Autobiography of Dorothy Day.* New York: Harper and Row, 1981.

DeVinck, Christopher. *The Power of the Powerless.* New York: Doubleday, 1988.

Dorr, Donal. *Option for the Poor.* Maryknoll, N.Y.: Orbis Books, 1983.

Dulles, Avery. *A Church to Believe In: Discipleship and the Dynamics of Freedom.* New York: Crossroad, 1982.

_____. *Models of the Church.* Garden City, N.Y.: Doubleday, 1974.

Dwyer, Judith, ed. *The New Dictionary of Catholic Social Thought.* Collegeville: The Liturgical Press, 1994.

Economic Justice For All: Pastoral Letter on Catholic Social Teaching and the U.S. Economy. Washington, D.C.: United States Catholic Conference, 1986.

Eliot, T. S. *Murder in the Cathedral.* San Diego: Harcourt Brace Jovanovich, 1935.

Foley, John. "A Song of Hope." *The Steadfast Love.* Phoenix: North American Liturgy Resources, 1985.

_____. "Wood Hath Hope." *Wood Hath Hope.* Phoenix: North American Liturgy Resources, 1978.

Friedrich, Gerhard. *"Kêryx. [hierokêryx,] kêrussô, kêrygma, prokêrussô." Theological Dictionary of the New Testament.* Ed. Gerhard Kittel; trans. and ed. Geoffrey W. Bromiley, 3:683–718. Grand Rapids, Mich.: Eerdmans, 1965.

Grünewald, Matthias. "Isenheim Altarpiece." Colmar, France: Musée de Unterlinden.

Haas, David. "We Are Called." *Gather.* Chicago: G.I.A. Publications, 1994.

_____. "We Have Been Told." *Gather.* Chicago: G.I.A. Publications, 1994.

_____, and Marty Haugen. "All the Ends of the Earth." *Gather.* Chicago: G.I.A. Publications, 1994.

Habiger, Matthew. *Papal Teaching on Private Property 1891–1991.* Lanham, Md.: University Press of America, 1990.

Haugen, Marty. "Canticle of the Sun." *Gather.* Chicago: G.I.A. Publications, 1950.

_____. "Easter Alleluia." *Gather.* Chicago: G.I.A. Publications, 1994.

_____. "God of Day and God of Darkness." *Gather.* Chicago: G.I.A. Publications, 1985.

_____. "We Are Many Parts." *Gather.* Chicago: G.I.A. Publications, 1994.

Haughey, John C. *Converting 9 to 5: A Spirituality of Daily Work.* New York: Crossroad, 1989.

_____. *The Holy Use of Money.* Garden City, N.Y.: Doubleday, 1986.

Hawking, Stephen. *A Brief History of Time.* New York: Bantam, 1988. A more difficult account. In the last half Hawking proposes his own very controversial and speculative theory to the effect that there was no "beginning" to the universe.

Hoffman Elizabeth, ed. "General Norms for the Liturgical Year and Calendar" and "Constitution on the Sacred Liturgy." *The Liturgy Documents: A Parish Resource.* 3rd ed. Chicago: Liturgy Training Publications, 1991.

Hollenbach, David. *Claims In Conflict: Retrieving and Renewing the Catholic Human Rights Tradition.* New York: Paulist Press, 1979.

_____. "The Common Good Revisited." *Theological Studies* 50 (1989).

Jastrous, Robert. *Until the Sun Dies.* New York: Warner Books, 1980. A simple account for beginners, now out of print, but probably available through local libraries.

"John A. Ryan Institute for Catholic Social Thought." <http://www.stthomas.edu/cathstudies/cst> (January 28, 1999).

John Paul II. "Encyclicals and Documents of Pope John Paul II." December 14, 1996. <http://www.cin.org/jp2doc.html> (January 28, 1999).

_____. "Homily of Pope John Paul at the Papal Mass at Oriole Park at Camden Yard." October 8, 1995. <http://www.popevisit.com/history/pope/Homily Camden Yards.htm> (January 28, 1999).

_____. *Laborem Exercens* (In Proclaiming Justice and Peace). Mystic, Conn.: Twenty-Third Publications, 1984.

Joncas, Jan Michael. "As the Watchman." *Every Stone Shall Cry.* Washington, D.C.: Cooperative Ministries, 1986.

_____. "The Church at Prayer." *Spirituality and Morality: Integrating Prayer and Action.* Ed. Dennis J. Billy and Donna L. Orsuto, 80–96. New York: Paulist Press, 1996.

_____. "Mary's Song." *On Eagle's Wings.* Phoenix: North American Liturgy Resources, 1979.

Jungmann, Joseph. *The Mass: An Historical, Theological, and Pastoral Survey.* Collegeville: The Liturgical Press, 1976.

Kammer, Fred. *Doing Faithjustice: An Introduction to Catholic Social Thought.* Mahwah, N.J.: Paulist Press, 1991.

Kramer, William. *Evolution and Creation: A Catholic Understanding.* Huntington, Ind.: Our Sunday Visitor Press, 1986.

Martos, Joseph. *Doors to the Sacred: A Historical Introduction to Sacraments in the Catholic Church*. Tarrytown, N.Y.: Triumph Books, 1991.

Mass of the Angels. "Sanctus." Cathedral Singers, Richard Proulx, conductor.

May, William F. "The Beleaguered Rulers." *The Public Obligation of the Professional*, Kennedy Institute of Ethics Journal 2 (1992) 25–41.

McBrien, Richard. *Catholicism*. Minneapolis: Winston Press, 1980.

McGinnis, Kathleen, and James McGinnis. *Parenting for Peace and Justice: 10 Year Later*. Maryknoll, N.Y.: Orbis Books, 1990.

Michel, Virgil. *Christian Social Reconstruction*. Milwaukee: Bruce Publishing, 1937.

_____. *The Social Question: Essays on Capitalism and Christianity*. St. Cloud, Minn.: Palmer Printing Company, 1987.

Miller, James Andrew. "Other Plans: Journal of an Illness." *First Things* (March 1993) 26–33.

Mozart, Wolfgang Amadeus. "Sanctus and Benedictus in C Major," K 258. *Music of Mozart's Missa Brevis*. New York: BMG Music.

_____. "Sanctus and Benedictus in C Major," K 258. *Score of Six Masses in Full Score*. Mineola, N.Y.: Dover Publications.

The Mystery of Faith: A Study of the Structural Elements of the Order of Mass. Washington, D.C.: Federation of Diocesan Liturgical Commissions, 1981.

Naughton, Michael. *The Good Stewards*. Lanham, Md.: University Press of America, 1992.

Neale, John M. Trans. from Latin. "O Come, O Come, Emmanuel." *Worship: A Hymnal and Service Book for Roman Catholics*. Chicago: G.I.A. Publications, 1986.

Nell-Breuning, Oswald. *Reorganization of Social Economy*. Milwaukee: Bruce Publishing Co., 1936.

Newman, John Henry. *An Essay on the Development of Christian Doctrine*. London: Longmans, Green, 1920.

New Revised Standard Version Bible. New York: Oxford University Press, 1989.

Nocent, Adrian. *The Liturgical Year*. Collegeville: The Liturgical Press, 1977.

O'Brien, David, and Thomas A. Shannon, eds. *Catholic Social Thought: The Documentary Heritage*. Maryknoll, N.Y.: Orbis Books, 1992.

O'Connor, Flannery. *The Habit of Being: Letters*. Ed. Sally Fitzgerald. New York: Vintage Books, 1980.

_____. "Introduction to a Memoir of Mary Ann." *Mystery and Manners: Occasional Prose*. Sel. and ed. Sally and Robert Fitzgerald. New York: Farrar, Straus and Giroux, 1969.

_____. *Three by Flannery O'Connor*. New York: New American Library, 1983.

Pärt, Arvo. "Sanctus." *Berliner Messe* score. Munich: ECM Records.

Pieper, Josef. *An Anthology*. San Francisco: Ignatius Press, 1989.

_____. *Leisure: The Basis of Culture*. New York: Pantheon Books, 1952.

Pius XII. *Summi pontificatus* (On the Union of Human Society). October 20, 1939. For the full text of this encyclical on the Internet see http://abbey.apana.org.au/Official/Papal/Pius12/P12summi.Htm.

Pritchard, James. *The Ancient Near East*. Princeton, N.J.: Princeton University Press, 1969.

Rengstorf, H. *"Apostolos." Theological Dictionary of the New Testament*. Ed. Gerhard Kittel; trans. and ed. Geoffrey W. Bromiley, 1:407–45. Grand Rapids, Mich.: Eerdmans, 1964.

Rouault, George. *Aimez-vous les uns les autres*. Richard L. Hillstrom Collection, Minneapolis. Photographer: Roger Rich, University of St. Thomas.

Ryan, John A. *Distributive Justice*. 3rd ed. New York: The Macmillan Company, 1942.

_____. *A Living Wage*. New York: The Macmillan Company, 1906.

Schmemann, Alexander. *For the Life of the World: Sacraments and Oxthodoxy*. Crestwood, N.Y.: St. Vladimir's Seminary Press, 1973.

Schor, Juliet B. *The Overworked American*. New York: Basic Books, 1992.

Schuck, Michael. *That They Be One*. Washington, D.C.: Georgetown University Press, 1990.

Schumacher, E. F. *Good Work*. New York: Harper and Row, 1979.

Schutte, Dan. "Come With Me into the Fields." *Glory and Praise*. Phoenix: North American Liturgy Resources, 1977.

_____. "Here I Am, Lord." *Gather*. Chicago: G.I.A. Publications, 1994.

_____. "I Found the Treasure." *The Steadfast Love*. Phoenix: North American Liturgy Resources, 1985.

Sharing Catholic Social Teaching: Challenges and Directions. Washington, D.C.: United States Catholic Conference, 1998.

Shea, John. *Gospel Light: Jesus Stories for Spiritual Consciousness*. New York: Crossroad, 1988.

Talley, Thomas J. *The Origins of the Liturgical Year*. New York: Pueblo, 1986.

Vatican Council II. *Dei verbum* (The Dogmatic Constitution on Divine Revelation). November 18, 1965.

Vatican Council II. *Gaudium et spes* (Pastoral Constitution on the Church in the Modern World). December 7, 1965.

Vatican Council II. *Sacrosanctum concilium* (The Constitution on the Sacred Liturgy). December 4, 1963.

Vawter, Bruce. *A Path Through Genesis*. New York: Sheed and Ward, 1956.

Vorgrimler, Herbert. *Sacramental Theology*. Trans. Linda M. Maloney. Collegeville: The Liturgical Press, 1992.

Wadell, Paul. *The Primacy of Love: An Introduction to the Ethics of Thomas Aquinas.* New York: Paulist Press, 1992.

Wuthnow, Robert. *God and Mammon in America.* New York: The Free Press, 1994.

Contributors

ADÉ BETHUNE is an art director of the Terra Sancta Guild and a
renowned liturgical artist. She is a partner in Bethune-Durta
Associates and a liturgical consultant. She lives in Newport,
Rhode Island.

DON J. BRIEL is director of the Center for Catholic Studies at the University of St. Thomas in St. Paul, Minnesota. He holds a Ph.D. in
theology from Université de Strasbourg.

KATHLEEN FOLEY, C.S.J., is director of the *Focus on Theology* program at
the University of St. Thomas in St. Paul, Minnesota. She holds an
M.A. in theology from the University of Notre Dame.

MARY DANIEL HARTNETT, C.S.J., is a former director of Field Education
at the St. Paul Seminary School of Divinity at the University of
St. Thomas in St. Paul, Minnesota. She holds an M.A. in education from the University of Minnesota.

JAN MICHAEL JONCAS, a priest of the Archdiocese of Saint Paul and
Minneapolis, is assistant professor of theology at the University
of St. Thomas in St. Paul, Minnesota. He holds an S.L.D. from the
Pontifical Liturgical Institute of St. Anselm in Rome.

ARTHUR L. KENNEDY, a priest of the Archdiocese of Boston, is professor
of theology at the University of St. Thomas in St. Paul, Minnesota. He holds a Ph.D. in systematic theology/philosophy of
religion from Boston University.

VICKI KLIMA is the director of the Worship Center for the Archdiocese
of Saint Paul and Minneapolis. She holds an M.A. in pastoral
liturgy from the University of St. Thomas.

MICHAEL NAUGHTON is associate professor of theology at the University of St. Thomas in St. Paul, Minnesota. He holds a Ph.D. in
theology from Marquette University, Wisconsin.

TERENCE NICHOLS is associate professor of theology at the University of
St. Thomas in St. Paul, Minnesota. He holds a Ph.D. in theology
from Marquette University, Wisconsin.

PEGGY O'LEARY, C.S.J, is coordinator of the *Focus on Theology* program at the University of St. Thomas in St. Paul, Minnesota. She holds an M.A. in education from Loyola University in Chicago.

CHRISTOPHER THOMPSON is assistant professor of moral theology at the University of St. Thomas in St. Paul, Minnesota. He holds a Ph.D. in theology from Marquette University, Wisconsin.

Index